OUR STORY

Jets &
Sharks

STORY

Then and Now

OUR

Jets &
Sharks

STORY

Then and Now

AS TOLD BY CAST MEMBERS FROM THE MOVIE
WEST SIDE STORY

Outskirts Press, Inc.
Denver, Colorado

Introduction

WEST SIDE STORY: Is there anyone who doesn't know this iconic film that transcends generations? It won ten Oscars including best picture of 1961, and The Golden Globe and New York Film Critics awards of 1961. In 1998 it made the AFI's The Hundred Best Films list. In 2002, Tony and Maria's star-crossed love story was #3 on AFI's 50 Greatest Love Stories. It climbed to #2 of Best Musicals, and on the list of the greatest songs from American movies, "Tonight" ranked #59, "America" ranked #35, and "Somewhere" ranked #20. The film has been deemed "culturally significant" by the United States Library of Congress and was selected for preservation in the National Film Registry in 1997. George Chakiris and Rita Moreno won best supporting Oscars, and Robert Wise and Jerome Robbins won best director. 2011 will be the 50th anniversary

Yet very little is known about the Jets and the Sharks their leaders and their girls, the rival gang members who are the backbone of the film. Not much is known of the amazingly gifted dancer/actors without whom there is no *West Side Story*. Little is known about their audition experience, or how each member was chosen, because of their unique qualities fit Jerome Robbins vision.

In this collective memoir, each gang member shares behind-the-scenes personal stories about the making of this classic film. Stories never before told. Stories that will make you laugh, stories that will inspire and surprise. They came together to be rival gang members in a movie. They hadn't a clue they were creating history. They were even less aware that this shared experience was creating life long friendships and that a new extended family was being born, a family that would bear witness to marriages, divorces, births, deaths, joys, and sorrows. Where are they now, and what are they doing?

Let them tell their stories.

Contents

lets

"Riff"/Jet — Russ Tamblyn

IN 1960, WHEN *West Side Story* was going to be made into a film, I wanted to do it more than any other movie that had come up. Unfortunately, I was under contract to MGM Studios and W.S.S. was going to be a United Artists film, so my agent Phil Gersh had to convince Metro to let me audition for it. My first meeting was a success, and they asked me back to do four more tests with other actors trying out for parts. Luckily for me, Producer/Director Robert Wise's agent was also Phil Gersh, so I had up-to-date info on how things were progressing. He told me the part I wanted so badly was between one other actor and myself. I would know in a few days, but the anticipation was nerve-racking. Finally, he called! "Sorry Russ," he said, "Richard Beymer got the part you wanted, but they've offered you the role of Riff." I said, "I'll take it."

After *WSS*

I AM NOW co-managing my daughter, Amber, whose career is blossoming rapidly. I'm also writing my autobiography titled *Dancing on the Edge*, and recently directed and choreographed Neil Young's rock opera, *Greendale*, for the stage. Besides the performing arts, I'm involved in fine art. For the past couple of years, I've had several pieces of contemporary artwork and films traveling across the country in an exhibition called *Semina Culture: Wallace Berman & His Circle.* This exhibition was at the Santa Monica Museum of Art, the Nora Eccles Harrison Museum (in Logan, Utah), the Ulrich Museum of Art (in Wichita, Kansas), the Berkley Art Museum and Pacific Film Archive (California), and the Grey Art Gallery (New York).

Russ Tamblyn

"Action"/Jet — Tony Mordente

IT WAS MATINEE day at *Bye Bye Birdie*, a rainy Wednesday at that. The doorman, whose name of course was Pop, told me I had a call from Robert Wise, the co-director of the upcoming film *West Side Story*. I acted very casual, but my heart started pounding. I was expecting the call; Jerry Robbins had told me that Mr. Wise was going to call for a meeting. I returned the call ASAP. He wanted to meet in the next hour. I of course said, "No problem." Well, one little problem: the dogs had to be picked up from the groomers. I had to get them before the groomers closed. My wife, Chita Rivera, had already gone to a press interview, and I told her I would pick them up.

So I took a cab, got the dogs, and proceeded to the interview. I walked in, introduced myself to the secretary, and sat down. The office was empty. In a few minutes Mr. Wise's door opened, and out walked Edward Villella, who, at the time, was one of America's great ballet dancers. Edward and I had met as students at The High School of Performing Arts. There I was holding the leads to two beautifully groomed French poodles.

Eddie looked at me and said, "Not the best image for a guy who wants to play a tough guy."

It took a few seconds for that to hit home. I thought I really blew it. So I just tried to act like the dogs were not there. Mr. Wise never mentioned the dogs. He glanced at them briefly and then looked back to me, stared for a few seconds before we went into the usual introductions and got down to business.

He told me that Jerry wanted me in the film and he was okay with that, but could not tell me which role I would be playing. If I was not happy with the role they chose for me, I would be free to leave the film. He told me about the testing procedure and asked if I would agree to that. Well, I was so excited, the dogs were shaking! I was thrilled; I would be a part of something that originated on Broadway. I would have said yes anyway! He said he would give me a call and wrap everything up. He said David Winters already had accepted the same conditions. I was so happy that David, who played Baby John to my A-Rab, would be there. I knew David would be an asset to the film. As it turned out, Tommy Abbott, Jay Norman, Carole D'Andrea, and I would be together again. I was happy, the poodles were happy, and Chita was happy.

Then came the dreaded screen test. I tested for Riff, Action, A-Rab, and Ice. Now I have to tell you, I was so nervous I don't know how I got through it, and I don't know how anyone gets a job from testing. I had no idea what all those people walking about did, and this was only the testing!!!! What would the actual filming be like? David told me to block out the activity going on around us. Easy for him to say—he loved the excitement and he did well in chaos. He said he would be fine with anything they decided, as long as he got what he thought was a good role. Consequently, he was like an old pro in front of the camera.

As for me, all I can say is I wasn't very good. Why they asked me to do the job is still a mystery. When I later began directing TV and had to read or audition an actor for a role, I was a happy camper being on the other side of the table. This process was so foreign to me that even testing for A-Rab, a role I knew like the back of my hand and could do in my sleep, made me noticeably nervous. There I was in front of a camera saying lines to someone standing off camera! Never having been to an acting class, I felt like a fish out of water, though I seriously doubt an acting class would ready someone for this kind of controlled confusion!

I never knew how much work went into shooting a scene, and the experience overwhelmed me. I had no clue, and still don't know why they would test me for Riff. Ice was a role they tried on Broadway, but they didn't like the way it worked, and it definitely was not right for me. Truthfully, I'm not sold on why they decided to use it in the film. Action was a reach; I thought maybe I could play that role, but deep down I wanted A-Rab, and not just because I would be comfortable, but also because I originated him, something that nobody did before me! After all, one of my French poodles was named A-Rab! Jerry had everybody in the show write his or her character's history, which really helped me get to know A-Rab.

Anyway I got the call, I was going to Hollywood, and I was going to be in a film! Now honestly, I never thought of being in a movie, and not for a second did I think I was going to have a film career. I wasn't stupid. The excitement was all about being part of the *West Side Story* film. I always liked traveling, meeting new people, and working with great dancers. Tommy told me he was doing it, we both knew Jay would be, and when you can dance and have a face like Ms. D'Andrea, who originated Velma and was my partner in "Dance Hall," I had a feeling she was going to be there as well and I was right.

I drove cross-country with Tommy Abbott in my XK150 Jaguar sport convertible. This was the perfect car to arrive in Hollywood with! The exterior color was pearl grey with red interior. On the way, Tommy and I were temporally detained for a few hours; we were charged with armed robbery! Two guys with long hair and one answering to the name of Tommy were the suspects. We had just arrived in Amarillo, Texas, which felt like it was 120 degrees. We had taken the car to be washed, oiled, and lubed and a very large state policeman on a motorcycle pulled up, pulled his gun, and said, "Against the wall, boys!"

This guy could make a cup of coffee nervous. We then had to wait for a detective to arrive. Seemed like hours standing with our hands pressed against a hot wall with a .357 magnum pointed at us. He finally arrived, exited the car, and asked us what we were doing there.

"Going to Hollywood to make a movie," we answered.

He just sort of snorted, "Oh, really!" He then ushered us into his car. I asked what this was all about and how long it would take.

"If everything is okay, it will take ten minutes. If not, it will take about ten years."

Very funny! We arrived at the scene of the crime and the gas station attendant, thank God, cleared us. We got back into the detective's car and he handed me his business card and said, "If there is anything you boys need while you're in town, give me a call."

That was supposed to make everything okay, I guess. The state policeman thought they should search my car anyway. But the detective thought we had been through enough. Was I glad about that! Later I told Tommy that I did actually have a gun in my suitcase in the trunk of the car. He smacked me on the head about ten times. Can't imagine what would have happened had they found that gun. We finally arrived in Los Angeles all in one piece. We found a place to live, called the production office, and they told us where Samuel Goldwyn Studios was and when to report for work.

After we signed our contracts, we went to check out the studio gym where we would be rehearsing. We walked in and there was this guy swinging from a trapeze. He flew down and lo and behold it was Burt Lancaster! Said he was just tuning up for a film. He said hello and asked us what we were doing there, and we told him. Then with that signature smile, he wished us luck.

"Great musical," he said. "Should make a great movie."

First day of rehearsal was very exciting. I met up with dancers I knew like David Bean, George Chakiris, Eddie Verso, and some of the new dancers—Bert Michaels, Bobby Thompson, Nick Navarro, Andre Tayir, and Rudy Del Campo. Most of the dancers had performed *West Side Story* in some company somewhere, so most of us knew the show. But the California dancers, as we called them, had to learn a lot of new material. Now that I think about it, they were used to making musicals; we weren't. We New Yorkers had a lot to learn. It'll be interesting to read how they felt when they met us for the first time. I thought we blended in very quickly. Bobby Banas recently reminded me of competition between the New York dancers and the California dancers. I don't remember that, but I'm sure it will make good reading. So I will let him tell it.

Maggie Banks was one of Jerry's assistants, and had tons of experience with movie musicals. She was a great help to me when we got to the filming. Everybody loved Maggie; we loved calling her Baggie Manks. I have no idea why!!!! We rehearsed for a couple of weeks, learned some new stuff, and re-staged old stuff; still, however, no word of who would be playing what role, or if you even had a role! Then it came: Jerry and Robert sat us down at the end of the day and gave us the news.

I have to say, I was disappointed to hear that I would not be playing A-Rab—David would—and I think David was disappointed he would not be playing Baby John; Eliot would. I got the role of Action. Remembering Eddie Roll was the best Action ever, I took on the challenge. I think I could have been better; we always think that. It was a gigantic undertaking for those of us who never had any prior film experience. Most were happy and some not so happy about not getting a role. But no one left the film. We all worked hard and played hard. A few injuries but we made it through. Here's a cliché for you: we all became a family.

Now I knew what everybody's job was on a Broadway stage. But there were a few changes on a soundstage, like stagehands became grips, and then there was a gaffer and lighting crew that lugged lamps or hung the giant overhead arcs. The first assistant director was equal to the production stage manager. He set the call sheet and made sure the cast and crew were ready for the day's work, and of course he had to have an assistant! So there was a second AD. He made sure we got to the set on time.

Then there was the camera crew, which was an army in and of itself. There was the camera operator, the first assistant cameraman who checked focus, and the second assistant whose job it was to hold the marker, called the clapboard. The clapboard had the name of the production, the date, the scene number, and the take number. Sometimes we did a lot of takes, and I mean a lot. There was a third assistant that put the tape marks down. Everybody got marked so we knew where we started, every place we stopped, and of course where we finished. Each one's mark was a different color tape, and it was critical we hit our marks for a lot of reasons—like focus, blocking someone, or being covered by someone just to name a few. Sometimes we used a lot of tape! On the streets in New York they used chalk. What a budget saver! Now this was all new coming from stage. On stage I never had to worry about any of this.

We rehearsed the "Prologue" for about three weeks. The "Prologue" opens the film. Then the "powers that were" wanted to try a screen test to see if we could shoot in the studio and not on some real Los Angeles or New York streets. We got our make-up call and wore regular rehearsal clothes.

"Just be on time!!!" said Mr. Relyea.

I had a six am make-up call. That was tough being a night person. And then as a group—a very excited group—we headed to a new world led by Second Assistant Director Jerry Siegel. The set was a version of the Broadway set, some steps and a long ramp. That was nothing new; we had been rehearsing on it for the last couple of weeks. I looked around and saw half the studio draped with black velour. They would film us dancing, and then fill in the background with shots of the city. It was called a process shot. This idea sounded really phony to me. But they thought it might work and be a lot cheaper.

Then suddenly, what looked like an army of ants building a hill, men started moving, coming from all directions—grips, lighting crew, camera crew pushing the dolly with that huge camera mounted on top, all moving with speed like they knew exactly where they were going.

In the middle of all these "ants" was one man standing still with folded arms and looking straight ahead. If there was any man who looked like what a filmmaker was supposed to look like, it was him, a chiseled face, squinting eyes, grey fedora atop his head, and a cigarette, non-filtered, dangling from his lips. After a few minutes Robert

Wise and Jerry Robbins joined him, not saying anything, just standing alongside him. I began to wonder who this guy was. I did know right away he was a boss. But I had to find out, the boss of what?

"Who is that guy?" I asked Bob Relyea, our first AD.

"Daniel Fapp, the cinematographer," he answered.

"Okay, what does his job entail?" I asked.

"Stick around and watch," said Relyea.

I did and learned that he was the man responsible for all that beautiful lighting and camerawork. After about twenty minutes, it all settled down and Danny spoke for the first time:

"Set's ready. Let's get a rehearsal."

I knew then this man would have to be effective in order for this film to be a success. Boy was I right! We rehearsed the first segment, and there were Robert and Jerry with the director's eye-piece watching us dance down the steps, both sort of in a crouch, and there was Danny about ten feet to their left, standing absolutely still, arms still folded, cigarette still dangling from his lips. We finished dancing and both Robert and Jerry looked at each other and nodded agreement, looked at the camera crew, pointed to the spot where they were standing.

But ten feet from the left, Danny spoke again: "Camera's here, guys!!!"

Guess who won? From then on, I knew who the guy to watch was. Without question, the film's and my own unsung hero, Daniel L. Fapp, Cinematographer! Not only extremely talented, but also a soft-spoken, well-spoken, friendly, and gentle man. When we were filming in New York, he and the camera crew bet on how many seconds it would take before the sun would clear the clouds… He always won!

One day, I was called out from rehearsal—I think we were working on the "Rumble"—and was told to report to the stage, where they were filming the "Balcony" scene. Anytime I could get out of rehearsal, I ran. Jerry asked me just to watch Richard Beymer climb up the fire-escape ladder and see if the staging looked similar to the original staging. It looked the same to me. The set was slightly different, but the staging looked the same. I was not made an assistant as yet but I did assist Jerry with the London Company, so I did know the original staging. Jerry's first assistant Howard Jeffrey was there, but Jerry always wanted more eyes checking things. Personally, I think he wanted more friends and familiar faces around at this very uncomfortable time.

He was talking with Danny when I arrived, and I asked Howard how things were going.

"Very, very slow—no, I would say excruciatingly slow and a little, no, a lot of discontent amongst the leaders," said Howard.

Jerry did not look confident, which was not ever the case. Robert Wise was sitting way to the other side of the stage trying to look immersed in the script and not be a part of the anguished chat between Jerry and Danny. Jerry looked like he was having some trouble getting what he wanted through to Danny. I assumed it was the lighting, not the staging, they were discussing. I heard Danny say he would make some changes—reluctantly I will add. He went back to his crew as Jerry walked back to Robert and had what looked like a heated discussion. Jerry then came to Howard and me and told us Ruth Mitchell, the original stage production manager of WSS, was in town and we would all be having dinner together that night. He then asked me what I thought of the staging.

"I like it," I said. "It's a little awkward but very natural for teenagers in love for the first time."

Danny then said he was ready for the first team, Richard and Natalie.

"Action!" yelled Jerry and they began. About twenty seconds into the scene Jerry yelled, "Cut," walked over to Robert; they spoke briefly, Robert waved his hands in the air and looked at his watch. Anyone could tell he was not happy with the goings-on. Jerry walked back to Danny and wanted more changes.

Danny just stared at him, reached in his pocket, and pulled out his cigarette lighter, handed it to Jerry, and said, "Here, you light it."

He then turned on his heels and headed for the exit with Relyea and Wise running after him. Well they got him to come back, Jerry relented, and they got on with the filming.

Howard looked at me and said, "I don't think it is going to be an easily digested meal tonight!"

He was right. But all said and done, Jerry really liked Danny, and Danny really thought Jerry was special. They worked brilliantly together when we were shooting "Cool." Jerry didn't often confer with someone when working something out, but he did with Mr. Fapp.

Here is another nice little story about Mr. Fapp. We were shooting "Cool," I think without question, the hardest number for the Jets. Not only difficult to dance, but filled with contained tension and then all-out explosive energy. At this point the Jets are losing control—their cool, if you will. Ice has to regain control, Riff is gone, and he needs to show leadership over a pack of loose cannons.

Now Jerry was working our asses off. When there was a cut for some reason, planned or otherwise, wherever we were in filming the number, we had to start from the top and get to where we were physically and emotionally in order to match the previous take. If he didn't think we were there, we started from the top again. Then he would try different versions of the number. We had versions A, B, C, D, and E. They were mostly the same steps, maybe other people doing them and perhaps different floor patterns. We had the same thing going on in the original company and the London company. I can tell you I was getting tired and so was the rest of the gang.

Danny noticed a little more than the usual early morning reticence. We were slow getting to the stage from make-up and slow getting to the barre for warm-up. Jerry was trying to get us up to speed; we were getting noticeably more irritated. And it was taking even more time than usual to get a sequence filmed because we were just plain worn out. Even when Eliot Feld got some sort of flu—I think it was mono—we shot around him, and so we never had a break. I looked around and I could see hands on hips, eyes looking straight down to the floor. Not the usual "Good morning, how was your night?"

These past few days we were working on a segment where we ended up on our knees—I was not looking forward to getting back down on my knees for the rest of the day. I never liked to use kneepads, thought they looked bad in our tight jeans. We did use them in rehearsal; I did not use them when we were shooting. I don't think anybody did. We started to use furniture pads under our knees during the time it took to light this segment.

Danny walked over to David Winters and I and asked, "What's up?" I just stared back, not answering, nor did David. Well, Danny picked up on it.

"You wanna finish this number? You better give these guys a day off," he yelled over to Jerry and Wise, who were discussing something.

He didn't say "gals" but he meant all of us! Relyea looked at Jerry and Wise; they both looked at Relyea. The entire Jet gang looked at the three of them, who looked very confused.

"Everybody gets a day off," said Danny before anyone could say anything.

Well, you have never seen a group of tired dancers move to the exit doors so quick. We never looked back to see if Jerry, Wise, or Relyea agreed or not! Thank you, Danny.

So what about all those versions of "Cool"? Well, I thought, who is going to know if I do the same version or not; I always did the same version in the original company, the London Company, and all the rehearsals for the film. One day we were watching the ladies rehearse their section, and we had some pretty ladies to watch. I have to say, not only were they pretty, but they were good, really good, dancers! Howard was cleaning up. Meaning, making sure everybody was on the same foot or arms were together, heads were looking in the same direction. Jerry came and stood next to me. Asked me how I thought the filming was going, was it looking good, about the set, did I like the way he'd changed some things? I didn't have to look at him to know that all of these questions were dripping in sarcasm.

Then he said, "I know you have been doing the same version from the first day of rehearsal of the original production, and in the London company, including now! So if you think you're fooling me, I just want you to know you are not."

I had no reply. I know I had the look of "awe." The man knew everything. We both started laughing—what else could I do, I was caught. When I think about Jerry, and I often do, I am always amazed at how he saw everything and forgot nothing, his great sense of what would play, what would work, and what wouldn't. Now back on Broadway, he never seemed happy with the final version of "Cool." The number he felt would be the easiest for him turned out to be the hardest. I know he was happy with the film version, and why wouldn't he be? It was sensational—the set was great, the low ceiling, the lighting, and the camera work, it just all worked. It was never meant to be a showstopper like "America" or "Krupke."

His enormous experience on Broadway, not to mention how many shows he was called upon to fix before they opened (they call that a "show doctor"), carved the film version of "Cool" into another brilliant piece in the monument that is Mr. Robbins' legacy.

His erratic behavior during rehearsals was not overblown; once he started kicking cigarette butts and moving his chair around, we knew somebody was about to get it. There was no question when he got frustrated, he could get nasty. But I believe it was because he demanded more, expected more, knew they had more to give and they had not executed his vision yet. He was not a perfect human being—well, to me he was. I am very proud to have been chosen by him to share a small part in the history of *West Side Story*. Not only to be able to do his work, but to be around the great dancers that I got to work with.

There are and will be more great choreographers, but I can assure you, none quite the likes of Jerome Robbins. Michael Kidd, Bob Fosse, Jack Cole—they all had a great signature style and inventiveness. If you saw a show, movie, or TV show, it wasn't necessary to read the credits to know who choreographed that dancing. But Jerry was different. Watch *West Side Story*, *Peter Pan*, or the ballet *Fancy Free*, his first ballet, with the score written by Leonard Bernstein, "Uncle Tom's Ballet" in *Anna and the King of Siam*, *Fiddler on The Roof*, *Dances at a Gathering*, all choreographed by the same man. All different in style but created from the soul of that one man.

There will never be another Jerome Robbins. I guess what I am saying is they fired Jerry way too soon. The "Dance Hall" still had to be filmed. Some were saddened and some celebrated the news of Jerry's leaving. I thought it then and I still think it was a big mistake. Now that I have directed, of course nowhere near the scale of this film, I don't know how it could have gone any quicker.

A little side note: someone told me after the film had been completed that during filming, the project had run out of money! The price tag, the final cost of the film, was somewhere near six to seven million dollars. The starting budget I was told was three million dollars. Can you imagine what it would cost now? I don't recall who gave me this information, so I cannot verify this story. But if true, the "suits" in the "big offices" must have liked the dailies they saw, because they gave us the money to complete the project. It is just a humongous body of work, and I don't think the producers had any idea of the scope of this monumental undertaking. I have mounted productions of *WSS* in summer stock, Japan, California, all with lots of dancers who already knew the show; it is just a very difficult show to put together.

The "Dance Hall" was not in the can—a film expression meaning not finished—when Jerry was let go.

The day after we got the news of Jerry's leaving, he called me and told me about the plan to make me an assistant, to put the finishing touches on "Dance Hall" and work personally with Natalie Wood. That also meant giving her private dance class at her home in Beverly Hills. I told him I was not interested. An added responsibility was not attractive to me at that time. I was having too much fun and didn't want the extra work. Jerry said, "Think about it"; he wanted it to happen. He would call me tomorrow. I talked with Tommy about the offer that night, and he already knew it was coming. He had spoken with Jerry that afternoon.

We had dinner that night with Betty Walhberg, the rehearsal pianist and musical dance arranger who held the same important position with the original company. I have some history with this elegant lady; she was one of my teachers at Performing Arts High School. She taught musical composition, sort of a "how to break down a musical composition and choreograph class." Mr. Bernstein once said he could not play the score as well as she did.

When I directed a company of *WSS* at the Burt Reynolds Dinner Theatre in Florida, with my daughter Lisa playing the role of Anita, the role her mother originated on Broadway, the hardest part of that job was finding someone who could play the score for rehearsals! There was no Betty in sight. Later on, Betty did some dance arranging for me when I choreographed a couple of TV specials. I was very lucky to get her; she was one of the most sought after in her profession.

So back to the movie, they both wanted me to take the post; I told them not to hold their collective breaths, that they had about the same chance as hell freezing over! Tommy wanted no part in having to choreograph something. He was just not ready to take on that kind of burden.

What I didn't know was that Natalie had also asked for me. Jerry suggested me to her so that was all she needed to hear, and she then spoke to Relyea. The next morning, Relyea, rather than asking me, told me I was to put "Dance Hall" on its feet with Tommy and Maggie. I was also to work personally with Natalie, teach her the staging with special attention on the "Cha-Cha." That particular section looks so easy, but if you ask the six other dancers who danced alongside Richard and Natalie, they will tell you how really difficult it truly was! We were very fortunate to have had such exceptional dancers.

I told Relyea I was not interested, but thanks for asking. When he offered me a substantial increase in salary, however, I changed my mind in an instant. I had a wife and child to support and dancers historically don't make a lot of money, and I hadn't lost that mindset.

Howard Jeffrey was not in the film, and opted to leave with Jerry. Besides the normal but difficult duties of a dance assistant, Howard had the added responsibility of working privately with Natalie. When he had arrived back in New York, he called to tell me she was fun to be around and very hard working. To be honest,

I had not spoken to Ms. Wood other than the normal civilities that happen when one works together. We had not worked in a scene together at that point. I do remember her being at some rehearsal and we chatted about the original show. She was very charming; as beautiful in person as she was on screen, a real "movie star." Her husband at the time was Robert Wagner. Great guy; we talked about cars. He had also owned an XK150 Jaguar convertible, so we had something in common.

After the film finished, I went to London to mount a production of *Birdie* and RJ (his nickname) was there, making *The War Lover*. We spent a lot of time together then, but when we first met, I felt more than a little awkward around them. I was young and just getting started, and they were two people at the top of their profession. Natalie was gracious and unpretentious and made me feel welcomed. We hit it off and became very good friends.

Seriously, folks, who wouldn't want to be around Natalie Wood? My God, how many dancers get to do that and make money? So here I was loose in California, working closely with Natalie Wood, while my wife and kid were back in New York! Now I have heard that Warren Beatty was hanging around the set. Some say they actually saw him. I never did. I can tell you I spent a lot of time with Nat and RJ at their home and at the studio but never saw him.

Bob Relyea, after forming Solar Productions with Steve McQueen, wrote a book about his experiences with stars and projects he had worked on. He, of course, has a chapter on *West Side Story*. Well I have to set the record straight, correct a myth he writes about. He writes that I reluctantly accepted the job of assisting on the film— true. He says that I complained about it at first, also true, but later enjoyed the job because I was having an affair with Natalie. I don't know who his source was, but that is not true and could not be further from the truth! Relyea also says Jerry and Howard were lovers, again not true—perhaps in the distant past maybe, some time way back in New York, but certainly not on the film.

I would like to add, if I have not said it before, Relyea was great!

Having directed TV for some twenty-eight years, I know when an AD is great. Not an easy job. Relyea formed a great relationship with all us guys. I would say he was more able to communicate with us than Mr. Wise and on a different level than Jerry.

But I digress, so back to "Dance Hall": we auditioned and hired some extra dancers to fill out the stage. I had to rework the competition section with Russ and Gina and also worked with Mr. Wise and Mr. Fapp in restaging sections to accommodate any last-minute changes in camera angles when needed. I did whatever was asked to facilitate getting the day's work finished expertly and on time. It's hard not to imagine how much better it could have been if Jerry were there—although we might still be filming the movie. Jerry took a long time filming the numbers, but what he did was masterful.

I did make one small change that was selfish, I replaced Ice with myself to dance with Carole in the "Blues" section, that little featured duet in the middle. Carole and I performed that little section opening night on Broadway and many performances after. I thought it was only fitting that the two of us be preserved dancing that section on celluloid for posterity. Tucker was perfectly okay with it. Jerry told Russ no tumbling in this film, but I put in some tumbling for Russ in "Dance Hall," and Gina Trikonis, of course, could do anything. I was seated next to Mr. Robbins at the premiere in New York. (A side-note of interest: Warren Beatty was Natalie's date for the premiere.) During the competition with Russ and Gina, Jerry nudged me, told me he liked it.

We had to shoot many, many takes of the "Cha-Cha" master—a head-to-toe shot with the full cast dancing behind Tony and Maria. Natalie had a little trouble holding her balance coming out of the turn. Like I said it looks easy, but it demands a lot of technical skill to perform successfully. The three couples shadowing them danced it beautifully. Jay, Tommy, and I especially remember Maria Jimenez. Rehearsing with that group was sheer elation to watch. I have a picture of Nat and me rehearsing for camera. I was dancing in for Richard and Maria is just behind me. That picture hangs in my office and I look at it every day. Nat gave it her very best under very difficult circumstances.

I said I did not see Warren Beatty on the set, but I did see Marlon Brando! The rumor going around was that he and Rita Moreno were dating, and I thought that was exciting. I seem to recall they had to stop shooting because Rita had cut her hand. The story goes she had a fight with Marlon and put her hand through a window! How would anybody on the *WSS* set know that? Hooray for Hollywood!

Rita had worked with Jerry in *King and I* and it was easy to see why she got into film. She was beautiful. We were shooting the "Rape" scene, where we throw Anita around pretty good. I have to say that I did miss Chita in this scene. She was electrifying. Hell, she was unbelievable in this show! Rita did pick up on how I felt, but I have to say made nothing of it.

This particular scene was emotionally demanding and extremely difficult for Anita. It can be really hard for actors to match these kinds of intense scenes from take to take. You sit sometimes for hours waiting for the lighting or some touch-up paint job on the set to get finished, and then you have to get back into the mood all over again. On top of that, nothing is shot sequentially. It's all shot out of order. So your first shot may be the ending of the film and the last shot the middle or the beginning. Stage is so different. You rehearse for weeks; have out-of-town tryouts, then opening night. You start from the beginning; run through the show in order, and two and half hours later it's over. Then it's the next night. As a performer, I preferred the stage because it made sense. This way of working didn't.

Rita was coming back to the stage for her close-up, where she spews vitriol at us Jets and tells us the lie that Maria is dead. She announced to Mr. Wise that she needed to get back up to where she was to match the master shot. Not so easy to just jump in. Remember the stage we were shooting on was huge, the size of a Costco! I might add that the only place with some light was Doc's, the drugstore set we were working on. The rest of the stage was dark and the floor had a lot of cables running throughout.

So she decided to take a run around the stage to get her breathing hard and back up to her emotional pitch. So she scoots off into the dark. Well we waited…and we waited…and we waited. No Rita. Relyea goes along the path she took to see what's going on…and he found her sprawled out on the floor. Seems she tripped over one of the cables. Fortunately it was only a minor ankle sprain, but the shoot was cancelled and we, of course, loved getting out early! The things actors go through to please an audience. By the way, I thought she was great in the scene. So did the Oscars. I've often been asked if there was tension between Rita and me during the filming with my being married to Chita at the time. The answer is no. Except for what we played in the scenes.

Well what about Chita? you might ask. Where was Chita? My wife was back in New York starring in a very big Broadway hit, *Bye Bye Birdie.* Chita is a genuine "triple threat," meaning one person who is able to act, sing, dance, and performs all three at a degree of excellence that so few can attain. Her talent is beyond rare. She created the role of Anita on Broadway, the role that would ultimately lead to her now legendary career on Broadway. We got married and had a beautiful daughter, Lisa, during the run of *West Side Story.*

We never talked about why she was not asked to do the film. To this day I don't know what went down. Maybe one day we will talk about it. I admit when Jerry told me Mr. Wise would call, I never thought about it and he never mentioned it. I do know she was happy for me and was all in favor of my going. Chita knew the love I had for *West Side.* She knew this was something I had to do even though it meant leaving her, Lisa, and the poodles back in New York.

"We will handle this, it will work," she said.

As it turned out, we went back to New York to film "Prologue" for a few weeks. I managed to fly back home for several weekends after the company returned to California. When Chita took her vacation week from the show, she and Lisa came to California. We had dinner with Jerry a few times. Larry Kert, the original Tony, came into town so there we were, like old times, Howard, Jerry, Larry, Chita, Tommy, and me. We laughed for hours. I never pushed Chita to visit the set. She did come to visit once; she knew a lot of the dancers and I introduced her to Natalie Wood.

Chita was amazed at how many people they had moving things around. We never had that many people moving sets around back on Broadway. I don't recall what was being filmed when she was there. I knew it would have been uncomfortable for both Rita and Chita if they'd happened to be on the same stage. I also knew they respected each other and would have enjoyed each other's company, but not at that time. Thinking about them now, they had similar personalities, both blessed with a great sense of humor and both possessing that rare value, something we all hoped to attain: professionalism. If Chita was not going to be Anita, Rita was the perfect choice. Chita loved meeting Nat and RJ. Chita and RJ still stay in touch.

Before I forget, a few interesting notes about George Chakiris. I first worked with George in the London Company, but he was not Bernardo, he played Riff. George had been in a few films as a dancer. Watch *Diamonds Are a Girl's Best Friend* right next to Marilyn Monroe. In my opinion, he was a good Riff, but a much better Bernardo. He was tall, very good looking, could dance, terrific singing voice—what a lucky guy! Did that read like professional jealousy? Oscar thought he was a great choice for the role too. He now is a very successful jewelry designer working with silver and precious metals.

Russ was a terrific choice for Riff. He was truly charming and a seriously sassy Riff. Years of film experience made Russ completely at home in front of the camera. He was not a trained dancer, he was a gymnast, but no one would ever know it watching *Seven Brides for Seven Brothers* and *West Side Story*. One day in New York, we had to delay filming because the neighborhood was having a parade. Russ and I were doubled over with laughter when Tucker joined the parade as a baton twirler! The funny part for us was how pissed off Jerry got at Tucker. We loved it when someone got caught! I am sure that his daughter Amber, a talented actress/poet, learned a lot from Dad. Sorry, Russ, she does resemble Bonnie, her mom, more.

I wish there was some "juicy" stuff I could tell. Like love affairs that started up during the filming. Like when Broadway shows go to tryout cities. There are a ton of affairs that start up and quietly die when they all get back to New York. This happens in national companies as well. I think there were a couple of dates here and there, but none that got talked about during break.

I did hear from both Banas and Gina that marriage was contemplated. Well, I had a huge crush on Gina, so much so that I couldn't even speak to her. I would go to the other side of the rehearsal studio on our short breaks so people would not see me blush in front of her. Especially when her big brother Gus was always around; he had to be…he was a Shark. That crush lasted quite a long time. I never even had the guts to ask her to dinner. Every once in a long time, when I catch the film on TV and see her, well, besides being an outstanding dancer, she was incredibly attractive! Every time I see her now, she grows more beautiful.

When *Ballet Theatre* was performing in San Francisco, some of the guys went up to spend some time with a few of the ballerinas and could not get back because the flights were cancelled due to fog. Mr. Wise was not happy! That was good for a few days of laughs. We always loved when the other guy got caught. Then there was a company of *Flower Drum Song* playing in Los Angeles. There were some parties, quite a few parties. I think they were there for two weeks, so there were two weeks of parties.

I have only two unpleasant memories. One was when Jerry left the film. The second was some tension amongst a few of the Shark ladies. As I mentioned earlier, there was no love lost between Natalie and Rita, and I think some of the Shark ladies sided with Rita. They seemed to take exception over my friendship with Ms. Wood. There was a Christmas pool, where you picked a name and exchanged gifts. I was given a book about hobnobbing with the stars. It was unsigned and I don't know to this day who gave it to me. I have to say I didn't find it funny. I hadn't snubbed anyone or treated anyone with disdain or used my relationship with Natalie to advance my position. I already had a role and I was asked to assist; I did not ask for the job. I thought it petty, or maybe someone wanted to show loyalty to Rita.

Another sad episode includes a very pretty young lady, Taffy Paul, who later became Stefanie Powers. Jerry hated Taffy's mom having to be around. It drove him nuts. But Taffy was a minor and one of the parents had to be there. Jerry said to Tommy Abbott and me that he was going to fire her just to get rid of the mother. Tommy and I objected but once Jerry had his mind made up, far be it from us to change it. She was so pretty and a very good dancer. Talk about six degrees of separation: she starred with Robert Wagner for years on the very successful TV series *Hart To Hart*. At that time Robert and Nat had re-wed.

The relationship between Richard and Natalie was tenuous to say the least. Nat never talked about it, but I felt it was there. It never became an overt issue during the workdays. I don't think there was any love lost between Rita and Natalie either. Again it was never discussed, just something I felt. There was never any inappropriate behavior on the set between them. Those kinds of things are not un-usual working in a large company.

"Gottles, glives gluns, what a cloup full of glickens," said he with unbelievable confidence and conviction. The real words that should be said are "Bottles, knives, guns, what a coup full of chickens!" That was Richard during the War Counsel scene. That was in rehearsal. I don't know what the rest of the guys did, but Tucker, David, and I doubled over. The laughter came out like a mighty clap of thunder. Richard started laughing. Once you got David and me going, there was little you could do to stop us except take a long break. Mr. Wise didn't think so, and so we went on to actually try to film the master. The scene was moving along pretty good until...you guessed it, it came to Richard and once again, not with as much confidence this time, he just turned the words inside out and upside down! We broke up. We tried to regain control, seems like Tucker got it together, but David and I were still iffy. Mr. Wise wanted to do a pick-up from the last couple of lines leading to Richard. David and I did not have control and out came the laughter once again. And that was before Richard even got to his lines. It got so bad that Mr. Wise not only asked David and me to leave the set, but the assistant prop master Beady Eyes as well. It felt so good to laugh; it was very difficult maintaining that kind of tension for so long, every day, all day long. It was especially evident when the two gangs performed in the same scene. Hate takes its toll, and we were just pretending! Well, we finally did get the master shot.

David and I were so glad they were moving on to a tighter shot of the Sharks' entrance. That gave us the badly needed time to pull ourselves together. When we got to the close-up of Richard saying those lines, Mr. Wise asked David and me to get lost. Good thing too—I was still not under complete control.

The same spontaneous outburst of laughter happened one other time. Again during a scene filled with tension. Tony has been shot by Chino and Maria has the gun. The rehearsal of this scene was endless. Jerry was gone and Mr. Wise couldn't find a camera angle he was happy with for the master of the gangs rushing into the schoolyard after Chino shoots Tony. Danny Fapp and Mr. Wise finally agreed upon the camera position, and we moved on. I think camera discussion was on the height of the lens, not so much the position. It was said that Mr. Wise was a master of editing while shooting. It was said you could just cut out the markers and splice the film together and get a finished film.

After I agree to help get Tony's body carried out, a Shark, Jay Norman, changes his mind and rushes over to help with lifting the body, and we all stop to exchange looks. For some reason, I suddenly found this funny and out came the laughter once again. I really had to work hard on controlling myself. The guys would have killed me if they'd had to keep doing this over and over again. I do remember losing control once again during my close-up when Maria looks to me for help. I look at this person who has now become a woman, and she looks at me as if to say that this should all end, that we should come together, so I choose to help her. The rehearsal was fine, but during the take, Nat started making faces, sticking her tongue out at me; of course she was off camera. Relyea called me over and said, "Not again, Mordente."

Of course I didn't rat out Ms. Wood. Her sense of humor tended to be very mischievous. For example, one day filming the "Dance Hall," Tucker and I were having lunch with Nat in her cottage/dressing room. Natalie decided it was time to play some sort of a joke on Relyea, who was having a tense day. So we came up with her calling Relyea from the cottage and saying there was a strange man knocking on her door. Bob said he would send security. Tucker and I started pounding on the door.

"Bob, he's breaking in, please come now!" she started screaming and hung up the phone.

Nat still had the white dress on that she wore in "Dance Hall." We knocked over anything standing in the room, threw the leftover lunch all over the place. She sprawled out on the floor. We spread ketchup on her dress and she held a knife to her midsection. Tucker and I hid in the small side sitting room.

Bob came running in and was confronted by this tableau! We heard, "Holy Shit!" We jumped out and Nat jumped up and we screamed…..."Surprise!"

Sorry to say Bob was not at work the next day. He was hospitalized with bleeding ulcers. He did have a history of this, but what an astonishingly stupid prank to play on someone. We did of course apologize profusely, and thankfully our apology was accepted! Bob of course blamed me! I don't think to this day he believes it was her idea.

Let me throw out a few thoughts about Richard Beymer. What I hear the most from people is that he was wrongly cast as Tony. I don't agree. I feel he wasn't helped a great deal. For some reason Jerry just backed off when it came to Richard. I watched some of the filming of the "Ladder" scene, where Riff and Tony talk about what was going down in the hood and Riff angles to get him to come to the dance at the gym. I don't recall either Jerry or Robert taking over the directing job. Maybe there was some confusion about when who was supposed to do what. I know Jerry took over when there was dance involved.

Richard was not very happy working on this film. Maybe because he received no help what-so-ever! He was out there totally on his own. He was never a problem on the set, even when Larry Roquemore really got into roughing him up during the "Rumble." He put some hurt on him for sure, but I never heard a complaint out of him. He made a few good films before *WSS*. *Diary of Ann Frank* comes to mind. I later worked with Richard in *The Longest Day*. I thought he was very good in that film. We never talked about *WSS* while we were shooting in Paris—city dropping here! He never comes to any of the reunion dinners; maybe he is not asked.

Now here is my take on Robert Wise. I never worked with Robert before or after *WSS*, so I can only speak to that body of work. I have seen many of his films, films that I truly admire. I never had nor will I have any pride when it comes to help. I'm sorry to say that as an actor in need of help, he gave me none whatsoever. His everyday line to the gangs was, "Don't lose your New York accent."

Maybe he thought we all knew the show so well that this was all he needed to say. I never heard him say anything different to any of the other actors. He never said a word to Rita during the "Rape" scene. Maybe he had a talk with her in the dressing room prior to the rehearsal or filming of that scene. It would be very interesting to hear her opinion of Mr. Wise's direction. He never gave us—at least me—any options to think about. He started as a film editor and later moved up to directing. So maybe he was just technically oriented.

I was used to choreographer/directors who told you what to do, when to do it, and why you were doing it. If you had any suggestions about what you were doing, they would listen and agree or disagree. There was a give and take. Not on this film. In my humble opinion, Relyea had a better understanding of what we were doing than Mr. Wise did.

Jerry certainly knew what he wanted us to do. So maybe for those reasons Mr. Wise backed off. But after Jerry was fired, he never truly stepped up to the plate and took charge. Now maybe he did give some guys notes and/or direction, but if he did I never heard about it. All I can say is, I never got any. I don't want to give the misperception that he was anything other than a very professional and pleasant gentleman. I did respect him as a co-director of the film. I guess I just expected more from him.

Now I believe it was he who came up with the idea for the opening shot of the film. In a helicopter with the camera pointed straight down covering the view of New York City, and then the zooming down into the playground and the Jet Gang. I was told that a special camera mount had to be built to accommodate this camera shot. Later, this mount was used on a regular basis for other films. No question, a brilliant shot.

But it was Jerry that got us into position and told us what our action was. I don't recall seeing much of Mr. Wise when Jerry was around except from a distance. It has been said that Mr. Wise was the one who gave Jerry the option of taking his name off the screen credits, or leaving his name there as the co-director of this musical epic. A very gallant, humble gesture, I believe. We all know what Jerry's choice was, and that he well deserved the Academy Award on his mantle. I am not sure how much editing he was allowed to contribute or if he was allowed any. I did hear that he gave copious amounts of notes to Mr. Wise. Whether Mr. Wise used any, we will never know. But you can only use what has been shot, and Jerry was responsible for most of the musical sequences. Have I said enough about Mr. Robbins? I could never say too much about that man. I don't think anyone could say too much about this very gifted person.

I am remembering the famous "rain dance" the first day of filming in New York. The first real day of filming WSS, it rained for three straight days. How great was that? We knew it meant more days of work. So a "rain dance" was performed the second day on the street uptown. So who came up with this fantastic idea? About nine guys take credit! Whosever idea it was, it worked. It rained, I mean rained, for about three more days. So a notice was posted in the make-up room at the hotel: *No more rain dances!!!!* I think that notice came directly from the notepad of Robert Wise. Remember that Mr. Wise was the producer as well as co-director. During the rain Jerry had the school opened up and he used the time to rehearse, so we really had no days off.

I lived in New York, so I did not stay at the hotel. I went to the hotel in the morning for make-up and wardrobe, and then was taken by bus to the set. One morning, I walked into make-up to find them feverishly working to cover up a cut on Tucker's cheek, received from a small tussle when cornered by Sharks in one of the hotel hallways. The two gangs were always trying to outdo the other. It was a way of showing togetherness and strength. It never was meant to really hurt someone. But that got another note posted: *No more horsing around.* They had to change the shooting schedule because Tucker (Ice) would never have matched the shots "in the can." You never wanted to be caught alone by the other gang. You did not want them to have some joke to crow about on set the next day to the crew.

While shooting the playground scene the Jets had a dummy, dressed in Shark colors, hung and burned in effigy from a fire escape. That really got them pissed off. Jerry thought it was great. Russ came up with the idea of having one of those advertising planes fly over followed by a sign spelling out "JETS." The Shark guys really loved dropping that yellow paint on us during "Prologue." It seemed like it took all day. We just kept getting washed up and re-made up, and changed wardrobe forever. At the end of that scene we chased Jerry down a block with cans of paint, but never did catch him. Bert Michaels expression when the paint covers us is great. Watch Bert in "Krupke"—great choice of character.

Some days were so hot the street tar got soft. During the "spit section," they had to put furniture pads under Jaime when setting up the camera shot. The tar was burning his shoulders and back. For me the worst was the morning ballet barre warm-up held on the sidewalk. We had lots of people watching. I felt really silly. Here were these tough gang members taking a ballet class. Forget dancing and singing down the street. The barre was not voluntary but compulsory; I never looked any of the watchers in the eye. And there in the background was the rubble soon to become Lincoln Center. We filmed on both the East and the West sides of New York.

The location team did a great job of finding us the most perfect locations. They hired some local gang members to assist with security. They made sure that no one did anything to hinder the work process. Good idea for the safety of cast and crew. After all, we were on their turf. Some were friendly; some were not so friendly. Just like the end of the film, some decide to walk together; some choose to stay on their own side. We had no trouble from them during the filming.

David Winters turned out to be very prophetic. After the first day of filming in New York and the rain stopped, he said we would never finish the "Prologue" in the time planned. I think they were planning on two weeks. He was right on the nose; we were there for about four weeks. We left New York City behind schedule. How did they ever think we could catch up when it took as long as it did just to film the "Prologue"? Perhaps they thought we would make up the time when we got back in the studio.

Faster isn't always better. Look at the quality of all the production numbers and then look at the "Dance Hall." I think there is quite a noticeable difference. No question it would have taken longer, but I guarantee it would have been worth it! It was good; it just simply would have been better.

After we got back to California, the two gangs did start to mingle. Jay and I got a great apartment together up on Laurel Canyon. We got into fast-draw. We bought guns and had quick-draw holsters custom made. How we found the guy who made them I don't remember, but the holsters are numbered and in a Western collector's magazine. I still have them. His name was Andy Anderson. His store was located in the North Valley. He designed and made lots of holsters for the stars in films and many TV westerns. They looked authentic Old West but were made for quick-draw. He also made Indian boots and leather belts. Jay and I of course had boots and belts made to order. We started out with gas-operated pellet pistols but soon graduated to the real thing, Single Action Army 45's. We shot up a lot of beer cans in the backyard and in our huge studio apartment. Then we took the pistols to a gunsmith and had the trigger filed for faster action. One needs every possible advantage!

From time to time I'll strap one of those holsters on and quick-draw, not as fast as I used to be. Then again, I'm not as fast as I used to be at a lot of things! We took the "Rigs," as they were called to the set. We practiced the art of fast-draw between takes. A few of the other guys got into it as well; sometimes it looked like we were filming a western. On Saturdays, along with those same guys, we started going rabbit hunting. I think it was in Bakersfield or Barstow. We did have fun. Jay at that time had cataracts in both eyes. So he wasn't able to see very well. I'm still not sure how he saw the rabbits! I think he just shot in the same direction we did. We did make sure he was always in front of us. There was a rumor that he shot a cow. Jay now has become a very fine and very busy carpenter. I miss not seeing him. I heard he is making jewelry boxes for George, Mr. Chakiris, who designs fine jewelry these days. Those Sharks they do stick together.

Here is another one; not so sure I should tell, but what the hell. I don't think RJ is going to be too happy with this one. He may not even remember it. Maybe Russ won't either! Anyway here goes… Nat, RJ, Russ, his wife at the time, Mark Crowley, who was Nat's personal assistant, and I were at Russ's home in Malibu Beach on Pacific Coast Highway. Crowley later became a terrific playwright. He had a big hit with his first play, *Boys in the Band*, based on his friendship with Howard Jeffrey. He then went on to become a writer on *Hart to Hart*, RJ and Stefanie Powers' hit TV series.

Russ came up with this game called Truth. The rules were you had to answer the question with the truth, no matter what the consequences might be. The game seemed to be moving along with some fun questions and answers till Russ asked Nat, if she were guaranteed the Oscar for *West Side Story* with one stipulation—she had to divorce RJ, just give him up—what would she do?

"Receive the Oscar," she answered.

I thought that RJ was going to go through the roof. He upped and ran out of the house. The house was on the Pacific Ocean. He ran to the rock-lined shore and tried to cool off. I went after him, giving some possible explanations for Nat's answer. He did not buy any of them. Needless to say, that was the end of the evening. We drove back to their house and RJ quickly left, but we didn't know where. I stayed with Nat while Mark went looking for RJ. After a few hours RJ returned and asked Mark and I to leave. He said he was okay and needed some time alone with Nat. We left in a hurry.

Natalie was at work the next day. Nothing was said. I saw RJ a few days later; he never brought up that night, neither did I. I asked Nat why she would give such an answer.

"That's the way I felt at the time," she replied.

Wow! It did appear from that day forth they were not on the same page. Not long after the film finished, they were divorced, but Nat did not win the Academy Award! Nat and I spoke on the phone often after the film, till she got busy and I got busy in London. I did see her one more time when I returned from London. It was at a performance of *Gypsy* starring the great Ethel Merman in New York. We hugged and kissed and promised to get together, but never did. She might have known then that she would be playing the role of Gypsy in the film. So much for letting Russ come up with a parlor game at your next party!

The "Rumble" set was breathtaking! The perspective was beyond belief. It was even better on film than actually standing on the set. There was that menacing, towering fence on one side, and a twelve-foot-high wall on the other end. This was the same wall that some of the guys would get up and over in one mighty leap. Not as easy as they made it look. The Shark gang entered from the fence side; some climbed over and some came through a drain into the fight area.

Now the Jets had to enter walking on top of this wall that not only was twelve feet high, but only about three feet wide. In trying to keep our balance so as not to fall twelve feet, we approached the wall rather tenuously on our first rehearsal. We did look a bit like "Flo Ziegfeld Show Girls." The Sharks, never missing an opportunity, started singing "A Pretty Girl…is Like a Melody." Have to say it was brilliant and a complete meltdown for everyone including the crew. Jerry laughed so hard, his cheeks got red and he looked like Santa Claus. Glad to say that none of us fell off during a take.

The knife fight moved along pretty well. We survived without a major injury. I mentioned before that Richard did get pummeled pretty good. Larry was whacking Richard with this chain, rubber of course, but that had to hurt. He did need some medical attention. Very hard to fake a fight; remember we did not have stunt doubles.

Through the years, *West Side Story* has yielded friendships that I treasure. Jaime Rogers and I met back when I was a student at the High School of Performing Arts. His sister Polly was one of my classmates in the dance department along with Jay Norman. She brought Jaime to school one day and left him in my care; still not sure why she trusted me! I think Jay and I dunked his head in the toilet, not sure why. He probably wised off to us! He still wises off to us! We have been family ever since.

Life after *WSS* for me was very fortunate. I was lucky to be hired to choreograph a few musical series—four to be exact. Add to that those many TV musical specials. Then I fell into a directing career. From sitcom to action adventure shows, then on to family value shows. Mind you, these shows were never on the scale of *WSS*. I learned a lot, but that kind of talent I ain't got! Very few have! I was still living the dream! After directing for twenty-eight years, I decided to retire.

An amazing number of dancers from *WSS* went on to build careers as choreographers and/or directors, like our friend David Winters, who resides in Thailand and is still making films. Eliot Feld started a ballet company. Last year Harvey Evans was still dancing on Broadway; Gina became a costumer. Some, however, went into other venues of business like Jay Norman, who lives in Florida and is doing fine carpentry. I know whenever I went to a job interview after the film was released, the first question was, "What was it like filming *WSS*?" Then the second question fired in: "What really happened between Wise and Robbins, and was there a lot of infighting with the cast?"

My answer was always the same: I was living a dream; I don't know what really happened between these two talented men. I don't remember any infighting and I don't remember any bad blood between the dancers. Maybe there was with Nat and Richard…maybe with Rita and Nat…but I never talk about what I don't know. Maybe in this book, there will be answers to some of those questions.

I worked on *Seventh Heaven* for several seasons, and every day I got asked questions about *WSS*. The best for me was to watch the faces of these young kids who ran up to me in the morning and said, "I saw the film last night, it is unbelievable… How did you do it?" That always brought a smile to my face.

I don't believe any of us can say that we did not cherish such an exciting period in our lives. But that is what this book is all about, seeing it through different eyes, feeling it through different hearts. I thank God I was singled out to be part of this history in the profession I chose, or did it choose me? I sure was in the right place at the right time. I have two lovely daughters, Lisa and Adriana. They still ask me about *WSS* or will sit and watch it with me. I've even heard from some relatives living in Italy I never knew I had.

I learned so much from watching all those that I worked for and with. My experience in front of the camera sure helped my work behind the camera. Some of us get together for dinners and recall the stories, told from different points of view; it is the best of times. The energy in the room when we are having a reunion dinner is incredible, and as many times as these stories get told, we still enjoy them. You always hear, "I didn't know that" or "That is not the way I remember it." I know for me, I was living the dream, making *WSS* into a film. We were all a part of something that will live forever—history if you will. It was never just a job. It was a way of life. – Action

Tony and daughter Lisa

"Snowboy"/Jet — Bert Michaels

ON WEST 44TH Street, there was a rehearsal hall called "Variety Arts" where a lot of Broadway productions rehearsed and auditioned. When in New York, I would work on my club act material there. I became friends with Phil and Toni who ran and owned the Business. One morning, I came by and Phil asked if I wanted to go to a gypsy run through of West Side Story, before its out of town try out. He gave me a pass, and I ran over and got a seat in the balcony at the Broadway Theatre. Jerry came on stage and said that there are no costumes, lighting or scenery and Betty Walberg was the entire orchestra, boy was she ever. His only other comment was that when we saw Tony and Maria on stage left, that that was where a balcony would be. Otherwise, that is all that there was and for us to enjoy ourselves. He walked off stage right and the gang stalked on and moved together settling against a wire fence. The snaps began. The music began and the excitement exploded. Never did I ever see such a bombardment of excitement burst upon a stage with an instantaneously visceral response engulfing the audience. Each successive number was a spontaneous explosion bringing the audience to their feet. We all stood as one by sheer shared impulse. I'd never had such an experience in a theatre before. The cast was magnificent. When

Tony ended the last piercing perfect pinpoint note of "Something's Coming" atop a ladder, his arm reaching for the sky we all went ballistic. The deafening applause was instant and immediate.

Afterwards, I went on my way ecstatic, never imagining that I would be a part, however small, of this magnificent piece of theatre, let alone be in its transition to the screen. I was just a night club comedy tap dance act, but ended up being one of the very few selected who had never done the show. I am still amazed today, some 50 years later, to see myself up there, with those incredibly gifted chosen artists, who became friends and an important part of my life. But, I too was chosen by Jerry. How, I don't know. He must have seen something unique in me during my audition. I am so very grateful.

I had just left the national tour of *The Music Man*, in Chicago, when in New York at an all night party somebody said, "Jerry Robbins is giving his last audition for *West Side Story*.

"Let's go," I said. So, still fully in party mode, I immediately went home, grabbed my dance shoes and clothes, which were a pair of beat-up blue jeans and a T-shirt, and off I went to the Broadway Theatre for the 10 am audition. With the exception of *The Music Man* tour, I played mostly nightclubs in Miami Beach, so I really had no idea who Jerome Robbins was. If ignorance is bliss, I must have been ecstatic. The audition was an amazing master class. I ended up downstage left opposite Jaime Rogers, a formidable dancer. We learned a combination that was fast and furious. It was the "Mambo" from "Dance Hall." Jaime and I looked at each other, bristled and challenged each other and the material. It was exciting. Next, we learned the "Scherzo," a dream sequence in the stage production that was cut from the film to allow them to financially shoot in New York. I was relegated to the "B" group, which I presumed meant that I did not impress anyone after the "Scherzo's" famous circle count in fives. Five against four, then three against five—five itched my teeth. Thank God the filming of the "Scherzo" was scrapped.

We "possible Jets" learned the big chorus from "Cool" and I nailed it, especially the knee spins and the slow sink at the end. We did it again and again. Tommy Abbott came over to me and told me that Jerry said I didn't have to do it when he noticed I didn't have knee-pads on. I told him I was OK. I would do it. I suppose that impressed Jerry because at the end of that five-hour audition, I was asked to the call back. Hello, "A" group! I don't remember what happened next.

We started at 10 am and stopped at 3 or 4 pm. By that time I was sober and wondering what had I just done to myself? Out of the estimated four hundred male dancers auditioning that morning, I was later told only forty of us were called back to the CBS Studios. It was whittled down again to twenty and again my knee spins and slide down, I think, got me a final camera read. This was at a studio above Schraft's on 57th Street. I had a bad cold and a case of almost laryngitis that day, and I could hardly get my lines out. They sounded as strange as I felt. We were all standing in a line when Jerry walked in. Bob Wise went over to him and we were seperated into groups in front of a camera. Bob Wise was on one side of the camera and Jerry was on the other feeding lines to several of us gathered in a tight group in front of them. "Not even garbage?" I remember gurgling out several times.

We were then told to go home and we would hear from them later. I headed to the door when Jerry caught up with me. He turned me around to face him and gently cupped my face in his hands and quietly asked me if I was going to be alright. I told him that I was going home, soak in a hot tub until I wrinkled and sleep for a week. He nodded OK. I turned away and walked home. It was the first and only time I ever witnessed any personal concern for anyone from him. I suppose he felt that he had to keep a distance from us to remain in control. I think he was right. He rightfully exercised total dictatorial control.

The phone ringing woke me the next morning. It was Jerry asking me if I wanted to do the film. "Yes! Thank you," I croaked, and immediately went back to sleep. I caught the plane to LA with Harvey

Evans a week or so later. I introduced him to scotch, and we have been friends ever since. We occasionally work together.

In 2006 we appeared together in the film *Enchanted*. We reprised our roles on the 2008 Oscars. Later in the year we appeared at Town Hall in New York doing "I Won't Grow Up" from *Peter Pan* celebrating the Musicals of '54. Not shabby for two seniors. Don Percassi, another friend and gypsy of note, joined us as a third theatre elder statesman. Does 50 years go by fast!**The Year of Filming** was filled with so many incidences, it's hard to pick out any one particular moment. As with all remembrances, everyone has a slightly differing version. Here are some of mine.

(1) An Important Incident

JERRY CHOREOGRAPHED A pastiche of many versions of the basketball sequence where the basketball ended up in Bernardo's hands. We counted 19 variations or so. They were combinations of 8 bars of version 4 and the last 6 bars of version 14, etc., etc. We all did one version after the other by rote until he was satisfied and we were numb. He finally settled on one, which was comprised of several different sections of each of the variations we had rehearsed. Then he said, "That's it!"

What was it? We rehearsed "the final" version several more times. We all girded ourselves to concentrate and do it right the first time for the camera and not incur Jerry's growling "back to square one."

As we got into position just before "Action!" was called, Jerry quickly said, "Reverse it!" and "Action!" was called. We did it by sheer panic and no one said anything afterwards, but we all thought we knew that we probably couldn't remember it to be able to do it again unless by muscle memory. So, I just blanked out and let my body do it. We did do several more takes, but again, the utter panic of trying to do it on the opposite side pushed the emotional intensity of the sequence to where Jerry wanted. Or, was he going to change it back to his first choice just before "Action" was called this time?

Emotional intensity gripped everyone, and it showed on the film. This was an Actors Studio trick, and it worked. I believe that the first take was the one eventually used. He used this type of pressure all through the filming.

(2) The Fickle Finger Points That A-way

DURING THE REHEARSAL for "Cool," my dance partner was a sweet, talented young dancer. Her name was Taffy Paul. Her mother was nearby because she was still underage—that in itself wasn't unusual. Then after a few weeks, they suddenly were gone. Was it something I said? No! I found out that they, the studio, didn't want to pay for an on-set teacher so, bye-bye Taffy. She and her mom had been very friendly and then, gone. Never to be heard from again, that is until the next year, when she was starring in the film *Experiment In Terror* with Harvey Evans, my friend and fellow Jet, as her boyfriend. Now my baby, Taffy Paul, was transformed into Stefanie Powers, the quickly emerging film star. She was fired and became a "star," and we "principal" players wafted into the ether as character actors do. I'm not complaining (yes, I am!), but this has happened, to not only me a number of times, but to many others. The axiom of "Get fired and become famous" would hold true.

(3) Star Hierarchy Underlined

THE FIRST FEW days at the Goldwyn Studios, we all were in a studio rehearsal hall. It was a Quonset hut type of structure. We were thrilled to be there but it was hot and muggy inside, and it was almost impossible to do a ballet barre first thing in the morning. On our second or third day we kept asking for AC, and were dismissed with, "Sure! Later!" Then in came Natalie. She was introduced to us in a group. She asked how we could work in this heat. We told her "they" said they'd get around to putting AC in later.

She turned around, walked over to the phone, called the office, and said, very businesslike, "This is Natalie."

She didn't even use her last name, just Natalie.

"I want air conditioners in the rehearsal hall, a table with coffee, some snacks, and cold water!"

We all looked astonished. She then hung up the phone, walked back to us, and sweetly continued the conversation as if nothing out of the ordinary had happened.

Something out of the ordinary did happen, for us. "They", the office, knew who was on the phone because right after lunch, there were ACs in the windows and we were cool. There were snacks, water, and coffee on a covered table. Now, not only "they" knew who she was, but so did we. Everyone seems to remember this somewhat differently, but I remember a version of all of us getting down on our hands and knees praising her. She was ecstatic and we were grateful. She admired who we were and was one of us now. It stayed that way. She was always sweet and respectful towards us New York performers. This lesson in star power was to be seen still again.

(4) Another STAR Power Lesson Demonstrated

HOWARD JEFFREY, JERRY'S official assistant, at one point, when we were rehearsing the schoolyard sequence in the rehearsal hall, got pissed that we weren't doing something good enough and started to chew us out at the top of his voice, including Russ Tamblyn. Mistake! Big mistake! (#9 on the film reference page.)

Russ suddenly bolted to his feet and in a strong loud clear voice that brought everyone's attention up front, he stalked over to Howard and boomed: "I am a star! I am a goddamn star! And if you ever speak to me, or any of us like that again, I will personally come over and kick your ass all over the studio and run you out of this town. Do you understand that? Do you understand that?"

Deafening silence prevailed. A studio full of production personnel and crew and nobody moved or spoke. We were all shocked. Was this Russ? Just-one-of-the-guys Russ? No, it wasn't! Howard deflated and started stammering trying to placate Russ. Russ stared him into silence.

Then, looking over the entire hall full of people, he again said to Howard, "Don't you ever speak to me like that again!"

He stared defiantly at Howard, who stood there humiliated. No one said a thing! He walked back to where we were sitting with mouths still agape. Russ stared around the room surveying the set, turned around, winked at us, smiled, and sat down, then defiantly looked back at everyone with his "dead face" stare, leaving no doubt who or what he was. We butched up! Yeah, Russ! Yeah, Jets! Jets! Jets! Jets!

What was interesting to note was that Jerry was among that group and saw the whole thing, but he never said a word. I don't know if he just didn't want to confront Russ—that may have been in the mix but I have recently read that Jerry had studied at the Actors Studio and was a fan of The Method Acting Technique. If he wanted to strengthen Riff (Russ) as our leader, then what better way than to conspire to have a real live public incident imbue that kind of "Leader Image" punched into the forefront of our consciences? This, of course, underlined Russ as our leader and protector. If this was the case, he didn't let poor Howard in on it. Nasty! Jerry, you crafty manipulator. He pulled the same Actors Studio trick later.

(5) Later is Now.

WE WERE REHEARSING the "War Council" when Lt. Shrank was to come in. We were sitting around easily talking when Jerry suddenly exploded and yelled at us, "Hey, smart ass!" We all froze! He then said, "That's what I want you to feel when Shrank walks in."

He made his point again. He always did. Our anxiety dropped, but we all felt that lack of ominous intensity when he wasn't there, and I think the film suffered later on for the lack of his driving presence. I thought about this after the tongue-lashing we got from Jerry on a particular Friday.

6) A Much Bigger Biggie!

ONCE WHEN WE Jets weren't doing our ballet barre seriously enough, Howard ran to Jerry who was with the Sharks on the roof-top set finishing up filming "America." We, the Jets, he bleated, were misbehaving…. Again, Jerry charged into the rehearsal studio, where we were attempting to warm up after the brutal six or more weeks of filming "Cool." Our kneepads were bloody, our knees scabby, and our bodies were aching. Anytime we did a plié the scabs and blisters would break, and bleed. We were physically and emotionally beat. We eventually burned our kneepads in a wastebasket on Jerry's front door, but that's another fragment of a story.

Jerry, raging, stormed up and down the line of us face-to-face growling, "Just because you have your faces on some film don't think that you can't be replaced! Anyone can be replaced!" he yelled. "Anyone can be replaced!" again and again, he growled at each one of us.

He then stormed out back to the Sharks. We all just stood there and thought, "What was that?" What it was, was that he was right. That was a Friday.

The next Monday at lunch break right after the first set of takes, at which Jerry was conspicuously absent, which was a relief, Russ called us over to him in the "Drugstore" set.

"Jerry was absolutely right. Anyone can be replaced!" he said. "Jerry was 'replaced' last Friday."

We were all stunned. We surmised that the studio had waited for him to finish filming the last big production number, "America," and then, with the exception of the "Dance Hall," which was already fully rehearsed, fired him. Two cast members, Tony Mordente and Tommy Abbott, as dance advisors, would oversee the "Dance Hall." Jerry was fired and won two Oscars, one for co-direction and one for choreography! It was too late for us to be "replaced." We just kept on wafting. Think! We coulda' been contenders. Well, maybe not!

Here are a couple of other incidents that deserve mentioning:

(1) A Slippery Slope to Fame

DURING THE REHEARSAL for "Officer Krupke," all the characters' positioning was open to improvisation with the exception of mine (the Judge), and a couple of other specifics that had been sketched out from earlier rehearsals. I was set in the window as the Judge. I decided to put on my coat backwards, and grabbed the rolled newspaper as my gavel. That worked well for a couple of rehearsals, then I spotted an aerosol can of shaving cream. At the next take, not telling anyone what I was going to try, during the very quick musical transitions between characters, I quickly sprayed on a white foam beard and mustache and slid myself onto the window ledge. The takes from everyone, including Mr. Wise, were total shock. It was just what I wanted. They let me go a bit until I spun upside down and the foam flew off in every direction. Everyone near got spritzed and that was the end of that. I wonder if there are any shots of that in existence. Mr. Wise said he wished that there had been a way to keep it intact and adhered, but there wasn't any time to experiment.

(2) A Grown Man Could Cry

IN REHEARSAL IN the schoolyard fight sequence, Nick Navarro came at me. I hid a very large rubber monkey wrench behind my back. When he was right on top of me, I swung it hard over his shoulder. He didn't know it was made of rubber. The monkey wrench bent over his shoulder like a wet noodle. He stopped dead in his tracks and just froze like a statue. I immediately carried him over my shoulder to another part of the set. After that rehearsal the wrench and most props were cut from this sequence. But I'll never forget the panicked look on Nick's face. The Jets and Sharks did have a special relationship, i.e.: "Let's not hurt each other. It's a movie and we may be dating later." In a few cases we did.

(3) It All Comes Home.

A GREAT BIG bunch of a lot of unexpected things can happen in 26 years when this incident happened. I got a phone call from my 10-year-old son asking me if I could pick him up after school. It was an all boys' school that cost a bunch of bucks and promoted exclusivity. That he would ask such a request of his father brought me to ask if anything was wrong.

My dear son, my independent taciturn boy, very seldom shared anything that might put him in a dependent position. He would never have asked me to be around his classmates. I didn't feel bad about that. Most preteens start to distance themselves from their parents. This turns into full rejection and disgust when the hormones derange your angels. They become embarrassed, no matter who their parents are and what their positions.

"Is anything wrong?" I asked.

"No!" came back the very calm response.

In fact, he sounded on the smug and confident side. How strange. So, I said I would pick him up. I waited outside on the sidewalk. He came out followed by more than a few friends greeting me with excited waves and "Hi, Mr. Michaels." I waved back and tried to look casual and adopted an unassuming attitude.

My boy said, "Hi Dad!" and accepted my hand on his shoulder. He looked back smugly, smiled, and waved good-bye at his classmates.

As we walked up the street I asked, "What was that?"

He told me that their class had been studying Shakespeare.

"Oh," I said, knowing what was coming.

First they studied the play *Romeo and Juliet* followed by seeing the Zefferelli film and today, *West Side Story*.

At which he said, "That Jet is my dad."

Of course, he got the usual "Oh Yeah's!" Even by the teacher, which then prompted the call to me. Vindication and reflected glory of some sort. He was so proud of me and me of him for claiming me for the first time. Thank you, *WSS*.

(4) Mom and Dad

MOTHER AND DAD connections connect us all; this time with mine only twenty years earlier.

In the summer of 1960 when I was filming *West Side Story* in New York, where Lincoln Center would soon be erected after we finished using the facades of the soon-to-be torn down buildings, my parents, Sam and Evie, showed up at the barriers on Broadway where the public could watch. They did not tell me they were coming.

An AD came over to me on a break and told me where they were. I ran over on the first break and we had very quick hugs and hellos. They were smiling and looked wonderful. It was an animated short conversation. I remember having to quickly run back to the filming. I can only imagine them beaming and telling the other people around them that I was their son. I don't recall if I asked them where they were staying or if we had dinner after the shoot or if we met afterwards or not; I hope we did. But it does give me a disquieting sense of comfort that because of living in LA, I didn't get to see them often. But that they could go to the movie and see me is now of comfort to me. I can imagine that when they did go, they couldn't help informing those seated around them that I was their son.

Gypsy was also out soon after *West Side*. I can visualize them sitting there and saying "Hello, my son" to me as they watched. How proud they must have been. What, regrettably, I never really told them and I only hope that somehow they knew, was how proud I was of them. How very much I owe them. Love you, Sam and Evie…Mom and Dad.

(5) Another Lincoln Center Tie

PAT AND I were on the #1 subway going uptown when we stopped at the 66th Street Station that is also the Lincoln Center Station when a group of young kids jammed into the car. I didn't pay much attention until Pat, who was sitting on the seat next to the door, called me over. The kids were rowdy but not threatening.

Pat told me that they were saying that all the Jets were fags. The Jets? Obviously they were students of the theatre department of the school located near the Center.

"I understand that you said all the Jets were fags," I said to one of the loudest kids.

He was shocked and for a moment didn't know what to say or do. He stammered and said that they, the Jets, all do ballet.

"Don't you take ballet?" I asked.

"Well, yes," he said.

"Isn't it hard?" I said.

He became confused at this old man's aggressively confrontational questioning.

Again, "Yes!"

After looking at his confused classmates, he looked at me confused. I then pointed to Pat seated directly to his left.

"That's my wife and I have two children and three grandchildren. I'm not a fag and I was a Jet," I said.

He looked really confused and shaken and said, "You were a Jet?"

"Well, I did the film," I replied.

He stared at me hard for only a moment, trying to figure it out.

"The movie?" he said. Then almost immediately he yelled at the top of his lungs, "SNOWBOY!" then charged me and grabbed me in a bear hug. He laughed and screamed, "I can't believe it, Snowboy."

All of his classmates laughed good-naturedly and started to shake my hand. They all recognized me. I still can't figure out how. He was all of 16 and yet he recognized me as I once was. Amazing!

I said that I thought that they must be doing a production of *West Side* at their school. He quickly started to ask me if I wanted to come see it. But his friends said that they might not have any tickets. I quickly thanked them but begged out, even though it might be wonderful. I think they were relieved. So was I.

The train came to our stop, and as we walked out the door I looked back and said, "Be cool. You never know who is standing next to you."

We waved and walked to the exit as they stared out the windows at us. I can only imagine the stories they told the rest of their production. It's New York!

I am constantly surprised at the recognition I get even after all these years. I don't look anything like that young man, not remotely do I resemble him. Yet, somehow year after year I get recognized under all manner of conditions and variety of places. I feel somehow him forever. Like my film-mates, I know we all are in the same position, especially in places where films are consistently considered treasures. Just as valid as any ancient artifact, and there we are and will be for the foreseeable future. As my in laws said, I am immortal.

(6) At the New Jersey Mall

PAT AND I were shopping at the grand mall, where Route 4 and Route 17 cross. At this moment I was on the second floor by the escalators while Pat went wandering off on the level shopping. That afternoon there were children's choirs singing on the first floor, and at the top of the escalators where I was at there was a young boy, about fourteen or so, singing his heart out accompanied by a boom box operated, I assume, by his mom. He was doing noted show tunes, some from *Hair Spray* and other current productions. He was very good.

While I was watching him, I noticed out of the periphery of my eye two middle-aged women. They appeared to be circling me. No! I'm just imagining it. No! No, I'm not. Finally, they cautiously approached me from a distance of eight or ten feet.

"Excuse us," said one of them. "Do you work in the movies?"

"On occasion," I said.

To which they excitedly got closer. "*West Side Story*?" they asked.

What? I thought. How in the world did they see that? They then said, again to my astonishment, "Snowboy?"

Again I said, "Yes!"

After which they charged right up to me.

"We thought we recognized you."

"How?" I asked. "That's forty-seven years ago."

"We would know you any place. We have seen the film over and over again since we were little girls."

Little girls? Little girls?????? I was 23 when we shot the movie. And they were little girls! But still.

"I don't think that I look anything like that young boy," I said.

"We'd recognize you anytime," they said with excitement.

How? I still don't know. They've watched the movie since they were little girls! Aggaa! We shook hands, then hugged, and off they went looking back a couple of times. Little girls? Middle-aged women. Who am I? How old? It seems I'm one of a very few in a position that gets this kind of being caught forever 23 looking 16 being 73. Wow! Every time I look in the mirror shaving this strange old man, I wonder where am I? I must have a beard down to my ankles by now. I can't imagine me as I was then, but they said different. Yagotta' believe.

(7) The FRENCH Connection

PAT AND I had been married a short time and were on our way to half-hour. Which is -show talk for the time performers are expected to sign in at the stage door so the company would know you're there to prepare for the performance. Suddenly, I blurted out that we were going to Paris, France. Pat looked at me, astonished. We had only been married a year or so and working in our first Broadway show, *Baker Street*. We gave our notice the very next week.

Tommy Panko, who had been the assistant choreographer to Onna White on *Music Man*, called us and was doing a show by the creator of *La Plume de Ma Tante*, a past big Broadway hit, and was now going to bring to Broadway his new European hit, *La Grosse Valise*.

The hitch was that we would have to rehearse in Paris, where he and his wife were playing in a production of *La Plume*. Tommy would bring the dancers from New York. The rest of the cast would be comprised of French and English actors. Did I mention we would be in Paris? So off we went. We stayed on New York time the entire time we were there. What has this to do with *West Side Story*? This! On one of the days we had off, we passed a movie theatre that was playing *West Side*. Was the dialogue in French or subtitled? We had to know. We bought tickets, and while we were being shown our seats, the usher recognized me and almost dropped her flashlight. I put my finger to my lips in the universally understood gesture of secrecy. She smiled and seated us.

The audience flew into wild applause at the opening fly over, and it didn't stop there. Neither Pat nor I can recall if it was subtitled or dubbed. The dramatic effect upon the audience was emotionally potent. They responded the same as an American audience would, as if it were playing in the States in English. They reacted as if they knew every line and song. I do remember that the songs were in our voices. The universality of the film attests to the emotional impact of a classic work of art. No matter where it is shown, Paris or Tokyo, it receives tears, laughs, and the realization of the love that we need to have to resolve any situation. What an honor. No one recognized me on the way out. I guess that puts me in my place. Only onscreen is the proper place.

(8)The Non-reel Gang on the Corner of the Street

WE REHEARSED AND filmed the opening sequences, and including dancing on the school playground and the adjoining street. It was a playground on 110th Street. We took over the street with trucks, film trucks, and all the equipment that goes along with a major film endeavor. The one thing that in that point of time was not of major concern was safety and security. We had some real cops and perhaps some professional security. But it was someone with smarts that hired the local kids to stand around and see that everything was OK. At that time no one referred to anyone that they were a gang. We had a gang of real JDs to guard a couple of reel JD gangs.

We were aware, only somewhat, that we were being watched with looks of "What is that?" as we did our AM ballet barre hanging onto a street railing. We also were kinda aware of them when we rehearsed. To put it mildly, we were more terrified of Jerry than any group of JDs.

The shoot proceeded and we sweated and worked very hard on the cement of the playground and the street with very intricate choreography that strongly resembled fighting and anger. It must have looked real because we only got respect from any of the occasional words we had with the kids except towards the end of the fight sequence.

One of the larger-muscled kids came over to I think it was David Bean—and he asked, "How did we learn to do that?" David assumed that he meant the double air turns and arm moves that resembled fighting, but was put to music. It now resembles Kung Fu moves, but back then it did look strange and threatening. David told him it was the warm-up ballet barre that we all did every morning before we rehearsed or shot a sequence.

The hulking kid paused and then quietly asked where he could learn to do that. He wanted to see if he could move like us. That was respect that made us relax. I don't think he realized what he was asking. We should have told him to ask Jerry. Can you picture that? I wonder what that conversation would have brought to the shoot. No one dared laugh or make fun of it. Wouldn't it be wild if he did and joined the ABT whether or not they liked it? This unlikely scenario did happen in real life when a JD that I taught dance to fell so in love with it, that the violence in his life disappeared. His dancing became so good that after graduating high school, he went to Denmark, auditioned, and joined the *Royal Danish Ballet*, eventually becoming a principal dancer.

(9) Heavyweights

DURING THE EXPERIMENTAL filming in L.A., Tucker Smith followed the new trends in everything. One of the newest ideas coming into prominence was the miniaturizing and slimming of everything. This was reflected in his acquisition of a very new, thin, expensive attaché case. During the breaks between takes, Tucker quickly went to a chair where his new attaché was placed, and carefully picked it up and put it on his lap. He opened it and took out a pad. Then he closed the case, placed the pad on top of it, and began to write. When "places" was called, he just as precisely reversed the process and returned to his place all butched up and continued the scene.

After observing this action over the next several times, David Winters, who happened not to be in that scene, slid over to where the case was. At the same time, Tony Mordente had walked over to where the camera crane was stationed. Sitting on the back of the crane were stacks of very slim weights that were used to counterbalance the weight of the camera and the operator as well as the directors. These weights were, by necessity, very slim but very heavy. I think that each of them weighed around 40 pounds, but were only a few inches thick and long. Tony nonchalantly, one at a time, picked up six or so of these weights, and struggling walked them over to David and the attaché case. David and Tony quickly placed them into the case after removing the pad and papers. I think all six of them weighed about 240 lbs. They then tilted the case back in its original position. We all saw this but no one said anything. We just watched as Tucker walked primly back to his chair and fashionable case.

He swiftly walked over to seat himself on the chair while reaching over and slipped his fingers under the case's handle. As he tried to pick it up, his legs flew up in the air as his body stayed parallel to the floor. The look of terror and shock burst over his face. His jaw dropped. He stepped back in abject horror, incomprehensibly not believing what had happened. He tried to pick it up again and couldn't move it. He backed off just looking at the case. He stepped back in disbelief until he looked at all of us now exploding in laughter.

Still wary, he slowly walked and carefully laid the case on its side, opened it and stepped back in disbelief at the contents. And then, surveying the landscape of laughing faces and then applause, he took out the weights one by one with Tony and David coming over to help.

To Tucker's credit he started to laugh too. He took a bow and then sat down prim and proper, picked up his papers, and continued writing as if nothing had happened. He, indeed, was cool.

(10) Who'da Believed It?

I MAY HAVE this tale jumbled but if I do my version is funnier. As I remember being told, Tony Mordente and Tommy Abbott were driving across the country from New York to LA for the filming in a Jaguar, when somewhere in the hinterlands they were stopped by a highway trooper. Now looking like teenage hoodlums having stolen such an expensive car, they were about to be tossed into jail. They tried to explain that they were ballet dancers on their way to shoot a movie about teenage hoodlums. The trooper, sizing them up, said, "Yeah, show me." And they did. There on the highway, they performed the "Blue Bird" variation complete with all the ballet flourishes while accompanying themselves singing the score.

Can you imagine the sight of two side-burn-looking "hoods," tough and scruffy, whipping off this show, obviously classic ballet variation? I told you my version is funnier. He let them go…quickly, Tony will probably have the accurate version in his chapter. It's the stuff sitcoms are made of. I wonder if that trooper ever saw *West Side* and recognized them.

Here are some other remembrances of note:

(1) Book by Its' Coveralls

IN THE PLAYGROUND sequence when we ran up the seesaw, the expressions on many of our faces was from the fear of falling off in front of Jerry rather than that of aggressive teen behavior. When it was time to do my solo from the Jet Song as I climbed up the fence during a rehearsal Jerry told me not to be Al Jolson. He also shook us up by replacing me on the teeter totters with Eliot for one rehearsal. I figured he wanted to relegate me to a minor position as a punishment. Maybe I did Al Jolson. He looked at it, then immediately put me back in the front after the rehearsal. We all were on edge as to what he would do next and to whom. That pushed the anxiety up several notches, at least for me.

(2) Modern art we were....street-level living graffiti.

AS WE EMERGED from the sequence where we were chasing some Sharks under a building sidewalk construction, we were met by some Sharks on top of the bridge pouring buckets of yellow paint on us. It took seven or eight takes, after which we were transferred to a nearby hotel to wash off, put on clean costumes, and do it again. After the fifth or sixth time the hotel refused to rent us the room, so the next take would be the final take. On top of the liquid being sticky, it also smelled terrible. Tony likened it to the smell of his daughter's baby vomit. On one of many takes, probably the fourth or fifth, Tony yelled immediately after we got doused, "They've finally added a mystery ingredient because I'm beginning to like it."

I broke up, thinking it was over. It wasn't! You can see me laughing on the print. A still photographer on the shoot decided that I looked like "Le Spectre de la Rose" and was going to enter his shot of me in a contest. He was a photographer of some note but it never turned up. I will try to dig up his name.

(3) Safe!

WHEN WE WERE rehearsing the sequence after Tony got shot on the playground, they placed a 4-inch-thick 4 x 6 green mat for Natalie to run to and slide on when she reached Tony's body. It worked so well that they forgot to remove it for the take and there it is. For a split-moment it is visible at the bottom of the screen. Apparently unnoticed until too late, and then who cares? I recently saw a very large still with Bob Wise kneeling beside them prominently displayed in the entrance hallway of the Directors Guild Theatre on 57th Street here in New York.

(4) Sergeant Pooper and His Band of Merry Men

RUSS TOLD US about being a recognized "Star" when he was drafted. The sergeant told him, in front of everyone, that he lived in make-believe land. But now this was real life—real and dangerous. He would not be given any special treatment, movie star or not! Russ being the everyday guy, was very "Yes, sir!" Then after being officially put in his place in non-make-believe land, his group was instructed to charge up the hill following the butch drill instructor, who roused all to follow his call to battle and yell, "Kill!" "Kill!" while stabbing the hillside with the bayonets on their rifles. Kill the daisies! Terrifying! Picture it! Russ, crazed and foaming at the mouth, yelling, "Kill the daisies!" I can only guess how he endeared himself to that DI with an Oscar-worthy performance.

(5) We Could'a Been Chumps.

DURING THE DANCE rehearsal on the set of the "Dance Hall," several large groups of teenage-looking extras were brought in to dress the set. They were costumed in non-descript green and non-descript other shades of bland. They were brought in to look as if there were other kids in the school beside Jets and Sharks, I guess. They blended into the background while we rehearsed the scene and the choreography. Then a moment of excitement arose, for me! At a point early on, this very pretty blond girl came over to me. She appeared not to be well. She was sort of slightly trembling and I thought, She thinks I'm a movie star. Oh boy, I'll be cool. An autograph? An invitation to share some inside stories on "our" filming? She speaks!

"Hi!" says she in a blond-girl, vulnerable voice.

Good start, I'm thinking.

She's shaking a bit and lowers her lids as she asks, "Do you know where I can get something to help?"—now looking into my eyes in earnest. "Something to help, I just need a little something."

"If you need something the nurse's office is in the next building," I said, concerned.

She looked at me strangely and so I reiterated.

"Yeah, she must have something to help you calm down. You don't want to lose the shoot," I said.

"No, I mean I really need something to help me a little to get straight. Just enough. Can you help me out?"

Whaaaaaaat? No longer was she a blond beauty, but a ticking bomb. It suddenly dawned on me she was asking me for drugs. I looked at her shocked and said, "Boy, are you in the wrong place. There ain't anyone here that's into that. Do you think we could do what we do consistently and be on that junk? Forget it, lady! Look at us. We are artistic, highly tuned athletes, and if I knew anyone here into that I'd call the cops myself after I beat the crap out of them. You better get out of here before anyone spots you."

I turned away, and trying to move in character, boogied over to some of the Jets and never looked back. I did see her across the set later. She looked very much unsick, and was still cruising the dance floor. I then realized that she was probably a reporter, or worse than that, an undercover nark trying to make a bust on the *West Side* movie set. What a scandal that would have been. New York teen punk dancers on the *WEST SIDE STORY* set shut down after police drug raid. BUSTED! Jerry would have eaten us up alive. I never saw her again on the set. I wonder if she ever approached anyone else. I never heard anyone say anything about it. Maybe she got a hold of…naw! He would have bragged about it, or we would have been playing rock hockey in the county hoosegow. Making little rocks outta' big ones.

(6) To Arms! Two Arms, of Course.

THEY WERE PUTTING the soundtrack together for *Spartacus* on the lot in an adjacent soundstage. During a sequence of the gladiators breaking out of their cells and climbing over the walls, which had lots of yelling, jumping, and tumult, the orchestra under the direction of Johnny Green blasted away the musical accompaniment. It was overwhelming. Several of us snuck in while this recording was going on. We stood in front of the orchestra, our backs against a black wall about forty feet from the conductor's podium, which was raised several feet off the floor.

Johnny asked to do another section again, and they did it even more energetic and full. Boy was it exciting, but not so much as when Johnny asked for the playback. They did, and we were blasted ten feet forward by the sound of the playback. No one warned us that the black wall we were standing in front of was actually giant speakers. We sailed across the floor like wisps of dust. We tried to keep our dignity and pulled ourselves together and sort of strolled out mouthing words like "gotta' get back" and waved to the musicians as we left. When we were outside, we were still mouthing because we couldn't hear anything! It took several minutes before we could hear anything again. This incident did lead to us almost getting thrown off the lot.

(7) Playing Big-Time Chicken

WE WERE SO overtaken by the *Spartacus* craze that whenever we were free off the set, several of us jumped on any of the two-wheel prop moving carts that littered the lot, and we had chariot races careening around the lot with two or three of us pulling the cart as several more stood on the carts yelling, "I'm Spartacus! I'm Spartacus!"

It got so bad that Billy Wilder complained that it was him or us. He would move off the lot. Close down his production if we didn't stop or leave the lot. I guess that Bob Wise calmed him down because we were told in no uncertain terms that we were not Spartacus! We wanted to issue a rumble challenge but somehow were dissuaded. That would have made a story. There will be other versions of this as well. Mine is still funnier.

(8) The Great Sailing Wall

WE ALL STOOD in awe when we walked on the set and saw THE WALL! It was big. We were to enter (Jets or Sharks. Who knew?) on top and then jump down. Several of us (not me) got up there and slid, hung from, and then dropped, etc., to the floor. Then someone just took a running leap, putting one foot several feet up on the wall and then pushing off to grab the top, and pulled himself up onto the top. I think it was Eliot Feld. Then everybody started to take a run at it, and to no one's surprise almost everyone made it up. That is, until Bob Relyea, the AD, came in and put a stop to the fun.

The set came alive with rehearsals, but the temptation to scale the wall remained, and the attempts continued when Relyea or Bob Wise weren't there. Someone imitated Relyea's commands to "Stop that! That's off limits." In fact, the imitations became routine to us so we didn't listen to it, but others did! It was so good that often we mistook it for Relyea.

It came to pass that after the set had been lit one lunch break, Relyea was heard to bark "86 the wall," 86 being the command to get rid of something. The problem was that he wasn't there. Apparently some of the stagehands had not been privy to our antics, and they started to move the wall…off its mark and out of its lighting. We all walked away. After the lunch break when Relyea came in and discovered the wall's new position, he blew up and asked who did it. The stagehands answered, "You did!" Arguing with union stagehands is a lost cause. We all walked back in as they were trying to replace the wall and hoping the lighting was still where Danny Fapp, our award-winning cinematographer, had painstakingly set it. I believe that it took them the remainder of the afternoon to accomplish that. Since Relyea suspected, but couldn't prove, who gave the order, he just had to gird up and tell Bob Wise that there was a minor but costly problem. With nothing to do because the "Rumble" had to be staged on the set, we were relegated to a ballet barre and class—a just punishment. Relyea never found out who imitated him. And that was that.

(9) No Do Re for Meia!

MIDWAY THROUGH THE rehearsal period, Mr. Wise came up to me and wanted me to sing for him, Jerry, and Mr. Tuttle. In the scheme of things we did have some vocal coaching directed by Mr. Tuttle, who was a living caricature of a turtle. We all had to stop from calling him that. He was a sweet, unassuming, middle-aged man who slouched at the keyboard as if he did indeed have a shell on his back. So I went to a small room with an upright. On the way there I met Tucker, who said that he had also been summoned to audition, but for what? They were testing the two of us to dub…Russ. Russ did every rehearsal and sang the number as well as needed. Tucker and I looked at each other in disbelief. Dub Russ? Why?So we sang the part of the Jet Song that Russ sang. I couldn't tell what they were looking for. So you hear Russ mouthing Tucker's voice. Yes, he got it and I am glad. In a moment, I realized that I sang my section right after Russ, so maybe Jerry was protecting me. It would have been too easy to spot and I probably would have lost my section, whereas Tucker sang "Cool" much later on in the movie and it wouldn't be noticeable. I only found out in 2009 that David Bean also sang for the same assignment. They said he sounded too much like Russ. He asked if that wasn't the idea. Tucker may have gotten more money for it. I got "no" and he got "dough." No one including Russ ever mentioned it till years later.

(10) A Face of a Different Color

WE REHEARSED FOR three months or so and did some experimental filming. I guess that they were deciding what film and process to use. When I walked on set one day after we had shot some experimental scenes, Danny Fapp grabbed me and put me in the light of a lamp. He turned my face one way and then the other, and I thought that "they" were deciding if I looked too strange to fit in with the others. But we all looked as strange as I, so I thought maybe I was about to be downgraded or fired. I coulda' been a star. Naw! I finally got the nerve to ask him what was wrong? "I just wasn't aware that your eyes turn a different color in different lighting," he said. My eyes turn different colors? He would just have to be aware of it, and it wasn't a problem. I hoped that wouldn't cut any solos I had. It didn't.

(11) The Dance Jerry Was Afraid Of

WHEN WE DROVE up to the 110th Street playground one early morning, I don't remember how it came about, but when we got off the bus we were told there was a chance of rain but it looked clear now, so get out and get warmed up. Well, devised by Mordente and Winters, we all decided to do a "rain dance." The sky was clear, but as we danced literally out of the blue drops came dancing down onto the playground. We all spoke to the raindrops like they were our children, encouraging them to come to Da Da. The crew just went on as if nothing was happening. Jerry looked at us and looked away until it started to come down like Faust. We kept on dancing. We were ordered back into the bus before our costumes got soaked. The rain stopped. We waited and were then told to come out. We did and it was clear until several of us started to dance again. The rain came down like a flood, we were put back in the bus, and Jerry was stuck on a lifeguard tall deck chair under an umbrella. There is a still shot of that. It stopped again and we were told in no uncertain terms not to do any dancing, unless it was for a rehearsal. When we did rehearse it didn't rain and we said it wasn't the rain dance.

WE GOT GOOD-NATUREDLY laughed at, but the next day we were told to stop when we formed a circle just outside the bus. Now I know everyone will probably have different remembrances of this incident, but whatever version is told, what was is that it did happen. We have stills and film of us doing the rain dance with Jerry sulking under his lifeguard umbrella. Ask Relyea. He has written a book, and although I haven't read it I betcha we are a chapter. A mention?

(12) Another Cameo in *WSS* Catapulted a Career

WHEN THE DANCE at the gym was rehearsing, no one paid much attention to the actor who played Glad Hand. He seemed to be just saying lines and following blocking and direction. No one paid him much attention until "action" for rehearsal was called. Then this unheard-of character exploded into life and added elements that caused us all to laugh at pedestrian lines that we all had heard before. Before, there was nothing but uninspiring lines to push the action. Now all of a sudden we were paying attention and reacting with interplay. His attack was fresh and invigorated the scene with that much-needed push. This continued throughout the scene and pushed the film industry into recognizing this unique talent. *West Side Story* again had birthed the wonderful career of John Astin. Big dividend!

(13) Would this have made a difference?

I HAVE RECENTLY been told that when they were looking for a Tony that the first among stars who were asked was ELVIS! The Colonel declined. He reportedly told Elvis that he could make more money doing his movies than this. ELVIS as Tony. Can you hear him singing "Tonight" with a twang? I'll bet he would also request, er, demand to sing "America." They would probably have found a way for him to do it. Jerry would have risen (?) to the challenge.

(14) 6 Degrees of Cameo

RECENTLY A QUESTION was asked on a TV show, "Whose father was in *West Side Story?*" During the playground sequence we, the Jets, saw Jerry gently put his arm around a young boy, handing him the basketball and giving him directions on how to act intimidated towards us when we strolled up to him. Specific emotional reaction needed in giving it over to Russ. He asked him, "OK?" He nodded. Jerry smiled, and then turning to us across the yard yelled, "JETS!"

This was our cue to rehearse the sequence. We obediently butched up and did the encounter.

After the rehearsal he asked the young boy, "Was that all right?"

The boy demurely nodded yes and again Jerry smiled at him, then turned his attention back to us and dismissingly yelled, "JETS! Back to starting positions."

The boy was not yet Macaulay Culkin's father.

15) After the Fact

I'M NOT SURE how this came about, but someone in the group decided to take "ACTING LESSONS." Most everyone had professional theatre and now film experience, so why did anyone want to spoil our presentation with knowing what we were doing I have no idea. We mostly were now just basking in imagined glory but hey, we're in Hollywood and might be here for the rest of our lives and careers. For some that would be yes, and for the rest reality was unobserved, me included. So, I auditioned for what was rapidly becoming the *West Side* version of "Actors Studio." A renowned actor, Jeff Cory, who was blacklisted and couldn't find work as an actor, was hired by stars to be their personal coach on shoots. He moved into a small Studio City storefront and founded his acting studio. It was cozy with real theatre seats and a stage. A stage! Oh, boy!

He held class most of the time, but his apprentice taught the classes when he was not available. Leonard Nimoy, pre–Mr. Spock, is whom I auditioned for. He was easier for us to reach out to. We soon became family. We took class for the next few years, the West Siders plus a few other wonderful people, but that's another book. Every Saturday morning we had class and coffee afterwards with Lenny— sorry, I learned later he liked being called Leonard, but with us he tolerated Lenny.

He was considerate and wonderful as a teacher. I learned so much from him. We all did. I did see him backstage at *Ulysses* visiting Carolyn Kirsch in her dressing room. But after all these years he remains a strong force in our lives. I used his lessons when I taught. He lives here in NY sometimes. The spread-finger Vulcan hand sign is a Jewish "hi" sign. We're everywhere! Thank you, Leonard, from all of us Westsiders.

(16) Well after the Fact

I DON'T RECALL anyone informing us that we would not be special guests in a reserved section or even bringing up the subject of the Academy Awards, but we, the cast, were never given any information. I think that they were afraid that we might show up on the night, so it was a non-secret. After all the hoopla was done with, we all never spoke about it. We ignored it like they ignored us. After all, as far as I knew, none of us thought about the classic important work we did. We were grateful that we were chosen out of the plethora of incredibly talented artists that were auditioned. BUT, I was aware of the ceremony that was planned. I remember proposing that we all make foot-square cement slabs with our handprints and names imbedded in them and suggesting that we take them to the Grauman's Chinese Theatre, where we would leave them out front. We would pick them up after the Awards, our temporary marks on the famous ground. This proposal was ignored. I suppose our post-adolescent gesture would have been embarrassing. I don't recall the Mirisch Co. or anyone throwing a wrap party. Did I miss that too? No Bob Wise. No Mirisch. Just Relyea telling us, that's it! We're all done. We all quietly went home, I think. I hope we had a rap party. If we did it must have been so wild. I don't remember. Did I have fun?

Today-In 1962 I did Yonkers (unaccredited) in the film *Gypsy* and another film, *Incident in an Alley*. Later, after moving back to New York I was fortunate to do another classic film *Saturday Night Fever*, in which I played Pete, the owner of the dance studio. In 1963 Harvey and I went to a summer stock resident theatre audition at the Masonic Temple on Hollywood Boulevard, where the Jimmy Kimmel show is now shot. Among those auditioning was a beautiful red-headed girl. She was singing, "I'M NOT AT ALL IN LOVE" from *The Pajama Game*.

"She sings like that and is a dancer? Wow!" said Harvey.

"That's the girl I'm going to marry!" I said almost immediately. Patricia was a dancer on the *Red Skelton Show* and had performed in many major television specials, even though she was only 19 at the time. We both did that resident star-featured summer stock theatre in Berkeley. We got married the following summer, and moved to New York in '64. We celebrated our 47th Anniversary this June 2011.

Before we were married we came to New York and auditioned for a major director/choreographer and he was thrilled, he said. We were hired. Come back after your marriage, we were told. When we called from our honeymoon in San Francisco, we were told come on in for a "cast look at" on July 3rd before rehearsals, just so the director could see us all together on stage. We did and without warming up or dance clothes, we were forced into an unexpected dance audition after which, with a group of dancers, we were told, "Thank you! Goodbye." As I was dressing to leave it was related to me by the author of the show, my cousin Sidney, that he was told I wasn't the greatest dancer in the world. All this time, I thought I was. Pat was with me so she also got "Goodbye." Hello Broadway! Quickly dismissed that didn't happen a lot, in fact it was the only time.

Pat, having been on the *Red Skelton Show* and dancing on many major television specials, had pretty much the same professional acceptance that I had. But back then, newly married and now thousands of miles from her home and her television series, we stared at each other. Then my rep came back to the rescue.

George Lee, a great dancer, told me on the street one day that I was being looked for in LA for a new Broadway show here. So we auditioned, already being told that we had the show called *Baker Street*. The choreographer, Lee Becker Theodore, had played Anybodys in the original stage production of *West Side Story*, so *A Baker Street Irregular I became*.

As a team, Pat and I were considered formidable assets. We were a big plus for any show since we were both very strong performers. We could act, sing, and dance and portray characters with emotional impact. When we did audition, it was pretty much by request.

Our next show was *La Grosse Valise*. The story behind it is rather amusing. The #104 bus is the vehicle of choice with most of the Broadway gypsies going to work for half hour at a Broadway theatre. It travels on the upper West Side down Broadway into the theatre district.

On one such day as Pat and I were on our way to a *Baker Street* performance, I suddenly blurted out, "We're going to Paris." Every once in a while I seem to know something before it happens. The next week we were hired to rehearse in Paris for a new show that was coming to Broadway.

On the way over on the airplane, we were given the script. Pat and I looked at each other and quietly said, "Save our money," which we did. This rehearsal became a delayed honeymoon in Paris. The show played one week at the now demolished 54th Street Theatre. The night we closed we put our suitcases into a new Cadillac that we were driving to LA for a car service. We took off for Christmas with Pat's family but when we ended up in LA, I was greeted with a telegram from Onna White telling me to get back to New York to go into *Half A Sixpence*, the Broadway show she had choreographed. I was to replace a friend who was let go because of a broken hand. He had hit a horse. Just when I thought I was out, they pulled me back in.

I had worked for Onna in the first national tour of *The Music Man*, so it wasn't out of the blue I was hired without an audition. One of the major payoffs of being in *West Side Story* is that I very seldom had to do an audition. Everyone figured that if I could be in that classic and work successfully with Jerry Robbins for a year, I could do anything anyone could throw at me, and for the most part, I could.

Pat and I later went on to perform together in the original Broadway productions of *Cabaret*, *Canterbury Tales* and *Mack and Mabel*. Pat did *Superman* solo and other Broadway and Off Broadway shows.

Other credits of mine are *Man of La Mancha, On Your Toes, Half a Sixpence,* and *Ulysses in Night Town,* where I was dressed as a nightmare priest who along with a half-naked Carolyn Kirsch beat the crap out of Tommy Lee Jones. In *Cabaret,* besides being the understudy for Joel Grey's MC (I did get on one ½ times), Pat and I were featured in "The Telephone Dance," where we locked lips kissing for five minutes going up and then down a set of spiral steps on stage left, seemingly without taking a breath. We were featured in the television show *To Tell the Truth* in connection with the "Kiss Dance" section in *Cabaret.* We also performed together in the 1968 Tony Awards in *Cabaret.* I would perform in the Tony Awards again in the 1971 25th Anniversary Show as a consolation prize by the producer because I closed in a Boston production of theirs.

Later, I was Gower Champion's associate choreographer for the show *Sugar.* I performed in *The Gifts of the Magi* twice and directed the Off Broadway shows *Leaves of Grass, Bitter Suite, Romance Is* and *One More Time.* For Jones Beach I choreographed Lucie Arnez's *Annie Get Your Gun.*

I've acted in or choreographed many major television commercials hawking everything from KFC to a new push button telephone, where I was hung on a meat hook for three days only to be slid into slimy sides of beef. On another I was tied in a chair and had to roll over and push the buttons on the phone with my nose. I had to pop my head out of a manhole cover with the lid still on my head and duck as a miniature puppet cop car chase eventually ran over me. I have no pride. It gets more embarrassing so I'll stop. I lie!

My first commercial was for a cereal called Crazy Cow, in which the milk turned to strawberry or chocolate. I was in a cow costume on a farm and on my way to the barn for the shoot, and I had to pass several large free-roaming bulls who stopped grazing and began to follow me. This paid for my daughter's birth. On the *Ball Four* TV series, I played a processor server chasing Ben Davidson, a seriously very large and famous football player of that era. The sight of him running in abject terror from me seemed to amuse everyone. This gig paid for my son's birth. I have most of this television work on video, which will make my children shudder when they rummage through my belongings after I'm gone. HA! HA! No! No! That can't be my daddy, no! I did over 250 major commercials in that period. I have no shame. I've been accused of being an actor, but I soon proved them wrong even though my union affiliations cards say I am (AGVA 1952, AEA 1954, Sag 1960, AFTRA 1964, SSDC 1972).

I was a member of the Blue Ribbon Panel for the Emmys for choreography. During one of the breaks between the viewing of the nominated shows in different categories in an adjacent hallway, Otto Preminger walked up to me and asked me what was that he just saw.

"I'll tell you if you tell me what it was that I just saw," I replied.

We both shrugged and meandered over to our next nominated showcase.

Patti and I choreographed and directed two major IBM Recognition Events, *Pictures of a City* with Ray Bolger and Allegra Kent, and *A Century of Opera* with the *San Francisco Opera Company* the following year. Choreographing for Ray Bolger was a challenge, a delight, and a privilege. It almost didn't come off.

"I can't go on," Ray said to me a few minutes before he was to be introduced.

What!!!!! "My shoelace is broken."

He was serious. I saw a musician. I went over to him, made him sit down, and to his open-mouth astonishment I removed his shoelace, walked back over to Ray, put it on, and he, not saying a word, went on and stopped the show. Saved by a shoelace. If that ain't show business I don't know what is.

Also as a team we choreographed *Dorothy Parker's Big Blond* with John Lithgow and Sally Kellerman for public television. I did an acting cameo in it when an actor didn't show up. Neither John Lithgow nor Sally Kellerman knew how to tango, and they were both supposed to be hot stuff. So Pat and I were hired to teach them. I was a good dancer on my own, but I am a lousy ballroom dancer. Pat is great. But we weren't going to let a little thing like that stop us from taking a job. Pat's mom, Mattie Ree, had taught ballroom dancing when she was a young woman in LA. So she taught me the tango and fox trot the night before we had to work with the stars. I am a great faker. John learned quickly and worked well with Pat. Sally was another story. Movement is difficult for her. But Sally got so confident and comfortable with me that she asked if I could dance with her instead of John, and they could just shoot her over my shoulder while John said his lines. He said that would be OK if they could do the same with Pat and him. The director's answer was "No!" We noticed that no matter what I did Sally looked great, but it didn't matter; she could never master the choreography. When it came to the actual shoot, Pat and I were on our knees with the camera at waist level. Pat holding Sally's hips as I held John's, guiding them through the movements all the while scurrying on our knees during the close-up shots. They seemed to be sailing across the ballroom floor during the scene. Everyone had to hold back from laughing out loud and spoiling the shot. I did get to partner Sally when an actor didn't show up and I was volunteered to step in. We did look great.

On an academic side, from 1971 to 2004 we taught theater and dance at a Performing Arts High School, where I was the Theater Department Coordinator.

In 1984 Pat and I started a special events company, Jhada Productions, which produces private and corporate events. Some of our sterling clients are PNP Paribas, Pfizer Pharmaceuticals, Tishman Construction and Reality Company, for whom we opened the entire 42nd Street E-Walk complex and did their company holiday party in the New Amsterdam Theatre, prior to *The Lion King* opening. For Tishman, we also produced the ground breaking for their Times Square Westin Hotel. The first ten years in business, we did two to four Bar and Bat Mitzvahs a weekend and then taught school during the week. It was a killer schedule.

For Lowes Movie Theatres, (now Regal) we produced the grand opening of their 42nd Street E-Walk Complex with the then Governor Pataki officiating. The event ended with a fifty-girl, Rockette-like kick line dancing on the sidewalk to a medley of "Hollywood and 42nd Street." This was preceded by a duet from *Rent* by its' two male leads. The event ended with a street-drenching confetti shower covering the corner of 8th Avenue and 42nd Street.

Since 1991 we have produced over 121 major film premieres. Many for Universal Pictures, IE: *American Gangster, Mamma Mia, Frost/Nixon, It's Complicated, The Green Zone,* and New York's biggest premiere to date for *King Kong.*

We also produced the *Friends and Family* private screenings for IMAX, which have included the *Harry Potter* series, the *Spiderman* series, *Batman* series, as well as the New York Premiere of *Polar Express* for Warner Bros.

Pat and I have two grown children, neither of which is in the business. Kristin did belong to a touring ballet company and a young person's acting company when she was in her teens. During this time she joined Actor's Equity Association. She performed in our company during her early teens and twenties but stopped upon her graduation from Barnard College, when she started working on her PhD in Psychology. Today she has two masters and a doctorate. Along with her husband Dr. Paul Marston she has given us three delightful granddaughters and a beautiful grandson. Oh, joy!

Our son Kadyn, after graduating from Hobart College, joined the Navy. He is now a retired Lt. Commander in the US Navy and works in the defense industry. We are so proud to have a son that is a veteran. He has a great love and empathy for the theatre and film, and I wouldn't be surprised to see him as a theatrical or film producer one day. Both of our children bring to us a sense of sanity and continuity, making our lives joyous. In conclusion, I want to add a shout out to a wonderful woman who is a devotee of the *WSS* film and is our #1 fan, Ms. Maggie Adams. The letter below refers to a time in '09 when Bobby Banas was visiting New York and Bean, Harvey, and I all got together. Maggie was in New York at the same time, but unfortunately we couldn't get together with her.

Dear Maggie,

Banas, Bean, Harvey, and I did some filming outside the 110th Street schoolyard this Saturday. We couldn't get into the playground but we may be able to tomorrow (Sunday). Banas will show you it when he gets back to LA. We took a brief look at the stills you sent and it became alive again. It is indescribable the feelings we experienced just looking in and remembering the events during that time. We somehow weren't reliving but *instantaneously* being in both moments right then. We looked in and saw ourselves doing the takes and we all laughed and laughed. We could actually see us fooling around and hear the conversations during those morning barres and rehearsals and the shoot. Our positions came back as if it wasn't almost 50 years earlier, but now! It's not as if we were cliché young again, but we were then and are now at once. WHAT AN INCREDIBLE TIME WARP. Did I confuse you? You should see it from this side. We all agreed it was time jumping.

We wondered what we would have felt if, back then, for a moment, we had looked out at the street where we now stand and were seeing us looking back at ourselves from there 50 years later. Could we have bridged the time and acknowledged each other and waved and smiled? I'd like to think we just did. What a gift! Now, as one, we all waved goodbye to ourselves. For if not tomorrow, this probably was it. Bye, guys! See you on the big screen and we'll recall today for another tomorrow. We are blessed as few ever are.

Maggie, we can never thank you enough for your love, and love it is. You are one of us. We all wished you were here but then again, you were.

On behalf of all of us, always your Snowboy, Bert

West Side Story was a defining moment in all our lives. It was a moment so full and rich that its impact continues on throughout all the rest of time. We are privileged. We are embedded in a magnificent pastiche.

PS. To all those very special ones who have left the set and we no longer have the privilege of being able to speak with and share our treasures of the past, know we love and miss you. You will ever be our brothers and sisters in art and love. Still, look! You'll always be there, as we all are, for our children, grandchildren, etc. And every time they see *West Side Story*, they will know our contribution and rejoice. Go, Jets! Go, Sharks! Fifty years! Hear the music! Dance!

Snowboy-Bert

Bert Michaels

"Tiger"/Jet – David Bean

Audition?

LONDON, JANUARY 1960. I left the company of *West Side Story* at Her Majesty's Theatre in the West End. Eddie Verso (who played Baby John) and I took off for six weeks to do Europe. Our return found a telegram from Jerome Robbins for Eddie; come to New York, it read, for a screen test of the movie version of *West Side Story*. I, on the other hand, had no telegram and was not contacted at all. We gave Eddie a big party and saw him off at Heathrow Airport with great hoop-la!

I decided to take a slow boat home, arriving in New York City in February. That's when I received word to report to the Samuel Golden Studios in Hollywood. The studio seemed empty when I arrived. I reported to the gym on the studio lot in rehearsal clothes. Howard Jeffrey, Tommy Abbott, and Jerry Robbins were working on dance combinations. We rehearsed what seemed to be hundreds of different versions of the stage production. Tony Mordente, Jay Norman, Jaime Rogers, and, I think, Eliot Feld were there. Nothing was ever mentioned about a contract. I actually didn't know if I was to be in the film. We just started rehearsing. We worked and worked on the

"Prologue," changing very little in the end. There were what seemed like hundreds of new variations, but in the end the dancing was very much like the original, which we all knew inside and out having performed the stage version. At the same time, Robbins auditioned hundreds of dancers.

I personally do not remember auditioning. Perhaps my audition for Jerome Robbins took place in 1954 at the Musicians Union in Hollywood. I was fourteen years old then, and Mary Martin was doing the stage musical of *Peter Pan*, directed and choreographed by Jerome Robbins. This was my first ever audition right out of dance class. I was not allowed to put my tap shoes on, as the hardwood floors had just been polished. We were given a few simple ballet steps, which I did in my stocking feet. For three days I did everything asked of me with gusto. I made Jerry laugh and I had a great time. Three thousand kids showed up for those auditions so the days were long—very,very, long. I was given the part of Slightly Soiled, one of the lost boys. We opened in San Francisco, and moved down to Los Angeles for a limited run before going to New York. So perhaps I was the only person in the film that actually never had to audition for the movie, but then again maybe not.

Peter Pan

THE ENTIRE CAST of *Peter Pan* was booked on an old Pullman train. My dad, Beanie, drove Cyril Ritchard's (Captain Hook) old '41 Chrysler back to New York. My two sisters (Janet and Roberta) and my mother came on the train with the rest of the cast. We opened at the Winter Garden Theatre for a limited run on Broadway.

My dad was a truck driver by trade and had a "Billy Elliot" notion of what the theatre world was all about. It was OK for me to take tap lessons, but ballet was for girls. With six children, I being number six, mine was an easy way of life. The girls did the dishes, cooked, took ballet while the boys mowed the lawn, played football, and I took tap.

As it turned out, my dad couldn't get a job in New York, and it was fate that Cyril Ritchard needed someone to dress him. During a cross-over in the play one night, I asked Cyril to ask my dad. He needed a job, and he did drive Cyril's car across country for him. Bam! The show was now a family affair. During the run in New York, we all became like one family. Often I went to Cyril's apartment on matinee days and had dinner with Cyril and his wife (Madge Elliott). Mary Martin was like a mother to all of the Lost Boys, and Heller (Mary's daughter) played Eliza and was our age. It really was Family.

Noel Coward

EVERY NIGHT AFTER the final curtain, Mary talked to the audience while the cast stood behind her. She was very gracious and at times introduced celebrities that were in the audience. On one of those evenings, she had a special treat for the audience. Noel Coward was there and had agreed to come on stage and say hello. As he walked out on stage, she turned to me and motioned for me to join her at the footlights. So there we were, the three of us standing in front of the cast and looking out at the audience.

She then said, "David Bean, meet Noel Coward!" Then turning to Noel Coward, "Noel Coward, this is David Bean." We shook hands. "Ladies and gentlemen," she continued, "Noel Coward's very first professional role of his career was that of Slightly Soiled, and I thought they should meet."

We shook hands again and I leaned into Mary and whispered, "He grew up!"

She repeated it to the audience to great applauses. I did both live television productions of the show on NBC.

In 1956 Jerry contacted my agent in New York for me to fly there and audition for a new musical he was about to do. A new musical called *West Side Story*. My agent told him I was not doing any more shows until I graduated high school. I missed the original *West Side Story* auditions and my agent, Milton Goldman, owed me big time.

In 1958, having graduated the year before, Jerry was putting together the London production of *West Side Story* and I was summoned again to New York for the auditions. I got the audition and the London production of *West Side Story*. We rehearsed in New York for two months before we opened in Manchester, England, October 1958. The London opening was December 12th, and was a huge success. Later that evening, at the opening night party, I was surprised when my new boss Binky Beaumont announced that Noel Coward was looking for me. Wow! I couldn't believe Mr. Coward would remember me.

"I didn't, dear boy, but I had supper with your godfather Cyril Ritchard last week, and he reminded me, should I see your play to look you up."

"Are you busy?" I asked.

"Not at all, dear boy, I'm off to the island in a week."

"George Chakiris and I are sharing a flat in Eccelston Mews and you must join us for supper."

He did and I cooked a beautiful leg of lamb. We sat up till four in the morning talking and singing.

After five decades of relating stories and anecdotes that happened during the filming of *West Side Story*, I truly believe my stories get more detailed and perhaps longer with age. Some of these stretches are necessary to captivate the audience and are incorporated into the story, so often it's hard to separate fact and lightly stretched.

For example: we worked with Jerry for three months prior to seeing a camera creating sixteen different versions of eight bars of choreography. A stretch? Perhaps. Physically it would be possible, but remembering sixteen different versions of eight bars of anything would be a stretch.

After weeks of rehearsing hours of dance combinations, the studio was about to screen test some of us for what we thought were specific gang roles. I did two days of improvisations in front of the camera with Bert Michaels and Tony Mordente.

Jerry sat next to the camera and fed us lines, like, "Hey ya hoodlum, how's ya ole lady doin'?"

It was great fun. We learned later they were testing new 70mm Panavision film and it wasn't a screen test. Go figure! By June, I was finally given a contract.

Filming

WHILE FILMING THE "Prologue" on the upper East Side in a playground on 110th Street, the Jets decided to have "The Jets are the Greatest" campaign, prompted by the Sharks hanging an effigy of a Jet from the top of a school chimney. We bought white bed sheets and painted "The Jets are the Greatest" on them. We spent hours writing "The Jets are the Greatest" on thousands of small pieces of paper. At a most opportune time we went up onto the rooftops of the surrounding apartment buildings overlooking the playground. On cue we threw the sheets over the side of the buildings so they hung from the roofs and at the same time threw thousands of cards onto the playground and the street below. A great campaign; however, the building owners complained we had broken all the windows on the roof transoms and the film company had to keep the peace by replacing them at an outrageous sum. Our First Assistant Director Bob Reylea of course sent us to the bus, which was where we always found ourselves when mischief raised its amusing head.

The Lincoln Center now stands where we filmed most of the "Prologue." Many hours were spent waiting for the next setup on location. It was during one of these periods that we all found activity in the form of a good ole-fashioned "rain dance." We locked arms in the middle of the street and did our "rain dance." It was harmless and a lot of fun—that is until the rain came, not just once, but nearly every time we did the deed. The original New York location schedule was set at six weeks, but we ended up being there for sixteen weeks. So, no more "rain dances." When a cloud appeared, we were sent to the bus to keep it from raining.

By summer we Jets were working on "Cool." "Cool" was very intense, and since the entire number was already choreographed, Jerry had us do it from the top straight through every time. At the same time

Jerry was also working on "America" with the Sharks. Since the Jets were not involved in "America," we did not attend those rehearsals.

Genius that Jerry was, at the end of the day, he brought the Jets and Sharks together on a soundstage. First the Sharks did "America" full out, which received thunderous applause by the end of the number. It was exciting and thrilling! In the original Broadway production, "America" was sung and danced by Anita and the Shark girls only. For the film Jerry added Bernardo and the Shark boys giving it the strength of a freight train. Now it was our turn. We had to do "Cool" full out, and we did. When we finished you could hear a pin drop. Every breath in the studio was held—total silence. It was a great moment. A brilliant move on the part of Jerry to keep the tension and competition between the Jets and the Sharks. It worked!

The Jet Song

RIFF (RUSS TAMBLYN) sings "The Jet Song" in the opening few minutes of the movie. For whatever reason, the powers that be decided to dub Russ's voice and asked some of us to work a couple of days with the legendary Saul Chaplin and record "The Jet Song."

"Don't get lyrical, David," Saul said. "You are in the streets...try it again."

So after rehearsing and recording the song several times, Jerry Robbins was called in to have a listen. The tape was played and Jerry started to laugh.

"It sounds just like Russ!" he said.

Well wasn't that the idea?"

"You did too good of a job, we'll use Tucker."

And so it was; Tucker Smith is the voice you hear on the soundtrack of "The Jet Song." Russ sang "Krupke" and I thought he did a great job. So go figure.

George Chakiris played Riff in the London company. During the run of the show, he and I shared a flat from late 1958 through 1959. George was like a big brother to me. I was 17 years old and in a different part of the world. I was far from home and my five brothers and sisters. Returning to Hollywood and working with a couple of the kids that were in the London production was great fun. George, Tony Mordente (A-Rab), Eddie Verso (Baby John), and myself (Big Deal). It wasn't long after rehearsals started that we found out that George was to be a Shark, he wasn't going to be Riff, he was to be Bernardo! And Eddie Verso was going to be a Shark as well.

This was a disaster. I wouldn't be able to talk to either one of them on the lot...

Jets were not allowed to frat with Sharks. To keep tension between the rival gangs, Jerry Robbins kept us apart. One evening I got a call from George and was invited out for dinner with Rita Moreno and a friend of hers. Perhaps take in a movie. Well that's two Sharks and an outsider to one Jet.

"You'll have to hide me if we run into anyone from the studio," I said.

I didn't want to be caught with a Shark and have to buy lunch on the set for punishment. (Lunch on the set was a catered affair for the entire cast and crew, about $1,200 worth.) George agreed and we had a great dinner and no one ever saw us. And Rita's friend...Marlon Brando!

Poker

WEEKENDS DIDN'T COUNT when it came to separating Jets and Sharks. Every Saturday night we played poker. Tony Mordente, Jay Norman, Bert Michaels, Andre Tayir, Bob Thompson, and Bobby Banas were among the players. Betty Walberg, our pianist, would sit in on occasion. She was a hell of a player. The game went on till nine Sunday morning and was a fun get-together. Stakes were fifty cents and a dollar, but by morning there were no limits. David Winters had a pet monkey that sat on his shoulder during the game and would occasionally pee on you.

Our little weekend game was kid stuff compared to the gambling on the set. The grips and a few of the dancers were reckless. Dice/

craps was the sport and it was nothing to see hundreds on the floor with nearly every roll of the dice. I did play cards (two-handed Poker) with Betty Walberg on most breaks, or when we didn't get locked on the bus for getting into mischief.

Robert Wise owned a few racehorses, and when they were running we all had a pool-type bet. The entire company could get in on it. One morning we were filming the "Quintet," I had overslept and raced to the studio in my topless Chevy and skipped make-up all together. The cast and crew were waiting as I walked on set.

Our director Robert Wise greeted me with "Nice of you to join us, Mr. Bean. I have good news and I have bad news for you. Which do you want first? Your choice."

Well being an optimist I took the good news first.

"Good," he said. "You won the pool. Congratulations."

"And the bad?" I asked.

"You bought lunch."

Tiger

THE CHARACTER I portray in the movie, Tiger, was not one of the Jets in the original Broadway cast. My character's name sort of grew from me. Arriving in Hollywood from London, I still had long red hair. Meaning it was trimmed but not like I had just been to a barber. We were all asked not to get haircuts when we started working. After three months my hair was naturally long. Jerry started calling me Tiger. When the script arrived there I was: Tiger.

One very warm sunny day, the Jets were all rehearsing in the gym and were asked to move outside and form a circle around Robert Wise, Jerry Robbins, Robert Relyea, the make-up department, and a bunch of assistants. First we faced them, then we walked 'round the circle. When they were directly behind me they stopped.

"Him," Jerry said. I turned around and was given instructions to report to make-up. Snip snip and my Tiger's mane became a Tiger's crewcut, which they maintained throughout the entire shoot. Every morning a Polaroid was taken to keep our hair and make-up the same.

Filming a shot of the Jets strutting down the street in New York for the "Prologue," Jerry took me aside and gave me a direction to comb my hair. You can see me do this on film. That was the first time I combed my hair in the film, and to this day I kick myself for not thinking outside the box. It's something I should have been doing every chance I got.

Transportation

WHEN I ARRIVED in Hollywood I stayed with my parents in Culver City. They lived across the street from MGM, and had we been filming there it would have been very convenient. However, Samuel Goldwyn Studios, where we were filming *West Side Story*, was in Hollywood, a bit of a trek, especially if you didn't have a car. For two months I took the bus west on Washington Blvd., transferred north on La Brea Ave. all the way to Pico Blvd., then walked to the studio. Well this got old very quickly.

Ah, enter my favorite uncle Marshal. Uncle Marshal is my mother's brother and we shared a lot of genes—red hair, fair complexion, and a keen sense of knowing how to get things. I needed a car so I called Uncle Marshal. We had a budget that only he could appreciate, and he came through with flying colors. It was a 1952 Chevy convertible with four good tires and running. All for a hundred bucks. It didn't take long to find La Gardiner Apartments in Hollywood, where several of the dancers were living. I soon became a taxi service. Make-up at 7am, the guys piled into the Chevy and off we went.

One early morning Jay Norman sat in the front seat and happened to spot a tiny hole in the canvas above his head. By now we were doing 45mph down Fairfax Blvd. Jay put his hand through the hole and stood straight up, increasing the hole by one body size. All the while waving his hands and screaming, "I like to be in America," at the top of his lungs. I never did replace the canvas top, but the gray duct tape nearly matched the canvas.

Speaking of cars, Tony Mordente (A-Rab), purchased a 1958 Jaguar XK 120 when we were doing the show in London. He had it shipped to the States and ultimately drove it to Hollywood. One afternoon David needed to use Tony's Jag for an errand and parked the car on a steep incline, while he ran into his house to fetch something. When he returned the car was gone. He apparently hadn't set the hand brake and it rolled back out of the drive and down the hill straight into the living room of a neighbor's house. I never saw the Jag again.

Chariot Races

THE LOT AT Samuel Goldwyn Studios was typical of most major studios—rows of larger-than-life buildings with domed roofs. Enormous sliding doors peppered with tiny little doors with a single red light over the top. Shooting schedules started early, like 8 am, and make-up was even earlier, like 6 am. We would arrive on the set, block the scene, and do a couple of takes till the directors (Jerry Robbins and Robert Wise) were happy. We would break while the crew set up a different angle of the same scene. Well this took forever. What to do? We could go to the cafe on the lot, play cards, read. READ? Are you kidding? Within minutes of the break we found light stands not in use. Each of these had three wheels, which allowed us to pump along like a scooter. Holding onto the center pole we could get up quite a speed. Racing was tricky because roads around the studio were sloped to the center, and we clashed frequently. The screams and laughter were wonderfully loud. Too loud, it seems. Billy Wilder had an officer on the lot and complained from his office a whole block away that he couldn't work from the distraction. Back to the bus!

B&B Properties

WHILE LOOKING FOR an apartment in Hollywood, Bobby Banas offered to let me share his. Bob and I had worked together in the 1954

Mary Martin production of *Peter Pan*. It was like old home week. We shared an interest in real estate and decided to form a partnership, "B & B Properties." We wasted no time setting out to find the perfect property. Making movies is wonderful—you get the weekends off—so Bobby and I would scour the LA basin looking for investments. A real-estate broker that would critique our findings and in general be our mentor tutored us. We looked at everything (some I'd like to own today). We looked at an obscure cliff property in the Hollywood Hills that went straight down from the road for fifteen hundred dollars. We must have looked at every empty lot south of Santa Barbara, for which we would write up a report and take to our mentor. Three months into this and we still hadn't bought a single piece of property.

One beautiful afternoon we were driving home from scouting a few sand lots in Ontario. The San Bernadino Freeway was getting busy and we must have been doing the speed limit when all of a sudden the canvas top of the old Chevy ripped apart. The sound was horrific, and as I looked over at Bobby he was cowering in his seat as the ripped canvas was beating him on the head. Like I said, it was a lovely day, and driving with the top down is what Hollywood is all about. Our business venture was a success of sorts; after all, we didn't suffer a loss on investment. We didn't have any. Our mentor, we later learned, did buy most of the properties we brought to him for himself.

The Gym

THERE WAS A gymnasium on the lot where we rehearsed, took class, and generally hung out. At the time the score of *Big Country* was popular, and it played while the kids choreographed dances to it. We took class every day when we were not shooting. We started early with a warm-up ballet bar followed by up to two hours of class given by Jerry. Eliot Feld, Eddie Verso, Jay Norman, Bob Thompson, Tommy Abbott, Tony Mordente, and Howard Jeffrey were all challenged by Jerry, and the dancing was brilliant. Interestingly, we never worked on anything to do with the film, just pure dancing. After lunch, the Jets would rehearse "Cool" and the Sharks went through "America," then we could go home.

In the corner of the gym was a high bar setup (gymnastic horizontal bar), complete with mats. In high school I was a member of the gymnastic team. I could kip up on the bar and press into a handstand and do back giants. One morning I was fooling around on the high bar and Burt Lancaster appeared. To my surprise and delight, he was there to work out. After warming up, he kipped up onto the bar and did an awesome routine. Who would of thought?

Many Takes

AS THE DRUGSTORE scene opens before the Anita taunting scene, there was a quick shot of all the Jets hanging around. I was to go behind the counter, put my hand into the candy jar while Bert Michaels says, "I'm hungry, where's Doc?" To which I reply, "He's upstairs gathering getaway money for Tony." So the lights were set and the camera position had been rehearsed, and what should have been a two-minute shoot went like this:

Snowboy: "I'm hungry, where's Doc?"
Tiger: "He's downstairs gathering getaway money for Tony."
Director: "Cut! Tiger, it's upstairs. Take two."
Snowboy: "I'm hungry, where's Doc?"
Tiger: "He's upstairs, githering gataway money..."
Director: "Cut! Tiger, you want to try again? Take three."
Snowboy: "I'm hungry, where's Doc?"
Tiger: "He's upstairs gathering getaway money for Doc."
Director: "Cut! Tiger, it's 'Tony,' not 'Doc.' Take four."
Snowboy: "I'm hungry, where's Doc?"
Tiger: "He's upstairs gathering gataway money for Tony."
Director: "Cut! What's a 'gataway,' Tiger?"
Tiger: "Oh about three pounds."
Director: "Take five."
Snowboy: "I'm hungry, where's Tony?"

Tiger: "He's upstairs gathering getaway money for Tony."
Director: "Cut! Tiger, that was perfect. Snowboy, it's 'Doc,' not
            'Tony.' Take six."
Snowboy: "I'm hungry, where's Doc?"
Tiger: "He's upstairs gettering...Oh Jesus (giggle)."
Director: "Cut!"

It took eleven takes to get this one small bit into the can. We were laughing so hard we could hardly speak. Even Mr. Wise enjoyed himself. He was laughing with us when he called a wrap.

Looping

ALL OF THE music, directed by Johnny Green, was recorded before any of the filming started. We were lucky enough to be allowed to sit in on all of the recording sessions. Johnny Green was an eccentric European who wore a white coat that made him look like a dentist. He offered to pull teeth for a small fee. I remember the first piece they did was "America"—without exception the most difficult music in the entire score. The orchestra tuned up and fiddled around a bit, and Johnny had them play it through once. He gave a few brief notes and asked for another go, which was recorded. Done! I was blown away. The talent of those musicians was enough to make your jaw drop.

Eventually the cast was called in to record over the playback, the "Jet Song," the "Quintet," and something one wouldn't think about which was the sounds we made when we were just on camera. Not necessarily doing anything pertinent to the scene, but because we were in the background, we recorded ourselves. It's called looping. A 30-second piece of the film was looped to replay on itself, and we would watch ourselves and mimic what we saw like taking a simple step, or snapping your finger, talking to someone. It wasn't difficult to do, but it was difficult to record. The Jets would take bets on how many takes it would be to get it in the can. If David Winters' number was four, he would somehow quietly do a time step in the middle of the take, forcing another try. Take four! Nobody won a bet and we laughed a lot and were yelled at, to be sure.

Fifty Years of Residual Positive Return

WEST SIDE STORY was released in 1961, and that same year I spent doing the English touring company of West Side Story. Robert Wise had interviewed me for his next movie, Sand Pebbles. But I had already agreed to do the English tour. Having worked on the film version really had little return personally in 1961. When mentioned in passing conversations, the reaction was generally somewhat vague like, "How nice," or "Interesting." At the time I thought nothing of it. I was dating Jean Deeks (Anybodys) from the show and spent an entire year on the road. We did Bristol, Oxford, where we rented a boat and lived on the river Isis. Mooring wherever, and having the geese wake us up far earlier than was normal for show folk. We played Manchester again, Leeds, Blackpool, Liverpool, Edinburgh, and Glasgow, where we lived in a caravan trailer.

In March 1962, shortly after the conclusion of the tour, Jean and I were married. Cyril Ritchard flew to London to be my best man. Our wedding took place at the Holy Trinity Church, which is located directly behind the famous Catholic, Brompton Oratory.

"Oh! The church behind the better one!" Cyril announced. Cyril could have been the Pope, he was such a wonderful, devout Catholic.

One week into our Brighton honeymoon, Cyril contacted us with an offer for the lead dancers in the Mike Todd Jr. production of Around the World in 80 Days, for St. Lewis and Kansas City. The plan was to bring it to New York City, but we never made it, closing in Kansas City.

We settled in New York City and continued a career in theater and television. By 1966 we had a lovely home in Westchester County, fifty miles north of the city, and our daughter Jennifer was born. To supplement our income, we invested in real estate and started a dual career of dancing and a retail business in one of the buildings we owned.

We opened our second art gallery/gift shop by 1970. Jean was busy with a thriving ballet school and all the while we were still doing TV, commercials, and Broadway. A German delicatessen was in one of our buildings. We bought the business on impulse and Jean found herself slicing bologna on a machine that terrified her. Jean was amazed how a Royal Academy–trained ballet dancer could wake up every morning and find herself slicing bologna in a delicatessen that she owned. It was not without its reward, however. Jean is a fantastic cook and over the next thirty-five years, a whole new world opened up for us in the food industry.

During this period I was doing a Broadway show *Hot Spot*, with Judy Holiday. Martin Charnin wrote the lyrics. Marty was the original Big Deal in *West Side Story* on Broadway that I replaced for the London touring company. Marty also wrote the lyrics for *The Prisoner of Zenda*, with Alfred Drake and Chita Rivera that Jean and I were both in. Busy didn't describe the world we lived in, and to calm ourselves we took a drive to Duchess County, two counties north of us, just to look at property and get the bugs out of our systems. It was great fun and we found ourselves with a weekend getaway, in the little town of Clinton Corners. On top of a forty-seven-acre hill, we became gentlemen farmers, raising Holstein heifers, goats, sheep, horses, and we even had a pig. We grew our own hay and 60 tons of corn each year, to feed all the animals on the Bean Hill Farm. The heifers were artificially inseminated at eighteen months, sold, and flown to foreign countries like Brazil or Iran.

Our daughter Jennifer was 12 years old when we moved to the farm. She and her mother had spent most of the summer on the farm, and it was Jennifer's idea to move from Westchester to the farm. She met some of the kids over that summer in Clinton Corners and asked could she attend Millbrook School and Daddy could commute to Westchester. I brought up a box of shoes and most of our clothing, and moving was that simple, as the farmhouse was already furnished. Jennifer flourished during the farm years.

We bought milking goats one Christmas. It was a shared task between Jennifer and I. The task was fun to begin with, but quickly we had too much milk and so decided to get a pig. Within a month we had a rat infestation. The whole barn seemed to be overrun with them. We purchased rat poison, and after a week we got notes left by the critters, *mmm that was delicious, another case please.* So we changed the strain of poison and it worked. Milking goats when rats had a fatal high on was more entertaining than when they were sober.

Without Jennifer, our world would not have been fun or complete. Jennifer is a seasoned workhorse; she certainly knows how to dig in and get the job done. Today she and our fantastic son-in-law James (a New York fireman) are raising our four grandchildren, a job beyond description. Jennifer was never pushed to take dancing lessons or to follow in our footsteps. From the time she was born she attended her mother's dance school classes, and at six she could demonstrate for the twelve-year-olds.

On one occasion we were in New York City and stopped at Lincoln Center on the chance of getting tickets for Jerome Robbins' *Dances at a Gathering*. They sold us the house seats and we were just settling in, waiting for the curtain, when Jerry slid in and sat directly in front of us. I tapped him on the shoulder and we had a mini-reunion. Remember, Jennifer was eleven years old and Jerry had not met either Jean or my daughter.

After the introductions, Jerry turned to Jennifer and very sternly said, "Listen, young lady, this is a very long and boring ballet, so don't fidget!"

We all smiled and the curtain went up. Within minutes one of the girls tripped and tumbled on stage. Jerry jumped out of his seat in alarm, and seeing that the young girl had recovered, sat back in his chair.

Jennifer, without hesitation, leaned over Jerry's shoulder and whispered, "You're fidgiting!"

Jerry stood up and kissed her. Timing is everything. She gets that from her mother. Sadly, that was the last time we ever saw Jerry.

By 1979 we purchased what became the Clinton Corners Country

Store, which we operated for nearly twenty years. Because of our close association with Britain, we established a British food mail order which turned out to be a great success and great fun. Of course we had to make many trips to England, which was a bonus as Jean's family lived there.

Flying

I STARTED TO fly by accident. On a sunny afternoon a great friend, John Lawrence, asked me to lunch. I was to meet him at the local airport. He was taking flying lessons and we'd lunch after his lesson. I was hanging on the fence separating the airplane from the non-fliers when a Cessna pulled up and out popped John.

"I just got a business call and can't do lunch. However, that chap is going to give you a lesson."

"Wooah, wait a second, I don't think I'm interested," I said. "I never made model airplanes as a kid. I'm fifty-two years old and I think it's too late, but thanks anyway."

"Dave, I've already paid the guy!"

"Well, what the hell, but I'll probably throw up on him."

So that was the start of a life of airplanes and flying. It took me two years to get my license. The hard part was learning how to learn all over again. Today I fly a Piper Cherokee 180 that I've had nearly 18 years.

WestSide Story has been monumental in our lives. Jeanie and I have been married for forty-nine years, and as a team we worked through 26 career changes. We have done everything we ever wanted to, so far. We did it by finding the passion in everything we took on. Passion is the spark that ignites a challenge. We can't recall ever doing anything for money. We put one hundred and eighty percent into every project. The dollars seemed to take care of themselves.

Without a doubt, *West Side* was a draw for our numerous businesses. The years passed and the associations broadened. *West Side Story* was not just a friend to us as an advertising tool; it became an icon that changed the physical presence of fans that weren't even born when the movie was made. Young and old seem to fall down when I am introduced as a member of the cast. I look back and think how fortunate I was to have worked with Jerry Robbins and to have shared in the creation of this historical film. Come to think of it, the only other historical film of this proportion I could have done in my lifetime would have been *Gone With the Wind*. After all, I was born in 1939 and could have been that baby that Hattie told Charlotte she knew nothing about birthing.

David Bean

"Mouthpiece"/Jet — Harvey Hohnecker (Evans)

The Audition

I HAVE TO get in this show! I just have to be in it, but how? How?

I'm Harvey Hohnecker from Cincinnati, Ohio. I'm nineteen and dancing on Broadway in *New Girl in Town*, a new musical choreographed by Bob Fosse and starring the incomparable Gwen Verdon. It's 1957 and they are Broadway's hottest couple. But soon after we opened Jerome Robbins, the reigning KING of Broadway musicals, was starting auditions for a new show called *Gangway*. I was very ambitious then and knowing of his genius, I wanted to work with him. Our producer, Harold Prince, was also producing *Gangway*—soon to become *West Side Story*—and we unofficially heard he would not take us out of one show to put us into another, so I didn't audition.

We were invited to see a run-through of *West Side*, and it was life altering for me. I had never seen anything like it, and I became obsessed with the show. I knew I had to be in it. Since Mr. Prince was a hands-on producer, I pleaded with him to let me audition as soon as they needed someone. He did; I got the job and became Gee-tar, the first Jet replacement. My dream had come true.

I stayed with the show until it was announced it was going to tour and wishing to stay in New York, I left *West Side* to do *Redhead* and *Gypsy* on Broadway. During *Gypsy*, I got a call to audition for the *West Side* movie. I had two screen tests, one general and one for Riff. Since Robbins knew I did the show, I did not have to dance.

Gypsy was a Robbins show as well, and once again everyone said, "He's not going to let you out of the show for the movie." But he did. So there I was, the luckiest guy in the world flying first class to Hollywood to be paid three hundred fifty dollars a week (minimum principal salary) for a job scheduled to last two to three months. Three hundred fifty dollars a week was a small fortune coming from Broadway, where chorus dancers were paid seventy-five dollars a week and principals one hundred fifty a week. Seated next to me was Bert Michaels, a fellow Jet.

When the stewardess asked for our drink order he said, "Scotch."

Suddenly out of my mouth came, "Me too."

So scotch, first class, and a movie-contract grownup at last. I'm going to buy my mom and dad a swimming pool.

What I remember of my first day of rehearsal was breakfast with Gus Trikonis, a friend from the Broadway *West Side Story* cast who was to be in the film as well but as a Shark. We were sitting in the commissary of Samuel Goldwyn Studios. Sam Goldwyn's is where we rehearsed and shot the movie. I remember my heart racing and my stomach being in knots.

"I am so nervous I feel sick to my stomach," I said to him.

"Order tomato juice instead of orange," he said. "It calms the stomach."

It must have done the trick, 'cause it's all I remember of that first day.

Early on in rehearsals, I was partnered for "Dance at the Gym" with a terrific young dancer named Taffy Paul. One morning she was not there, and knowing Robbins' reputation and temperament I thought, *Okay, the first firing...but why? She was terrific!* I soon learned she was very young, still in school, and because of her age she held up production, so they let her go.

A year later I got a small part in *Experiment in Terror*, a film directed by Blake Edwards for Columbia Pictures. I was to play the boyfriend of one of the leads, a newcomer named Taffy Paul. I was thrilled. We had a great time filming and formed a warm friendship.

One day after filming she said, "I want to change my name."

And I said, "So do I!"

So I became Harvey Evans and she became Stefanie Powers. I don't see her much, but what fond memories.

Back to *West Side Story*: before we began filming we spent endless days and hours rehearsing all the dance sequences. For the audience to accept street gangs singing and dancing, the "Prologue," which would open the movie, had to be "just right"—so we rehearsed and rehearsed till we dropped. Plus we had some fifty versions of it and had to remember them all, not knowing which one we'd be asked to do on the spot.

Then off to New York we went to shoot "Prologue." Since I lived there, instead of sharing a room at the Warwick Hotel with my good friend Tucker Smith, who played the role of Ice, I chose to stay in my apartment. Tucker was the most dearly loved, outrageous, and gregarious cast member of us all. Now remember we were still basically kids. Not just kids, but pranksters that liked causing mischief.

While we were in New York, the movie *Psycho* had just opened and a bunch of us, including Tucker, went to see it. Well some cast members got into Tucker's room when he was in the shower. One was done as Norman Bates' mother complete with knife. I unfortunately missed this event, but Tucker's screams and his passing out was the talk of the set for days.

While filming at the playground on East 110th Street, a Catholic parade, which included a huge statue of the Virgin Mary, passed by. Tucker, never wanting to miss getting a laugh, ran to the front of the parade pretending to be the drum major leading it. Tucker was always a morale booster. I'm sorry to say he is no longer with us, but he remains in my thoughts and thinking of him always makes me smile.

Because of rain and Robbins' fanatical perfectionism, the scheduled "few weeks" of shooting in New York turned into two months, putting us way behind schedule. Though it took a long time to film, I feel the "Prologue" is the best thing in the movie and well worth the time it took.

Early on the studio brass kept saying, "We don't know if the public will accept this kind of a movie; if it will even work."

So, I thought, *Okay, maybe it'll be a little art house movie.* Meanwhile, I was having fun making it.

So back to Hollywood—but wait. I'm confused. Are we in a garage or on a roof? Are we doing "Cool" or "America"? Now remember, fifty years have gone by and the *ROSHOMON* effect has taken over, so this is my own personal recall of these events. I can't remember what was scheduled to shoot first; I think "America." During the filming of "America," the Jets were to rehearse "Cool" on their garage set. However, over the weekend Rita Moreno was injured in an accident in her home and could not shoot on Monday. Delays cost a studio thousands of dollars, so the Jets were frantically called overnight to start filming "Cool" the next morning.

To make the number more effective, a claustrophobic garage was constructed with very low ceilings, which meant the heat from the lights had no place to escape. It was like dancing in hell. While filming "Cool," Robbins and Robert Wise, the co-directors, disagreed about something, but it was only the second time I had seen them disagree. Whatever tension went on between them, they were always gentlemen on the set. Thank God, because with the pressure we were under to be perfect, any added tension on the set would have been unbearable.

Now back to the garage. Because of the heat, when we finished a "take" we ran outdoors to cool down and gasp for air. The temperature change was dramatic and Elliot Feld, who played Baby John, got pneumonia and overnight, "Cool" was put on hold.

So back to the rooftop and "America." Frantic overnight phone calls went out to the Sharks. But one, who shall remain nameless, was not answering his phone. Remember, this was way before cell phones. Where was he? Some of us *thought* we knew but would not say. We knew we were behind and we knew thousands of dollars were being lost, but we also knew *he* had met a pretty starlet on the lot and was maybe at her place, but our lips were sealed.

Eventually he was found, "America" was filmed, and then "Cool." And all I could think was, **Thank God I will never have to do that number ever again!** It remains the hardest dance in my fifty-five years of performing.

But Robbins obviously did NOT feel that way. Being an organic director, everything had to be as real as possible. So for every scene that was filmed after "Cool," we would have to do "Cool" again to be in the right emotional state for that scene. Once we knew for sure that "Cool" was behind us, we Jets ceremoniously burned our kneepads outside Robbins' office.

As I mentioned earlier, the movie was shot at Samuel Goldwyn Studios, located at Santa Monica Blvd. and Formosa Avenue. It was the home of many United Artists directors, including Billy Wilder and William Wyler. The set was always welcoming celebrity visitors like Gary Cooper and Jack Lemmon.

As opposing gangs, we were encouraged to be loud, competitive, and rowdy, and so we were. At lunch one day, a group of us "borrowed" a sound-equipment platform on wheels and had a *Ben-Hur*-style chariot race around the lot. Chaos and much reprimanding followed.

We were told that Billy Wilder said, unless those kids start behaving, he was pulling his office and pictures off the lot.

Filming went on for nine months and I realized as we turned a corner, right before "The Jet Song," we suddenly were seven months older.

"NEVER LOOK AT THE CAMERA," they said.

Although we knew the movie was being filmed in Super Panavision, we saw nothing imposing about the camera. It certainly didn't seem large. Then we were invited to see a preview at the

Chinese Theater, and oh my God! The biggest screen I'd ever seen! Our little movie was HUGE, and huge it remained. Except for one casting flaw, I think it's a terrific movie. The movie the studio brass didn't think would work went on to win ten Oscars, including best picture. Hopefully it will be seen by generations to come. And folks, it was made for a big screen, so see it as it was meant to be seen—on a big screen. Television doesn't do it justice. But big screen or not...just see it! Besides, our residual payments are down to pennies.

The Show Business Family of *West Side Story*, or How One Job Begets Another

SHOW PEOPLE BOND together unlike any other profession. Maybe it's because to be a good actor you have to be honest and naked in front of each other to be accepted. Once accepted, however, it's for life. Some think we are greedy, egomaniacs, and fiercely competitive killers. Some are, but most are not. My family consists mostly of people in the business. Many of them from *West Side Story*, and we are united forever.

Before *West Side Story*, I danced with fellow *WSS* Jet (Joyboy) Bob Banas in the movies *The Girl Most Likely* and the *Pajama Game*, and after *West Side* in *Mary Poppins*. Consequently, we share a strong bond. The movie with Stefanie Powers led to my getting a part on the soap opera *The Brighter Day*. When it ended I danced on the *Judy Garland Show* and *Bing Crosby Show*. Soon after, Tucker and I were offered a return to Broadway for *Anyone Can Whistle*, written by Arthur Laurents and Stephen Sondheim. How could it miss, right? It did.

Show biz families are loyal and Gower Champion, who was the choreographer of *The Girl Most Likely* film, cast me as Barnaby in the national tour of *Hello Dolly!* Through Michael Stewart, who wrote the book of *Dolly*, I got George M and later Barnum. The University of West Side may have even led to Hal, Stephen, and Michael Bennett casting me in Follies.

I still live in New York, just blocks from the actual West Side movie locations. It's been some fifty years, and I still get opportunities to work on Broadway. I find myself reuniting with other *West Side* alumni such as Martin Charnin in *Annie Warbucks*, Larry Kert in *La Cage Aux Folles*, and Bob Avian in *Sunset Boulevard.* Bert Michaels and I had dancing roles in the Disney movie *Enchanted* and found out our brains could still recall and our bodies could still perform some of the "Prologue."

Fifty-plus years down the road, I have a new appreciation of Jerome Robbins. I was recently involved in a New York play reading where we had to perform part of *Romeo and Juliet,* so I had to reread the play. My jaw dropped as I realized the parallels between Shakespeare's text and Jerry's choreography. When Romeo and Juliet first meet, there is beautiful dialogue about their hands (my hand is not worthy of touching yours). In *West Side Story,* when Tony and Maria meet, it is a dance called the "Cha-Cha," and the music is "Maria" done with a light cha-cha beat, with finger snaps.

In a beautiful bit of stage magic, Jerry has three couples mirror what Tony and Maria are doing and feeling. When they do touch, it's only with their hands, one arm extended high and hands intertwining. I did this section in the show and I understood the lyricism, but now older and wiser, I could put more meaning into it knowing where Jerry got it.

Another revelation was a step the Jets did in the "Prologue," where we crossed the street as a gang. Our direction was to own the turf. The step was strong, one leg swinging wildly to the side owning the street. I got it then, but once again, I could do it better now. I would visualize a male dog urinating on the street to claim its territory.

In another piece of brilliance, Jerry, Robert Wise, and Boris Leven, the set designer, had the garage set for "Cool" built with a very low ceiling, as mentioned before, making the garage very claustrophobic, which was perfect for the number. It made us feel the weight of the world on our shoulders.

Jerry was a method choreographer; you had to do more than smile, you had to act. All his steps were based on what the material dictated, and that is why he was so above all other choreographers. You will know right away who choreographed it if you see a Bob Fosse number;

not so with Jerry. His work on *West Side Story* was totally different from his work on *Fiddler on the Roof* or his *Dances at a Gathering, The Cage,* or *Gypsy.*

He was a genius, and although known as the ultimate taskmaster who went to extreme measures to get the results he wanted, he had a soft teaching side. If he felt you had a desire to learn, he encouraged that. During the filming of the movie, he talked about doing a ballet of Stravinsky's *Les Noces* and coincidentally, the composer was conducting it at UCLA. Jerry invited a few of us to go and we got to meet Stravinsky.

My niece Kara Hohnecker, while in high school in Cincinnati, told me that they were discussing *West Side Story* in her class.

Kara raised her hand and said, "My uncle was in that."

The teacher said, "No, dear, I'm talking about the movie."

Kara said, "Yes, he was in that."

The teacher still did not believe her so Kara shut up. I'm not going to say what I think of that teacher for not believing my niece, but I do realize how much that movie has meant to so many people…especially to me. I have done many Broadway shows and a few movies, but nothing will top *West Side Story*. I'm proud to have been a part of it.

I am still in "the business," but my mom and dad never got the swimming pool.

Harvey Hohnecker (Evans)

"Joyboy"/Jet — Robert Banas

I WAS FINISHING my breakfast one early weekday morning when the phone rang. I bolted to answer it before my dramatic answering machine voice kicked in. A woman on the other end of the line asked, "Is this Bobby Banas?"

Hesitating a bit, I replied, "Yes it is, whom am I speaking to?"

She said her name was Maggie Banks, calling from Samuel Golden Studios, and she wanted to know if I was available to run down alleys and climb chain-link fences while they tested some new film for the movie *West Side Story*. As I paused a second, I thought someone was pulling my leg—got to be a joke. Sometimes buddies of mine have set me up, having someone call about an audition with instructions to go to a certain location, and when I got there, no one knew anything about said audition. Of course I reciprocated whenever I had the chance.

"Well?" she sternly asked.

I decided to play along and answered, "Yes!"

She followed up with, "This doesn't mean you'll be doing the film of course." She gave me instructions as to the day, time, and location, advising me to wear tennis shoes and jeans. I realized then it was for real and not just a joke.

Not long after running and climbing fences in some nearby alleys, I got a call about the real **Audition**. It was being held at Samuel Golden Studios at Formosa and Santa Monica Blvd., in Hollywood. I couldn't believe my eyes as I entered the front gate. I had no idea that there were that many male dancers in Los Angeles. Every dance studio within a hundred miles must have sent their recruits. I had gone to many auditions before, but never had I encountered such a multitude in LA. I did *Peter Pan* on Broadway, and upon it's closing, I decided to audition for Bob Fosse's *Damn Yankees*. Now that was an audition. There must have been close to five hundred or more male dancers circling the block. I got down to the last twenty-five and was axed. Ouch! But I did do the movie.

As we were herded into a rehearsal hall shadowed by two giant soundstages, there was such a frenzy taking place, you'd think everyone was going to receive a free TV or car. I headed to a spot in the room to drop off my gear and greet some of my buddies. Everyone started warming up, stretching, splits, back flips, tours in the air, and one guy was on the floor doing push-ups. As I scanned the room I noticed a lot of new faces, some with New York accents who seemed to have an above-it-all attitude.

It would seem that some of the Broadway cast would be our competition this day, or at least figuratively speaking. I wondered how many from the Big Apple were promised jobs. How many dancers did they really need? One, two, or had they already selected everyone? From what I understood, Mr. Robbins held auditions in every major city in the US, and this could just be a publicity stunt to hype the movie. Oh well, I could always use a good competitive workout. I had a feeling the audition was going to be long and dragged out, and everyone, including myself, would be out for blood.

I had worked for Mr. Robbins twice before, once on Broadway, as an Indian in the musical *Peter Pan*, with Mary Martin and Cyril Ritchard, and as Keeper of the Dogs, in the film *The King and I*, with Deborah Kerr and Yul Brynner. As I glanced over to where he was standing, I noticed he was preoccupied with the pianist and talking with his assistants, and I wondered if he'd remember me. Just then his assistant, Howard Jeffrey, stepped to the front of the room and announced, "Everyone learn this combination."

Well, you might of thought it was a cattle stampede, with everyone rushing to the front of the room. Though I was close to the front at one point, when the dust cleared, I now found myself in the back row. Oh boy! I thought, what a bunch of hungry dancers! As the large group struggled with the combination, guys were bumping into one another and me. I felt as if I were dancing in a phone booth trying to give it my all. Finally after being kicked, stepped on, and pushed, Howard announced he would break us down into smaller groups. Now, I could bust out of that phone booth and fly through that combination and show them what I really was capable of.

Mr. Robbins glanced my way and gave me a quick smile of acknowledgement. He now knew I was there, but would I meet his expectations? I had never seen the Broadway show, though I had heard great things about it. I wasn't quite sure what he was looking for. All I could do was give it my best shot and hope for the best.

I remembered his many moods while working with him before, the way he went about challenging and taunting you to see how far he could push. He gave a few steps and demanded you put everything into it, then stood back judging if your execution was that of his vision. Then after unfolding his arms and ditching his cigarette, he interrupted with, "Try this instead of that."

I knew where he was going with this. "Take two steps forward, turn left, and jump with the right leg in second." Then it was with the other leg and in reverse. The next day you'd be put on the spot with, "Let me see version three again."

My eyes rolled and closed very tight, trying to visualize version three. I didn't dare ask what it was. To ask was asking for trouble. Somehow I would do three, four, five, and back to number one. It was "dance roulette." Robbins worked his dancers like parts of an elaborate mechanical clock, molding them a part at a time, till he had assembled the ultimate timepiece. He x-rayed each dancer, finding and exposing their weaknesses, then fired them up to do the almost impossible. He read you like a book a page at a time. He verbally ripped your heart out when you were not giving it everything you had and then some. He was so demanding he became very mean and ungrateful at times, but the end result was beyond comprehension. He was a genius.

I had five callbacks after that initial audition, and each time the group of about fifty guys got smaller and smaller. Robbins began to play chess with us, moving us around to different groups—maybe four or five. Then it was two groups, The Jets and The Sharks. He then shuffled us like a deck of cards, slicing in between two other lads, then to the end of the line, back and forth. Then the group you were in would have to do a combination again and again. Then slicing you again between two other guys. Then a little conference would happen as Howard and Jerry locked horns, pointing to individuals and whispering about that person. Somehow we all knew this was the final day and they were making their final decision.

The whispering always got to me. I felt very uncomfortable when they stared at me, and I knew they were comparing me to another possible choice. I wondered was it my looks, my dancing, or attitude? Howard then stepped forward holding a piece of paper, which I assumed was the list of Yes's and No's. As I held my breath, he began to rattle off some names. Mine was not mentioned.

"Thank you very much," he said to these gentlemen.

They quickly grabbed their gear and looking back at us remaining dancers, exited the rehearsal hall. He then called names to form two groups. The Sharks were the Hispanic or darker-looking dancers, the Jets whites with light and dark hair. I predictably landed in the Jet group. Then they had the two groups stand shoulder to shoulder and began that irritating whispering again. They had one or two guys step forward then back in place, then a little more shuffling. My nerves were pretty shot by then. It seems there were more of us to be let go. *Crap!* I thought. *When will this end?* Then first one group was told to do the combination we had rehearsed—a pause, then whisper. Then

JOYBOY"/JET — ROBERT BANAS

it was the second group; by this time my stomach was growling and my feet were killing me. Howard stepped forward again, and in a stately manner announced two names and again said, "Thank you very much." He then turned to the remaining physically and mentally exhausted dancers and said, "You all have the job!"

I was stunned...didn't know whether to cry, yell, or jump for joy. I believe I did all three. We were informed that some of us would be testing on film for parts. Wow! A part with lines—how great can that be? We were told the studio would call us about the rehearsal schedule. Rudy del Campo and Nick Navarro, fellow dancers, also got the job. The rough day showed on our faces and bodies, but underneath it felt like sunshine, rainbows, and dancing on clouds.

Mr. Robbins was known to fire dancers after he had hired them. He liked to keep you guessing right to the end. I do remember that happening on the movie *King and I*. It was the second day of rehearsal and we were taking morning barre. Chad, I believe his name was, happened to be in front of me the day before, but was absent that morning. I turned to Thatcher Clark behind me and asked, "What happened to Chad?" "Jerry didn't like the way he was doing the warm-up and fired him," said Thatcher.

During the weeks of auditioning, I had accepted a three-day job as a background dancer on the film *Pepe*. Then I got my call to start rehearsals Monday on *West Side Story*. Seemed okay, as Friday was to be my last day on *Pepe*. I arrived home after finishing up only to get a call from the studio I had just left, telling me that they had to reshoot the scene I was in and to report to the studio Monday. *Say what?* I tried to explain I was to start rehearsals on the movie *West Side Story* and I wouldn't be available. They said I was obligated to appear or it could be a problem. Huh! I guess they meant I could be blackballed from the union. Boy, what a disaster! I was sure Mr. Robbins would not be thrilled with me not showing up my first day of work, so there went my chance to work on the film. I finally got enough courage to call him. As I told him my predicament, I waited expecting him to say, "That's it, Banas, you're out, take a walk."

But instead he said, "It's okay, but you'll have to catch up and learn everything you've missed."

"Yes sir, I will, I will learn everything and catch up!"

The day I arrived at the *West Side* rehearsals, everyone gave me a weird stare as some of my buddies wondered what the hell happened to me.

Then Mr. Robbins said, "Let's start with the chase." Seems he was putting the "Prologue" together in bits and pieces and everyone got into position. "Banas, over there with Mordente," he shouted.

"Who the hell is Mordente?" I said under my breath.

This short Italian kid motioned to me to follow him. I was right behind him and I kept running, jumping, trying to keep up. That Mordente (Action/Jet) was pretty fast; I had to double step to keep pace. Mr. Robbins came over to me at lunch and asked how I was doing.

"I'll have it all by the end of the day, sir," I replied. But by the end of the day, he had changed it so many times it didn't matter if I had learned it or not. He changed it many, many times over, again and again. All I remember of that first day is when I got home, I slept like a bear...

I was pooped!

I noticed during rehearsal that the East Coast dancers were stand-offish towards us West Coast dancers. The East Coast guys gathered on one side of the room in the mornings when we arrived and on our breaks. They seemed to be well-rounded dancers and probably had more stage experience than most of us, but this was a new media called "hurry up and wait." And judging by their overwhelming exuberance, they had a lot to learn about film work.

I knew two of the East Coast dancers, Harvey Hohnecker and David Bean. I had worked with both before. Harvey and I did several movie musicals together including *The Pajama Game*, and David and I did *Peter Pan* on Broadway together. They were cool, but the others gave the impression that the Hollywood dancers were beneath them. They just weren't very friendly at first. I thought I was the only one that felt this way, but later discovered Nick Covacevich picked up on it also.

Then at lunch several days later, someone started showing off with some turns or some flashy dance combination. All of a sudden everyone took notice, then like clockwork one after another casually got up, did a few exciting bars of dance finishing with some wild trick. Nick did his famous t-fall, a lay-out landing flat on his back. Rudy did his double-knee tours in the air, landing on his knees, and I did my Russian knee turns. It was one trick after another, spurred on by the last trick. Each side trying to top the other, but there were no winners that day, and it was no longer a divided room. Everyone now realized we were all special dancers that had been handpicked for our talent, energy, and abilities and could handle whatever was dished out. It didn't matter what coast you hung your dance belt on, but could you cut the mustard?

I got a call a few days later about a screen test for one of the parts in the film, and I guess Nick (Toro/Shark) got a call also. He asked if we could run lines prepping for the test, so we met at his place. One evening, his lovely wife asked me to stay for dinner and I agreed. During dinner Nick got up from the table and left the room for a moment.

His wife, who was an ex–Miss America, turned to me and in a soft voice said, "What's happening at the studio, Bob? Nick comes home with these scratches all over his back?"

Bong! I knew Mr. Casanova (Nick) was rubbing kneecaps with a young starlet, and she liked to scratch backs. I quickly and without hesitation blurted out, "Oh! that's the rumble we're rehearsing, it gets pretty violent, some of the guys forget it's make believe. I got hit in the mouth the other day with a fist, and no apology." I think she bought it.

No word on the screen tests we all did. Who cares! We were working under a SAG contract "and the living was easy." But as we were becoming friendlier and getting settled in, Mr. Robbins began preaching that we were rival gangs and we were not allowed to associate with the opposing gang on or off the lot, period! I recall being lipsticked leaving the studio after rehearsal one evening. Gus Trikonis (Indio/Shark), was the target of my fellow Jets, who overpowered him, removing his trousers, and were about to tree-bound them, when two elderly ladies from Pasadena came to his rescue, flailing their purses at the would-be thugs. "Watch your back and don't travel alone," was our everyday motto. You never knew when or where you would be attacked with water balloons, flying fruit, liquid goo, flat tires, and a ransacked dressing room. Even when there was an event at one of the soundstages, like a birthday celebration, we got wind that the other side was planning some prank, and we met the challenge.

There was a truce when it came to the social parties. This was a time to let it all hang out and let off some steam. The Jets and Sharks bonded like brothers of the hood. We all loved to shake our booties and enjoyed the evening. There were always some very cute gals that loved to party and made the evening well worth it. I would hit the dance floor till I was dripping wet, often brought a change of clothes. There was a lot of drinking and smoking going on, but everyone was well behaved. We were dancers, and dancers are known for their excess energy. We had lots of it, and it had to be let out!

Around the corner from the studio was this western discount store, and the New York kids went wild, like *Wild Wild West*. They bought guns and holsters, and on weekends would go plinking in the desert. Tin cans went flying every which way, and a bunch of New Yorkers were practicing quick draw. Bert Michaels (Snowboy/Jet) had a German Luger and once accidentally discharged it near my head. I was about ready to shoot a hole in his shoe with my 9mm revolver, but was afraid I'd hit his big toe. I had ringing in my ears for a week, kept thinking everyone was whispering. I was surprised no one got shot. Thank God!

On days off the Urban Cowboys headed to Griffith Park to make their Cowboy Western dream come true by saddling up some horses. They rode their butts off envisioning cattle roundups and chasing Indians. I believe that store went belly up after the movie ended.

Card playing was another pastime on the set and the weekends, sometimes lasting to the wee hours of the morning. David Winters (A-Rab/Jet) was the number one "Ace." I remember him thumping his thumb in some kind of nervous rhythm on the card table, while waiting for his turn to lay down his cards and grab the pot. He was a stand-out, often bringing his latest beauty girlfriend to rehearsals. His wild interpretation of A-Rab in "Cool" was unforgettable. David worked as a choreographer after *WSS* and hired me several times to work for him. I was most appreciative. I liked his style and I felt very comfortable doing it.

Well, after rehearsing the "Prologue" for weeks and weeks, it was time to go to New York to start shooting it. In keeping with Robbins' doctrine of the gangs avoiding one another, the Jets and Sharks boarded separate planes. The location where we filmed the opening of the movie is now The Lincoln Center.

When we got to New York, David Bean (Tiger/Jet) and I were roommates. We stayed at Cyril Ritchard's apartment off Central Park. We both had worked with Cyril, who was the captivating Captain Hook in *Peter Pan*, on Broadway. Cyril was on tour and was most gracious to let us stay at his place. It was a spacious apartment overlooking beautiful Central Park, and we had it all to ourselves. We flipped a coin for bedrooms and started unpacking and putting things away. We decided to grab a bite to eat before turning in.

I woke the next morning and noticed a bag in the hallway, thinking David forgot to put it away and I didn't really think much of it at that time. When we went to visit some of the guys staying at the Warwick Hotel, we heard that the script supervisor had complained the airport had lost his bag and he had to buy all new accessories. He was pissed. A couple days passed and the bag was still in the same place. I finally told David to move his bag, as I was tripping over it every time I entered the hallway.

"What bag?" he asked.

"The one that's been in the hallway for days," I said.

"Not mine, I thought it was yours."

"What? Not yours? Holy shit! This belongs to the script guy, and when he finds out...we are dead."

We looked at each other and started to laugh, we couldn't believe what happened.

"This isn't funny we've got to return it to him, like now," I said.

We grabbed the bag and took a cab to the Warwick, got his room number, and headed for the elevator, bumping into some of the gang from the movie. We got off on the fifth floor and as I was about to knock on his door, David spins around, ready to run. I knocked, dropped the bag, and we both ran like hell. To this day I don't believe he knows who or what happened to his bag. He now knows.

Filming

OUR CALLS WERE early—the sun wasn't even up when we met outside of the Warwick Hotel for our bus transportation to the location site. Everyone was either holding a hot drink, donut, sweet roll, or newspaper. Some leaned and others sat against the wall. There was chitchat and greetings as each new person showed up. There was excitement in the air; I could smell it, feel it, and my stomach confirmed it. We all tried to be cool but I sensed everyone was on edge, knowing this was to be our first day of shooting on location.

Then above the sound of street traffic we heard our assistant director, Robert Relyea, trumpet, "Let's board up, gentlemen, it's time to go to work!"

You could almost hear the adrenaline in everyone kick in as we grabbed our rehearsal bags and targeted a seat on the bus. The trip was a skip and jump to the location. As we peered out the windows of the bus, we came to a stop at our new home for the next three weeks. It was deserted, no sign of inhabitants, except for the studio crew and equipment. There were barricades at both ends of the street, and this thundering sound of a wrecking ball, several blocks away, knocking down building after building. Here we were at last, now the real work began. We all seemed eager to get going, and as we exited the bus we were greeted by Maggie Banks (assistant), Howard Jeffrey (assistant), and the master himself, Mr. Jerome Robbins, smiling a welcome.

Before we even had a chance to explore our new surroundings, we were told to prepare for a ballet class. So without hesitation we found a support to hang onto, like a railing, a trashcan, car, street sign, you name it. Then we started a slow warm-up. The people who had gathered at the barricades watched with curiosity as Robbins called out pliés, positions, and tondues. What a sight! I'm sure our audience at the barricades watching supposedly tough, vicious, gang members taking a ballet class on the sidewalks were thinking, what kind of gang prepares for a rumble by taking a ballet class before going into battle? We did!

Wow! It suddenly hit me, here I was in New York City where I was born, shooting a musical movie about gangs, and I flashed back to when I was six years old and was a member of the "West 136th Street Gang," and not by choice. I vividly remembered being touted by older gang members to rob a candy store with another young companion, Alvin. He would distract the owner, Joe, while I meandered my way to the back of the store, where I proceeded to pilfer whatever my grubby little hands could grab. Once my pockets were full, I slowly headed for the door while Alvin made a penny purchase to further distract Joe. Successfully pulling off our caper, we hastened up the block, turning the corner to be greeted by our greedy overseers. We were lucky to get a stick of gum or maybe a Tootsie Roll.

I can remember the rumbles we had on the roofs of the brownstone apartment buildings. We had to participate or else, meaning you got the crap beat out of you. We didn't have automatic weapons; we had fists, bricks, stones, clubs, and knives. Us younger guys were mostly lookouts and delivered messages. Sometimes we got into the mix to prove ourselves.

Then one day the word was out—another street gang was going to invade our street, something about payback for something one of our gang members did. We didn't know which end of the street they were coming from, so I was lookout at one end and Alvin the other. Both of us perched on top of a tenement roof. We were to light a flare when we saw them coming. Well they came from Alvin's end of the street. Our gang was divided into two groups in case they came from both ends. Upon seeing the flare, everyone rushed to Alvin's end of the street and the plan was to get them to chase a small group up to the roof top, where the bulk of our gang lay in waiting to ambush them. Well it worked, and we won that day. The next encounter we were not so lucky; one of our guys got pushed over the side of the building and was killed. It was soon after that my parents decided to move, and I'm mighty grateful they did. If they hadn't, I might be dead now…but instead, here I was hanging onto a railing taking a ballet barre and pretending to be a JD in a movie, on the streets of New York.

Now as we did our pliés and tondues, we noticed a couple of homeboys hanging around the street. Come to find out the studio made deals with them to make sure we were not interrupted while rehearsing and shooting. They were to receive tickets to ball games and other special gifts for their services. They must have been on a break one day when Mr. Robbins was viewing a shot on the large camera crane, holding his viewfinder to his eye. Out of nowhere, a brick came flying over his head, barely missing him, and he didn't flinch. I think the street gangs might have challenged us, but once they saw us dancing down the street, I'm sure they must have felt no contest!

We watched Mr. Wise and Mr. Robbins conversing about our first shot with Danny Fapp, our cameraman. Robbins wanted perfection at any cost so we did many, many, many takes. I'm sure Mr. Wise, our co-director, was biting the bullet, as he was a veteran of movie directing and Robbins was not. I guess the way they worked it out was Robbins would do the musical numbers and Wise the acting scenes.

Well we seemed to be moving along very slowly, until we got to the chase scene with the Jets, myself included, in hot pursuit of a lone Shark. We ran across the street heading for a heap of garbage, losing sight of our prey as we reached the peak of the mound. Down below, a hidden group of Sharks lay in wait and began pelting us with a barrage of the rottenest smelly fruits and vegetables and none of them missed their target. After a few takes, our clothes were getting real messed up, and it being summer the odor was becoming pretty intense.

They then decided it was time to move up the street and do a different setup. As we started to rehearse the new setup, **Bam!** We heard this loud crash. We spun around only to see this huge truck had broken through the barricade and was speeding to the exact area we had just left. It barreled into the mound of garbage and stopped. We all rushed to see what had happened to the driver. He was alright and explained his brakes had failed and he couldn't stop, and seeing the mound of garbage decided to ditch the truck there. Well, if we had done another take, we could of all have been a tossed salad. Hold the dressing!

After a few good days of sunshine things were moving at a steady pace, but then it started to cloud up. I'm not quite sure who the culprit was that suggested we do a rain dance. But there were a lot of volunteers. The formation was a large circle with arms over each other's shoulders. I could see it as the remake of *"Fiddler on the Street."* We began to chant some nonsense and started what was a bastard version of the four swans from *Swan Lake*. As we continued to move in a circle, small drops of rain began to fall, increasing minute by minute, till it began to pour buckets and we all ran for cover. After several hours of a mighty deluge it finally cleared up and it was back to work, but not for long. On our next break we wanted to test our powers with the rain gods and started the rain dance once more. Yep, you guessed it: down it came again. This time they decided to let us go home and hope for a better tomorrow.

Well the next day didn't look too promising. There were more clouds but no rain. After our morning ballet class, we decided to give it another shot. Down it came again; we had the power! It rained most of the day, and reluctantly they let us go after rehearsing indoors. I couldn't believe our luck. We all felt the longer it rained, the longer we got to stay in New York. They say three's a charm, and believe it or not we got it to rain the third day.

The next day, we knew "the powers to be" were uptight because we were supposed to have finished at this location by now. Plus that wrecking ball seemed to be getting awfully close. As we exited the bus, Mr. Relyea, in his military sergeant's voice said, "All right, gentlemen, listen up, no more rain dancing, or else."

Some of us started to giggle and moan in disbelief. Under breath I heard, "Or else what, we'll never work in Hollywood again?" We reluctantly abided by his wishes, and the rain gods must have heard his plea because it stopped.

Our next location was a playground on 110th Street. A welcoming committee met us, a mixed group of locals, young kids, teenagers, and adults, all curious to see a movie being shot in their neighborhood. One young Asian girl, who looked to be about sixteen or seventeen, came dressed as if she was going to church. She greeted us every morning when we arrived on the bus. I guess she was our first "Groupie." We even adopted a cute six-year-old boy that had lost his parents and was being raised by his aunts. We chipped in money to help him and his aunts out. Frankie was a young teenager that became our runner. He got us drinks and food since we could not leave the playground. He said he had a punchboard (a game of chance) route and collected money for his bosses.

Once we all settled into our new location, both the Jets and Sharks started to mix it up again. This time Tucker Smith (Ice/Jet) was taken down with the intention of shaving his private area. He resisted and got some cuts and bruises. The Sharks caught hell as Tucker had a close-up the next day, and they couldn't shoot it because it wouldn't match what was already "in the can"—film talk for "finished." So then we hung a dummy from the school chimney with a Shark card around its neck. They responded with sheets hanging from the buildings facing the playground printed with large letters "Sharks." Then we sent hundreds of small cards with "Jets printed on them from the tops of the facing buildings streaming down to the street, like a ticker-tape parade.

The following day we were at the Warwick Hotel waiting for Nick Covacevich (Toro/Shark) to show up so we all could go to dinner, when Jose De Vega (Chino/Shark) walked in with cold cream all over his face—pretty scary! We decided to scare Nick. Jose entered the bathroom and hid behind the shower curtain. A few days prior, we had seen the Hitchcock movie *Psycho*—get the picture? Nick knocked, we let him in, and we engaged in small talk. Then someone said, "Lets go. I'm starving." As we got ready to head out, Nick, as predicted, headed for the bathroom to check his hair and out popped Jose with his white face. Nick turned pale, gasped, and fell against the bathroom wall. "What the hell!" he stuttered, our laughter drowning him out. We picked him off the wall, revived him, and headed out to dinner.

One day, we were rehearsing a scene on the playground, with Riff, our gang leader (Russ Tamblyn), and a group of Jets that encounter several kids playing basketball. In the scene the ball accidentally rolls out of play and Riff picks it up and throws it back after a little hesitation, while giving a dirty look. Well Mr. Robbins didn't like the way Russ and the gang were doing the scene and came down on the guys with some pretty harsh words. He was very upset; for what reason, one could only guess.

He then turned to the young kid that dropped the ball and almost in baby talk said, "Allen, take your time, and don't rush, you can do it."

Well, we all looked at each other thinking, what the hell? "Allen baby!" Well he finally got it right, and so did the Jets.

Then we were on a break when we heard chanting and saw a crowd starting to gather on the sidewalks in front of the playground. Well it was a small parade heading our way. A beautiful statue of the Madonna was being carried on a stretcher by mafia-looking gentlemen dressed in sleek dark suits. Streaming down the guide lines supporting the statue were hundred dollar bills. We joined the neighborhood crowd on the sidewalk to view this unusual event.

Tucker Smith (Ice/Jet), wishing to seize the moment, moved in front of the parade and pretended to lead it as a drum major. Well he was quickly restrained with good cause. Most of the well-suited gentlemen surrounding the Madonna looked pretty tough, and I wondered if some might be packing. As the last part of the small parade glided by, hunched over on the curb with his feet in the gutter was this shabby-looking guy who had just been stabbed. The crowd dispersed very quickly and an awful eerie feeling came over everyone. A couple of bystanders came to his aid while everyone else just walked away quickly. Wow! I thought. It could have been Tucker!

After rehearsing and shooting all day, David and I sometimes hooked up with some girls while on the way home on the subway. We had some great parties at our apartment. One such party went really late, and a very attractive Asian gal Paula needed a ride home. I volunteered to take her home in a cab knowing that after dark, strange things happened on the streets of the Big Apple.

One such incident. Several years before *WSS*, I was in New York visiting my cousin in Greenwich Village. One evening I was having dinner at my cousin's apartment joined by Tony Barberio, a friend from LA, whom I'd met the day before. It must have been two or three in the morning when Tony and I thanked our gracious host and finally said our good-byes. Well as we searched the streets for a cab, none was to be found. So we hit the street. That time of morning you don't walk on the sidewalks. Anyone could jump you coming out of the shadows of a doorway or alley.

Walking up 9th Avenue, we encountered what seemed like a scene out of a Fellini movie. We both stopped and stared in total disbelief. There in the gutter was a male midget on top of a woman going at it! No joke! It was so bizarre I thought I was hallucinating. Tony was just as disbelieving. As we moved up the street and the sounds of sex faded behind us, we both turned and took one last look to verify what we had just witnessed was real. It was.

Now back to getting Paula home. I hailed a cab out front, and when we arrived at her place she invited me in for a drink, and I couldn't refuse. We began a relaxed conversation talking about what I don't remember. I must have dozed off 'cause when I opened my eyes the room was pitch black, except for this beam of light shining through the window. The sheet of light was directed to the bed where she lay with her beasts exposed, casting a sensuous silvery veil across her nipples. It was such a beautiful sight I couldn't stop staring. I remember slowly putting on my coat, cautiously moving towards the door, quietly turning the knob, opening the door, taking one last look over my shoulder, and closing it. I never saw her again till many years later; we both had changed, but that image of that night was still etched in my head.

Time flies when you're having fun and much—much—later than sooner, it was a rap in New York and we were now behind schedule. Once again the Jets and Sharks boarded separate flights knowing "Prologue" was "in the can." Now it was time to rehearse and shoot "Rumble," "Cool," "Krupke," "Dance Hall," "Quintet," and the Finale. It was great to be back and to see the girls again.

Gina Trikonis (Graziella/Jet) and I were becoming very good friends, she invited me over for dinner, and boy could she cook. She was Greek Orthodox and I was Russian Orthodox, so you might say we had something in common besides dance. We attended services at St. Sophia's Greek Orthodox Church on the corner of Pico and Normandie Avenue. What a spectacular church it was—everything trimmed in gold, looking like an opulent palace. Built in 1952 by Charles Skouras, brother of Spyros Skouras, who was president of 20th Century Fox for 20 years. George Chakiris (Bernardo/Shark) and Telly Savalas both were members of the congregation. Gina and I danced the night away at our social gatherings; what a dancer and she could cook!

When I heard Natalie Wood was doing the movie I was excited to see her, as she was my dance partner when we were kids in the Michael Panieff's Children's Ballet Company in Hollywood. Stefanie Powers and Jill St. John were also in the company. Stefanie was hired to do the movie *West Side*, but was let go because the part she was hired for was evidently promised to someone else if that person didn't get the part she was originally up for. Complicated? Yes, and I'm sure there are many different versions of this story.

Now back to Natalie: she had invited me several times to watch her work on several films, and a couple of weekends we went horseback riding. She invited me to a taping of a TV show she was doing. There was a contest with audience participation, and the one with the best tongue twister won a prize. Well talk about a fix. I was given one to say just before the show and during the live show, I was called on to give my pre-rehearsed twister, winning a pair of roller skates. But I had my eye on a pixie camera and told her about my other choice. She went to the producer and I got my pixie camera. What a gal! One weekend we were on the driveway of her house. She jumped onto this pogo stick, showing how proficient she was, and I was amazed.

"Here, why don't you try it?" she said.

"Yah, sure," I replied. Now I don't ever remember jumping on one of those things before and I figured what the hell, it couldn't be that hard—little did I know. I figured I couldn't let this girl show me up, so I hit it with one jump and off I went. I got about four bounces and feeling overconfident decided to increase my jump, and that was my biggest mistake. As I pushed down to get more elevation, something went wrong and I fell backwards, hitting my head on the bumper of the parked car. Needless to say, I was seeing all kinds of stars, and a bump the size of Catalina was forming on my head. Natalie just stood there shocked, then she started to laugh and I joined in, even though my head was about to explode.

I hadn't seen her in awhile and wondered if she would remember me. The last time we spoke I had asked her to my senior prom; she said she couldn't go. Found out later she was seeing someone on the film *Rebel Without A Cause*. When I finally caught up with her, she was rehearsing a scene and I didn't want to interrupt. She then took a break and we were able to talk briefly. I asked about her mom and her sister Lana and said I was glad she was doing the movie and wished her well. She thanked me and went back to rehearsing. I will always admire her as an actress and dance partner.

The Jets and Sharks became closer as we continued with rehearsals and hung out in small groups. I had an 8mm movie camera and was shooting some of the scenes I was not in and had someone shoot some that I was in. It seemed everyone was taking photos—an unusual sight as most studios frowned on having cameras on the set except for hired photographers.

The production numbers that stood out for me while rehearsing and shooting were "Rumble" and "Cool." The "Rumble," when first rehearsed, was a little too realistic. It seems the prop guy handed out some real brass knuckles to my counterpart Jay Norman (Pepe/Shark). He was only too happy to show me how they worked—Bam! a right to the mouth! "Must be a method actor." But that was remedied with a rubber replacement. Larry Rouqemore (Rocco/Shark) hit Richard Beymer (Tony/Jet) so hard in the gut he was out for awhile. Then like clockwork after each take, someone yelled, "Dog Pile!" Everyone charged the center of the set knocking each other down, then piled one on top of another, yelling, "Jets, Sharks, Geronimo!" Then someone yelled, "Hold it, guys, I lost my caps" (a smile enhancement). Then back to shooting it again. Even though the "Rumble" was choreographed, it was hard to duplicate the same moves each time 'cause you'd be bumped, shoved, and attacked by someone else.

Now "Cool" was another story. It was like dancing inside a heated sardine can, hotter than hell and not much breathing room with a very low ceiling and hot lights. Maybe more like being buried alive! We felt contained, cramped, restricted, and asphyxiated, which certainly mentally and physically enhanced the choreography. We really wanted to bust out and explode to destroy ourselves. In "Cool" you could feel the tension start to build right from the beginning with "Easy, Action. Easy!" Tony Mordente (Action), David Winters (A-Rab), and Tucker Smith (Ice) gave hot fuel to this number. A lot of the guys complained of raw and blistered knees from the knee spins that we must have done a hundred times. The more we moaned, the more we did it. The girls' trio was outstanding—Gina Trikonis (Graziella), Carole D'Andrea (Velma), and Patti Tribble (Minnie) added that feminine fire to the number. Eliot Feld (Baby John) wasn't feeling his best, but Robbins kept the heat up and drove us to do it again, again, and again, till that last snap and body slump—definitely my favorite.

The "Jet Song" bonded us every time we sang it. It made us feel like a destroyer cutting through dangerous waters hunting the enemy and ready to obliterate them. I for one felt a force of might and strength come over me, that together we were invincible. I remember when we sang the song at the playground in New York, we had to mouth the line, "'Cause every Puerto Rican's a lousy chicken!" I guess the studio felt the natives living in the neighborhood would certainly try to prove us wrong. Just before the song begins Mr. Robbins gave me a line, "The Greatest!" as I leapt across the bench. I really got into the song as you could tell by my facial expressions. I was a Jet through and through!

"Krupke" was a fun number and we played it to the hilt. It gave the guys a chance to act out their version of family ties, social and domestic injustices. Bert Michaels (Snowboy), David Winters (A-Rab), and Tony Mordente (Action) scored high in this number with their comical social characters. David Bean (Tiger) did a convincing comical Krupke. I was one of the blurs in the background pleading for mercy, and went spastic on the line, "We're disturbed."

In the drugstore scene, Anita (Rita Moreno) comes to Doc's candy store to give Doc (played by Ned Glass) a message from Maria to Tony. As she starts to get a word out she is heckled, verbally abused, and taunted. It got pretty wild as we grabbed and pulled at her skirt till she fell, and Baby John was picked up and lowered on top of her, the frenzy building to a mock sexual climactic ending with Doc coming to the rescue. Rita did a fantastic job portraying this reluctant messenger of hope who after being humiliated and fondled, decides to turn it into a terrible tragedy, saying Chino had killed Maria. Tears streamed down her face, her voice trembled, her delivery so real, it stunned and shamed us all. She certainly proved her acting ability and made it one scene that really sticks out in my mind.

A bit of trivia: Rita Moreno was visited on set by Marlon Brando one day, and all the girls were besides themselves. I had worked with him on a film he had directed, replacing Stanley Kubrick. It was the last release in Vista Vision for Paramount Studios in 1961. The name of the film was called *One Eyed Jacks*, an action western. Choreographer Josephine Earl hired me along with a small group of dancers to do a "Bon Bon Dance" in the town square, during a colorful fiesta celebration. The job was to last three days, but the script was not finished and was being written day by day. Very unusual! Night shooting prevailed and there was a lot of celebrating with liquid libation. I was bored sitting around waiting for something to happen and decided to join a nickel-dime card game. Well, there was this guy that seemed to be winning almost every pot. I couldn't believe it. I just put in my last bet to call and he lays down a straight flush, smiling as he rakes in the money, uttering, "This is copacetic!" Not knowing the meaning of the word at that time I responded, "No, no way, this is pathetic!" I was cleaned out.

Well, after three weeks, we finally did our festive dance in the town square. Brando, they say, shot six times the amount of film, and his first cut was allegedly five hours long. Of course the studio cut it way down and Marlon wasn't too happy, even though the movie was well received. I never saw the "Bon Bon Dance." I'm sure it was the first to be cut.

The end of shooting for *West Side Story* was fast approaching, with "Dance Hall" and the Finale yet to shoot. We were in the midst of rehearsing "Dance Hall" when the door swung open and in walked Mr. Robbins, looking a bit overwrought. Everyone stopped and looked up. With arms folded he positioned himself a few feet in front of us, and almost shouting, he started this barrage of demeaning put-downs, saying we could all be replaced and that we were not doing our job to the fullest. His face was turning red! What set him off? Could he really replace all of us, or was it his "method acting" approach to get us up to speed? We were all bewildered. I never saw such an outburst of temper except the time he came unannounced to a matinee of *Peter Pan*, at the Winter Garden Theater, in New York.

The animals of Neverland were making their crossover in front of the curtain when the ostrich's beaded necklace broke and scattered all over the stage. Now the next scene was the Indian dance, with Saundra Lee as Tiger Lilly. We the Indians waited for the curtain to open, not knowing beads were scattered all over the stage. We began the number and then it happened: first one and then another stepped on a bead, lost their balance, hit the deck or bumped into an unsuspecting Indian. The formation we were to keep was no longer there with us slipping and sliding all over the stage. Now the inevitable thing happened—someone started to giggle and it spread like wildfire. No one could hold back, try as we may. The number was a complete disaster. Indians strewn all over the stage. The number finished, followed by an intermission.

Bam! As though a fire alarm had gone off, the loud sound of the back stage door slammed shut. Everyone in hearing range froze. We all knew that was the sound of God (Mr. Robbins). And at the blink of an eye everyone scattered in all directions to hide—bathroom, behind scenery, hallway, under tables; I hid behind a wardrobe rack. Saundra hadn't heard the door slam and was coming up the stairs from the dressing rooms below. There he was standing at the top of the stairs, hands on hips looking like Mr. Clean. Well what followed echoed throughout backstage, and I'm sure those in hiding were shaking in their costumes. He didn't mince words and had poor Saundra in tears. Talk about someone being crucified; she took the brunt and we were spared the verbal whiplashing. We had a clean up rehearsal for a week after that.

But here at the studio no one was spared his tongue-lashing. Robbins spun around, headed out the door, and disappeared. We later found out he had been fired, axed, terminated. The studio felt he was taking much too long with rehearsals, setups, and shooting. At first, no one believed it, thinking he would come through the rehearsal door any minute, but he never did. The word was that Howard Jeffrey decided to leave with Robbins, as he was his number one assistant. Robert Wagner wrote in his book, *Pieces of My Life*, that Natalie threatened to leave the film unless Robbins was reinstated, but Jerry and her agent convinced her not to desert the ship. So things continued to move on as though nothing had happened, with Robert Wise taking the helm. Tony Mordente was asked to help with the remaining musical number and did a commendable job. As they say in the biz, "The Show Must Go On," and it did.

Did the film suffer because of Robbins' absence? I don't really think so. Most of the extraordinary musical numbers had already been shot, and had his seal of genius on them. We did feel somewhat let down and maybe a bit disoriented because our leader was not there to guide us to the end of this unforgettable journey. We all knew what was expected of us and met that challenge. It was not so much to honor him, but we respected his creative process and had integrity about our work and contribution to it that we felt compelled to give him his vision even without his driving presence and guidance.

"Dance Hall" was a hot mambo and competition that drove the frenzy to a war counsel. Riff and his girlfriend Graziella take on their counter with an overpowering energetic routine, while being egged on by a zealous crowd.

The Sharks answered with a definite attitude of strong movements. Everyone was up to full speed, then came the transition when Tony and Maria notice each other, the excitement surrounding them is blurred out, and the tempo slows. I was not involved in this section known as the "Cha-Cha," but those that were will undoubtedly be writing about it and you will be able to read firsthand what went on.

In the Finale, not only were both gangs mourning a death, but we were coming to the sad end of a family of brothers and sisters. I'm sure we all felt the same. I could see it in everyone's face. I felt it too. Tomorrow, what about tomorrow? No longer coming to the studio, no rehearsals, no scenes to shoot, no longer a Jet or Shark. That was it—the end. Why did it have to end? With new close friendships, and memories never to be forgotten, why couldn't it have gone on forever? Yes, we know...nothing is forever. It was a very sad, sad day! Now what? Some of the gang from the East Coast decided to stay and try their luck here, while others were anxious to return home to New York. I believe the hardest thing in this business is when a job comes to an end and not knowing when or where the next one will come from. *West Side* was my longest film job—six months—and my longest only Broadway show *Peter Pan* lasted six months also.

I remember my very first job. I was graduating from Hollywood Professional School, where I had my tuition paid for by an anonymous benefactor. I was told he was a writer that lived in New England. He evidently had seen me dance somewhere and thought I had talent and stage presence and wanted to help. I found out who he was and thanked him for believing in me and hoped to repay him. I had a dance scholarship that required me to take four classes a day, and by going to HPS, which was a half-day private school, I could meet school and my dance class obligations. I had decided to attend UCLA Theater Arts classes after graduation to further my theatrical training in acting, choreography, and directing. But the summer before fall classes started, I attended a dance audition for the stage production of *Carousel* at the LA Civic Light Opera, headed by Edwin Lester. Well I was so excited and couldn't wait to strut my stuff. I made the cut and was asked to read for a part. I got the part of Enoch Snow Jr. I was on my way, my very first professional show and a small part. Who could ask for anything more? Jan Clayton and Bill Johnson starred and Jan was a great help; she kind of looked after me, helped me learn the ropes as this was all very new to me. I was eager and willing and I caught on very quickly. Our show was coming to the end of our eight-week run, four in Los Angeles and four in San Francisco. Well here was another family that worked together for a total of three months, and it was closing night at the Curran Theater in San Francisco. Well I cried like a baby, saying good-bye to all, not knowing if we would ever work together again. But by the second and third show I had hardened; farewells were hugs and handshakes, no tears. Not a drop! But it was different with *West Side*. It really got to me and it was hard to let go. This was no ordinary job, and neither were the people involved. They had become true friends who were very much part of my life, and still are.

After

THE MOVIE CAME out in October 1961, and it wasn't until *West Side* swept the Academy Awards and Critics' Honors, did everyone associated with the movie begin to gain recognition for their contribution. If you went on an interview and were asked what you had done recently, and mentioned *West Side*, you were given special attention. Sometimes someone before me gave it as a credit and when asked if I knew that person, I answered, "Never saw that dude before, he sure didn't do the movie."

Friends and relatives bragged and people came up and asked, "Did you really work on the movie *West Side Story*?" It certainly gave you an edge, opened a lot of doors, and helped all our careers.

Another movie released in 1961 was *Babes in Toyland*. I had the pleasure of working with another talented choreographer, Tommy Mahoney. It starred Tommy Sands and Annette Funicello. There was a gypsy celebration that took place in the center of this magical town square. Miss Patti Tribble, who was (Jet/Minnie) in "Cool," was one of the Lemonade Girls on pointe. I was a Russian gypsy dancer who played a concertina, while doing knee spins in a circle. Later I was to come flying over a crowd of townspeople doing a Russian split in the air. Well all went well during rehearsal. While shooting, I sprung off a hidden trampoline and came flying overhead when some nut job decided to step out in front of me. I twisted in the air to avoid landing on him and came down in a mangled heap. Clunk! Boy was I in pain; I was rushed to first aid and was told I might have to give up my dancing shoes, but that wasn't going to happen. I'm still looking for that idiot.

I had done a few musicals on stage, TV, and film, before *WSS*, like *Li'l Abner*, *Let's Make Love*, *Carousel*, *Rock Around the Clock*, *The Girl Most Likely*, *Damn Yankees*, *and Plain and Fancy*, to name a few. In 1964, Peter Gennaro, who choreographed "Mambo" and part of "America," was the choreographer of the *Judy Garland Show*, and I was a dancer on the show. He had to go to New York for something one week, and the assistant took over. We were to do a contemporary dance to a recording of Shirley Ellis's "The Nitty Gritty." The assistant didn't have a clue what to do. Everyone said, "Let Banas do it, he frequents all the local dance clubs." My partner was that beautiful and talented Gina Trikonis from *West Side*, and I delivered. That same year I did the movie, *Unsinkable Molly Brown*, with Debbie Reynolds, Grover Dale (Broadway*WSS*), and Gus Trikonis (Indio/Shark), choreographed by Peter Gennaro. Alex Plasschaert and I did a trio spot with Debbie, dancing on the bar to "Belly Up to the Bar Boys." Debbie was a delight to work with—so much energy, hard to keep up with. I also worked with her in *Say One For Me* and *How the West Was Won*.

Debbie Reynolds and Ruta Lee head up a wonderful charitable organization called The Thalians. I had staged a couple of shows for them. One was at the Sherman Oaks Galleria, in which I choreographed a show called "Follow the Yellow Brick Road." The event took place on the ground floor with a small stage and chairs set up all around facing the stage. Just before the show started, in walked the fire captain and his crew, saying we could not continue as there was not enough space to exit if a fire ensued. Ruta Lee convinced them to stay and enjoy the show while the exits were cleared to their satisfaction. The show went on without a hitch. I was awarded a yellow brick with my name on it. Brick? Yes, a brick!

Harvey Hohnecker (Mouthpiece/Jet) and I (Joyboy) were both chimney sweeps in that wonderful movie *Mary Poppins*, choreographed by Marc Breaux and Dee Dee Woods. They were a terrific couple to work for, and the "Chimney Sweep" number, danced on the London rooftops, was a standout. I also had worked for Dee Dee Woods on the film *Li'l Abner* in 1959, with cinematographer Daniel L. Fapp, the same guy that made all the Jets and Sharks look so great in *WSS*.

Because of *West Side Story*, many of the guys became choreographers and/or directors. I got hired by some of them, and even hired some when I choreographed a show. Tony Mordente hired me for a *Danny Thomas Special* for TV. Tony went on to direct a bunch of TV series. David Winters produced, choreographed, and directed.

I worked for David on *Hullabaloo*, *Dave Clark Five Special*, and a movie with Patty Duke called *Billy*. Andre Tayir had me assist him on a TV pilot called *Shivaree*. Gus Trikonis also directed many TV series. Eliot Feld started his own dance company.

After *West Side*, I started teaching and formed The Bob Banas Dance Company. It gave me the chance to explore choreography while experimenting with new ideas and giving "wannabe's" a chance to live show biz. We did performances every chance we got. I injected pantomime, singing, tap, ballet, comedy, and jazz. My objective was to give my students a chance to perform and gain self-confidence while experiencing the limelight with a live audience. Some went on to become professionals, while others cherished their moments onstage for the rest of their lives.

Lalo Schifrin had a rock version of "Bolero," which was a great rendition of that song, and I wanted to choreograph something special to it. I wanted to use a parachute and add balloons filled with helium to float the chute. I found a beautiful silk parachute at a uniform manufacturer downtown and then calculated how many balloons filled with helium it would take to raise the parachute. So one weekend the company met at my place and we tried to make my dream come true. I had rented a helium tank and bought four three-foot balloons (one extra just in case), figuring that would lift the chute. The chute had quite a few guide lines, and this was great because the dancers could use them to control the chute once it was up. We had a show coming up at the LA Garden Festival, and I wanted to unleash this crazy idea of mine.

We were to perform outdoors but there was one factor I hadn't figured on, and that was the wind factor. So we began to fill the balloons, and once they were filled we started to cover them with the chute, thinking the shape of the chute and guide lines would surely hold them in place. But as the chute began to rise, a small gust of wind pushed and leaned it on its side; one by one the balloons escaped and floated up and away, never to be seen again. I was utterly disappointed, kicking the metal helium tank in frustration. Ouch! The rest of the afternoon was spent with everyone getting high on helium and talking like Minnie Mouse. I was racking my brain—how was I going to save the day? Then it hit me.

One of our company members, Bruce Piner, who was about six feet tall, was going to be my lifesaver. He would be the focal point. He wore a black wig with one-inch long strands of felt material. His face was covered with a plain white mask, and he stood in the center of the parachute with his head extended from the center opening. He looked like a strange ghostly character in a very large white gown. As the music started he made his entrance in a slow, gliding movement heading for center stage. He slowly scanned to the right and then the left. The audience was completely bewildered. Then the chute began to rise open, revealing six female dancers in pure white unitards with mylar head gear, and mylar covering their ankles and wrists. These futuristic damsels started bellowing the chute up and down, coordinating their assigned guide lines, turning and twisting as the chute breathed upward and floated downward. The routine that followed was more of a mathematical Einstein equation with the dance movement combined with the guide lines acting as the foundation for the number. Bruce was reacting as though he had spewed forth and given birth to this erotic sensation. The number ended with the dancers disappearing under the parachute and Bruce slowly gliding offstage mimicking his entrance. After the show people were asking, "What were you trying to say?" I really wasn't trying to say anything. All I wanted to do was to use the damn parachute.

I have worked with many wonderful stars through the years, and it's difficult to tell all the captivating stories it's been my pleasure to experience. But one does stand out. In 1960, before *West Side*, I had called George Light, casting director at 20th Century Fox, about an audition that was coming up for a movie called *Let's Make Love*, starring Marilyn Monroe. At that time if you went on an interview, you would be paid a few bucks for carfare. I had a date coming up with a cute gal and needed gas for my car. I thought if I got on the list for the audition, my problem would be solved.

George immediately shot me down. "Banas," he said, "You're too short, we need six-foot, blond, blue-eyed guys."

"George, I'm not a midget!"

"Sorry, kid."

"Wait a minute, George, I've got a hot date and need gas for my wheels."

"Yah sure!"

It went back and forth till he finally gave in, as he could see I wasn't going to take no for an answer. Well the day of the audition it so happened two other midgets (my size guys , Jack Tigget and Alex Plasschaert, showed up. I wasn't feeling so guilty now, thinking George couldn't find the giants he wanted.

The choreographer was the famous Jack Cole, whose reputation preceded him. He was noted for his knee work and quick multi-movement to the beat of the music. He had nurtured the likes of Bob Fosse, Mat Mattox, Gwen Verdon, Carol Haney, Buz Miller, and I believe Bob Hamilton. He started the audition with jump passé in the air. Then after a quick elimination, he asked the three midgets to take the floor and showed a combination that was fast and sharp. The three of us looked at each other as if to say, "What was that?" We knew we wouldn't dare ask him to repeat it. The music started, and as if we were connected at the waist, somehow we all remembered the moves and finished on the beat. He was caught off-guard; I think he thought we would blow the combination and would be cut. He looked a bit shocked and abruptly told us to sit down. Well the three of us made the final cut. I'd like to add that no one did Jack's work like he did.

We started rehearsals without Marilyn, and the studio hadn't decided on a leading man to play opposite her. We were working on a song called "My Heart Belongs to Daddy." The set platform we worked on had four steel poles, and sticking out at different levels were steel pegs that you could step on to climb up. We practiced swinging around the poles, then climbing up the pegs and dropping to the floor. Now that doesn't sound so hard, but the music was a bit bright, and four guys were swinging through the poles while four others were climbing and the remaining darting in and out between the others. Talk about a traffic jam, not to mention when you hit one of those pegs sticking out, you bruised and cut your forearm. Someone asked, is that a tattoo?!

Then one morning there she was, the beautiful blonde Marilyn Monroe, leaning against the piano while we all stared in amazement. She turned and smiled as Jack introduced us. With him taking her place, Jack then assembled us in position for a run-through. After we finished the number, she applauded and seemed very anxious to take part. She began by sliding down one of the poles to start the number and walked through the other poles while we slowly moved all around her. Jack gave her sexy arm and body movements as she moved sensuously through the crowd of her excited "teddy bear" dancers. Jack just knew what to do to make her look like she was doing a lot more than she was. She would turn and look, and two guys were expelled into the air. Another turn and arm gesture, two more guys spun around and dropped to the floor. We made runs, jumps, and dives in front, back, and overhead, never touching a hair on her head. She controlled the number.

They finally got Yves Montand to be her leading man when we were ready to shoot the number. We were all excited and wanted to do our very best. The number started off pretty good, then Jack came over to give us a pep talk.

He didn't mince words; he said, "Destroy yourselves!"

The next take I took him at his word and went flying off the platform into the set wall, almost knocking it over. He smiled and gave me a look that said, "Destroy yourself, not the set." Marilyn's dresser leaned in to her before each take and whispered, "Pull in your tummy." But I didn't notice any reason for that; she looked terrific to me. There were a few days she didn't show up. So they shot around her. We sat around or were off in a corner rehearsing some choreography, while dialogue with some of the other principals took place. Tony Randall, Milton Berle, Frankie Vaughan, and Wilfrid Hyde-White were part of the cast. Tony Randall was very social and fun to be around. Milton was always on and not very funny. The rumor was that Marilyn and Yves were becoming very close friends. When there was no more to shoot without her, we had to come to the studio just in case she would show up.

I got bored waiting and decided to visit some of the soundstages. I found one that was empty except for a huge Titan crane. Temptation got the better of me and I decided to play cameraman. I climbed up on the rig and started to move it. Just then someone walked in and yelled, "What the hell are you doing up there?"

"Well ah, I ah was just seeing if it worked, and ah it did!" I stuttered.

"Get down from there right now, you're not to be in here, period." So much for my cameraman career.

Well our beautiful blonde bombshell finally returned, and we were ready to begin filming again. The number progressed in an orderly fashion, and at one point in the number, Marilyn grabbed Alex and I by the hair, pulling us toward her bosom as she sang a line and then proceeded to swing around one of the poles. She grabbed the pole and began to spin like a top, losing her balance.

Someone yelled, "Cut!"

She recovered, then turned to the director, George Cukor, and in that soft sexy voice said, "George, I don't want to say anything, but I believe someone has a bit of grease in his hair."

She then slid her contaminated hand up and down on her thigh to rid her hand of my hair pomade. Yes, it was I that was carted off to make-up for a shampoo. When I returned we picked up where we left off and started with the ending, where we all surrounded her in a huddle.

Jack came up to me and said, "Bob, jump on Herman's back and kiss Marilyn."

I thought he said "jump on Herman's back and miss Marilyn." Why would I miss her? Then it dawned on me he meant kiss her. Oh my God! I was asking the guys if anyone had a Life Saver. They began to laugh and so did I. I kept thinking what is my motivation, is it a kiss of overjoyed excitement, a playful gesture, or just a plain kiss? I'll just kiss her and that will be that. As we all got in position for the last section of the dance, I was ready and willing to kiss Marilyn Monroe. The music started and I moved to get in place; most of the guys had already surrounded her like a football huddle. I darted toward Herman at a fast clip, leapt onto his backside, leaned forward, and planted my lips on hers. I thought it was going very smoothly but when my lips touched hers, mine slid across her face because of the lip-gloss. She looked at me as if to say, "What was that?" I just couldn't let it go.

I turned to George, the director, and said in a low voice, "I don't want to say anything, but I believe someone has a lot of lip-gloss on."

She broke up and so did everyone else. The next take I nailed it. When we finished the number, all the guys lined up outside of her dressing room to get an autographed picture. She was most generous and signed them "Sincerely Yours, Marilyn." It just so happened I was the last one in line; she looked at me with a cute little smile and signed my photo. I took the photo which read, "Love and Kisses, Marilyn." I melted. Wow! First, just to be working with her, then an unbelievable kiss, and an autographed picture to end all autographs. I was definitely the luckiest guy in the whole wide world. Still am; it seems some things are never planned, they just happen! Thanks, Jack.

My parents had a lot to do with my career. They encouraged my sister and I to take dancing during World War II. We were staying with our grandmother on a small farm in Windber, Pennsylvania. My father was a military policeman at the Mckeesport Steel Mills, and Mom worked for Curtis Wright inspecting airplane propellers. Since Grandma was widowed, my parents thought they could help her out financially, and we would have a great place to grow up.

Dad found out about this dance teacher Agnes Shontz, who had a dance studio in downtown Winber. She taught tap, ballet, baton twirling, and acrobatics. She decided that my sister Faith and I would do ballroom dancing. I'll never forget us dancing to "The Tales of Vienna Woods." Faith, my sister, wore a beautiful white gown, and I a tux. I guess Agnes had a vision of Rogers and Astaire when they were kids and we were to mirror them.

The war ended and Dad headed to Los Angeles looking for a long lost brother he was trying to locate. There were no places to stay and he slept on bus benches. There were very few jobs, but he fell in love with the weather and finally found a room to rent. His leads finding his brother came to a dead end; he missed us and said get out here as soon as you can. California, here we come.

Well it was pretty crowded with the four of us in one bed and not much privacy for anyone. Dad finally got a job with RCA and Mom at Kress's Five and Dime Store as a cashier. They found a boarding school (California Children's College) for Sis and me, as it was still very difficult to find an apartment. The school was coed and almost military run. Roll call was at six am. We had a warm glass of water, then a break to make our bed and put our room in order. Then came inspection by the floor supervisor. If they couldn't bounce a quarter on your bed, it was torn up to be made again. You then had fifteen minutes to dress and report to the dining room. Serving monitors brought the food to your table. A tingling bell sounded as everyone bowed heads for thirty seconds of silent prayer. Then it was time to chow down. The morning meal usually consisted of orange juice, scrambled eggs, bacon, hashed brown potatoes, milk, and toast.

Both Sis and I were voted president of student council. I became editor of the school paper and started a victory garden. On Thursdays Sis and I accompanied vice principal Miss Huntington to Christian Science services and a trip to Coast Ice-cream Parlor for a treat. There was this girl Roberta Lyons that loved to get my goat.

She would come up to me and say, "What do bees make?" Of course I'd say "honey," and she would then kick me in the shins while blurting out, "Fresh!" I think that was her way of saying she had a crush on me. I hate to think what she would do if she hated me. She was big for her age, almost a foot taller than me. She had freckles, curly red hair, was built like a lumberjack, and ruled the playground.

My sister and I began dancing again with Peggy Vanne at Perry's studio on Highland Avenue, in Hollywood, run by Barbara Perry. Barbara was delightful, always smiling and greeting everyone as they entered the studio. Peggy Vannes' mother was quite a character. She sat at the door as you entered to collect the money for class. She wore a wide-brim hat, her dress hiked up to her knees with dark brown stockings gartered above her calves and her legs spread open in a very un-ladylike fashion.

We were studying tap with Peggy, and Faith was a natural. She picked up the steps even before Peggy executed them. She had the whole combination while I was still struggling on the first step. Things started to change as she became more interested in boys and she was getting too heavy to lift. So I decided to go solo.

There happened to be an audition for a ballet scholarship at Jack Walken's Dance Studio just down the street, and I thought I would give it a try. I had very little ballet training and thought this would be a great way to continue to learn more. I arrived early and climbed the steps to the second floor. Mr. Michel Panaieff was giving the audition and a few boys were there warming up already. He asked us to do a combination he showed and watched us very closely. He whittled it down to two of us.

He then asked if we could do a pirouette and I said yes, not knowing if I could. The other kid did a couple. When it was my turn, I began to get nervous and started shaking. As I prepared to turn, I tripped myself and fell to the floor, rebounded quickly and pretended nothing happened. I started again and got halfway around and fell to the floor again. I was so embarrassed but kept telling myself I can do it, I know I can, just one more try, I know I can do it. So I tried again and down I went.

Mr. Panaieff started to laugh; he couldn't believe his eyes. I rebounded with a few bruises, red face, and a lot of determination. As I wound up once again, knowing I could at least get one simple turn, that's all I needed, he said, "Stop, please stop, you've got the scholarship, don't kill yourself."

I guess he thought I needed help, and with all my gung-ho spirit I might have some talent. Another boy named Don Zoutte and I were to be the extent of the male dancers, who were to be part of the Children's

Ballet Company. As I mentioned before, some of the young ballerinas in our company were Jill St. John, Stefanie Powers, and Natalie Wood.

I would like to say that Michel Panaieff was generous, inspirational, giving, and a great mentor. His classes were challenging and so much fun. Many times I shared a barre with Oleg Tupine, Freddie Franklin, Alexandra Danilova, Vera Ellen, Leslie Caron, and many other dance world celebrities. I learned a lot from this man who taught me to never give up.

In early September 2001 I received an invitation to the 40th anniversary celebration of the film *West Side Story*, to be held at Radio City Music Hall in New York October 6th, 2001. Reception at 5pm followed by a screening at 7pm. You must remember that the Twin Towers had just been bombed, and flying was out of the question for most people. Rita and George had already agreed to go, but none of the West Coast gang players were eager to make the trip. I wanted to go not only for the movie, but to see Ground Zero. The only other person that went was Maria Henley (Teresita-Shark) .

When we arrived in New York, we met Mike Erick, producer of our latest DVD at that time. He had a limo and offered us a ride. I was the last to be let off and the driver got lost trying to find my hotel, which my son had arranged for me. It was an airy and comfortable hotel.

The night of the screening, excitement was in the air. Mr. Wise, Rita Moreno, George Chakiris came down the red carpet, followed by fellow Jets Harvey Evans, David Bean, and Bert Michaels, and I was behind the camera shooting. I was surprised to see Richard Beymer, and I asked him if he would join us after the movie to get a bite. He said yes but never showed. Marni Nixon, who dubbed Natalie's singing, seemed to be representing Natalie. During the opening introductions, a rep from Classic Films talked about the film but never mentioned Natalie; when George and Rita took the stage, they didn't mention her either. Then they brought the Jets and Sharks on stage and I was about to shout, "Don't forget Natalie Wood!" But we were hustled offstage very quickly. I guess people can get so wrapped up in themselves they forget their fellow thespian.

After this screening, we all went into the audience to greet friends and loyal fans. There were young kids and older people all hugging original programs and production photos from the movie begging for autographs. An ex-student of mine came up to me and thanked me for helping him—he was now working in a Broadway show. A mother announced that her young daughter was doing *West Side Story* and playing the part of Maria. Some people had tears in their eyes, others reaching out to shake your hand and expressing how much they enjoyed the film. It was unreal!!

We all gathered at Joe Allen's afterwards and passed around a poster with everyone autographing each other's. It had been a long time that some of us had seen the movie on a big screen. It sparked conversations about rehearsals and filming. It was great to see those that could make it.

It seems as one ages and times change, you start to slow down and the body you so recklessly abused now decides to resist your outburst of youthful energy. I have always loved gardening and have at times ventured into landscaping for friends and family. I took two semesters of Landscape Architecture at UCLA, but realized I would have to apprentice with a company for a year or so before striking out on my own. I would be cooped up inside drafting and not breathing the sweet smell of a fragrant garden. I found that working outdoors was so soothing mentally and spiritually, plus physically rewarding. My interest was driven to something more specialized...the rose!

I had been growing miniature roses for some time and would give out small bouquets to friends and sold them for special occasions. Then things changed when out of the blue my lovely dance partner in "Dance Hall," Roberta Deutsch, asked if I would take care of her roses, and of course I said yes. Shortly after, her interior designer Barbara Barry became my second client. Barbara recommended me to her friend Nancy Stanley, in the Hancock Park area. Things took off after that and now I have clients in Toluca Lake, Studio City, Brentwood, and Malibu. Don't forget to smell the roses!

If not for *West Side Story*, I would never have been able to take this fabulous journey meeting all the wonderful people and friends along the way. I have been very fortunate to work with some of the most creative choreographers in the US: Jack Cole, Bob Fosse, Toy Charmoli, Dee Dee Wood, Marc Breau, Gower Champion, Peter Gennaro, Rod Alexander, Helen Tamiris, Ernie Flatt, Onna White, Miriam Neison, Gene Nelson, and the one and only, the unforgettable Jerome Robbins. He stood alone because of his ability to bring to life movement that made you react with deep emotion.

Yes, Mr. Robbins, a great big tremendous Thank You! You gave others and myself the opportunity and trusted our ability to fulfill your vision of a stupendous work of art. With respect and gratitude, I salute you. You will never know how many dancers'/actors' careers you have helped catapult because of this classic film. A film that will forever live in honor of the legacy you leave behind. Not to mention the countless many you have moved and inspired by this iconic work of art to become an actor, singer, or dancer. For those of us who worked so closely with you in creating *West Side Story*, you will always be known as "Big Daddy" to us. – Joyboy

Robert Banas

"Graziella"/Jet - Gina Trikonis

MAMA AND ANESTOS were seeing me off at New York's La Guardia Airport. Just the day before, Jerome Robbins' secretary called and said: "Jerry wants you in LA tomorrow, and bring your green jumper."

So here I was, on my way to Los Angeles to be in the film version of *West Side Story*. It was such a life-altering moment that the navy LANZ jumper with matching jacket, lace-collared white blouse, and black T-strapped heels I wore, are seared in my memory forever. The year was 1960 and unlike nowadays, people dressed to travel.

"My little sister is going to be a movie star," teased my younger brother Anestos, ruffling my hair and laughing. "I'm gonna miss you," he said.

"Stop it," I said, grabbing his hands. "No movie star, just a dancer. I'm gonna miss you too, but I'll be back before you know it."

"Say hello to Gus for me."

"I will."

My brother Gus, who played Action in the Broadway show, had been in LA working on pre-production for weeks. Consequently, I thought Jerry had changed his mind about me. When Jerry's secretary asked if I could make it, of course I said yes. What was I going to do? Say no, I needed more time? You don't say no to Jerome Robbins.

My muddled mind went into total brain freeze and I felt as if I were swimming through molasses, finding a suitcase and packing what few clothes I had, all my dancewear, my favorite books and the green jumper I had made, though for the life of me I didn't know why he had asked for it.

Mama's eyes filled with tears when she hugged and kissed me. "Be a good girl, *kouroolamoo* (my sweet daughter), and may God be with you and keep you safe," she said while engaging in the automatic Greek custom of making the sign of the cross over me and spitting three times to keep the evil eye away. And when Mama asked as an afterthought, "Are you wearing your cross?" And I answered, "Yes, Ma, I'm wearing my cross," I was clueless my cross would become part of my costume.

"I'm proud of you," she said, crushing me to her breast. "Call as soon as you get there so I know you're safe. And tell Costa I love him and to behave himself."

As I walked towards the gate, I found myself wishing Papa were still alive to share this moment, just as I had wished he were alive to see Gus and I on the Broadway stage, but he died when I was ten.

"The arts feed your soul," Papa said time and again. "Without them only half of you grows; without them you shrivel up and die inside."

I grew up with this—the arts were an integral part of life in my parents' rich culture, and though poor Greek immigrants in this country, they brought that vibrant culture with them. So the arts became an important part of our education. Papa took me to my first ballet class when I was seven. The teacher put my feet in second position. I circled my arm and took my very first plié to Chopin with tears streaming down my cheeks. I knew then this was what I was born to do, but that's another story to be told another time.

As I boarded the plane, I realized I had been holding my breath, not daring to feel any emotion. When I finally allowed myself to exhale, my body began to shake and unstoppable tears streamed down my cheeks—tears of joy, sadness, relief mixed into one. I looked out the window, grateful no one was sitting next to me, and as I watched my New York fade away under a thick cover of white clouds, I wondered how long I'd be in LA, how long the filming would take, and when I would return. Little did I know, sitting in first class, I was flying towards my unimaginable future—leaving my mother, my brother, my family, and my hometown behind forever.

But let's start at the beginning of this extraordinary journey. When I first met Jerry, I didn't know who Jerome Robbins was. It was 1958 and I was a naïve seventeen-year-old right out of The High School of Performing Arts Dance Program. I knew nothing of his reputation as a tyrant and a taskmaster, but more importantly I knew nothing of his genius, so he did not intimidate me. Peter Gennaro, whose jazz class I was in and who co-choreographed *West Side Story*, thought I was right for the show and told me to go to the replacement audition, and so I went to the Winter Garden Theater to audition for my first Broadway show having no expectations. The entire train trip to the theater, I downplayed how excited I truly was and my inner dialogue went: *I'm not expecting anything—there's no way I'm going to get it—I really don't care—I'm going because Peter said to go.*

I remember so vividly when I arrived at the stage door, I closed my eyes, crossed myself, took a deep breath, exhaled, then opened the door. The unexpected assault of cigarette smoke and loud chattering voices nailed my feet to the floor! I-could-not-move! My mouth went bone dry and I wished I had a mint, a Life Saver, a piece of gum, anything to wet my mouth. An army of butterflies filled my belly and marched up to my throat, my fingertips turned ice cold, and the sinking feeling in my chest made breathing almost impossible. Like mold sticks to walls, cigarette smoke stuck to my hair, my skin, my clothes, and with my heart trembling, I made my way to the wings, where dance bags were tossed on the floor and the all-too-familiar smell of sweaty rehearsal clothes, dance shoes, and Jane Nate After Bath Splash rose from the bags and clung to the air like smoke from tobacco.

I looked about, enthralled by my surroundings, and my terror eased. I had entered an unfamiliar yet bewitching world of black, musty curtains and huge lightbulbs, cradled in cages, attached to standing poles that lit the bare stage. I had never seen anything like them. Their harsh light made things seem distorted and somewhat surreal, and I felt as if I were just outside my body observing it all. The proscenium became a horizon separating the stage from blackness. I heard a piano coming from the orchestra pit, but couldn't see who was playing.

Sets hung in the rafters held in place by ropes, weights, counter weights, and sandbags. A drugstore set butted up against the back of the stage. Dancers who looked as if they had been doing this forever stretched, jumped, and warmed up. Others stood about or sat smoking, talking, and sizing one another up. And there I was in my shredded-at-the-knees, cut-off-jean jazz pants, white socks, and black jazz shoes. I felt so out of place, I felt invisible, as if I were nothing more than a small shadow with a ponytail that no one looked at or noticed, and I thought, *What am I doing here?* My body wanted to bolt and it took all my willpower not to turn and run.

Then I saw him—though I didn't know who he was. A shortish man with a graying beard and a cigarette dangling from his mouth walked across the stage and stopped. He wore gray cords, white shirt with sleeves rolled, desert boots with gummy soles, and a cap.

"Listen up," said his assistant, Howard Jeffrey, following behind.

Howard was of medium height with long legs. He had large round blue eyes, and dark, closely cropped nappy hair. He wore a long-sleeved boat-necked blue and white-striped T-shirt, blue jeans, and white tennis shoes.

"Line up," he said.

Jerry stood with arms crossed and legs apart. His cigarette tip burned red while smoke circled his face. "To the right, to the left, left, left, right," said Howard as Jerry looked at the line and whispered.

"Right," he said when he came to me. And so it went, dividing us into two groups.

"Thank you for coming," he said to the left. "The rest, wait."

Little did I know that this ordinary-looking man standing on the stage was about to dramatically change my life. What I will never forget is how he felt. He felt like this huge, spinning, crackling ball of energy that was way too big to be contained in his small body, so his neck and hands shook. His light eyes, which looked as if they were on fire, reflected this intensity. Now, he didn't simply stand. He leaned in like a tiger about to pounce, and he didn't smile once during the grueling audition. He just watched with those fiery eyes, while dancer after dancer was eliminated and only one other dancer and myself were left.

We continued to dance side-by-side, combination after combination, again and again and again. The choreography was now in my muscles, so I stopped thinking of the steps. My body knew what to do and thinking got in the way—the dance and music simply took over, bending my back, kicking my legs, snapping my fingers. My heart pumped, my drenched white T-shirt stuck to my skin, and after the umpteenth time of doing the "Cool" variation, Howard finally said, "Rest."

I doubled over holding my thighs, my ponytail stuck to my neck, my lungs gasped and heaved, and I thought if I had to do one more step I was going to drop dead on the spot. A minute before Jerry left, Howard leaned in and said something that made him laugh. He looked directly at me and flashed a smile that lit up his face and made his serious eyes merry. When our eyes connected, the confusing thought, *Who are you? I know you*, ran through my mind and my body like a lightning bolt. Howard walked over to the other dancer, put his arm around her, and shook her hand, and I thought, *Oh well, she's got it.* Though disappointed, I knew I had done my best. And hey, I hadn't fallen on my butt, embarrassing myself, and I got down to the last two, which was a huge surprise and accomplishment since I wasn't expecting to get that far. At that point, I was thrilled to still be standing and breathing! Then Howard came over to me and I was expecting to hear "Sorry," but he said, "Congratulations."

"What?" I said.

"I said 'congratulations,' you got it."

I was filled with such joy, and being a Greek, I wanted to throw my arms around him and hug him, and I couldn't decide if I wanted to laugh or cry. He said things like "You start rehearsals tomorrow… costume fitting…"

Naïve and inexperienced as I was, I struggled to control my voice from shaking as I asked, "Excuse me, but who was that man?"

Howard looked at me, smiled, and said, "That's Jerome Robbins."

"Jerome Robbins," I repeated. Unbeknownst to him or to me, this stranger named Jerome Robbins had just opened the door to my future and invited me to walk through. With that simple word "Congratulations," I became part of an amazing ensemble of young dancer/actor/singers in a Broadway show that changed the face of musical theater and my life forever.

My character's name was Minnie, Baby John's girlfriend. David Winters, who played A-Rab in the movie, was the original Baby John on Broadway. Though *West Side Story* is about gangs and gang violence, it never entered my mind at the time that I was living *West Side Story*. You see I grew up in Chelsea, a neighborhood on New York's West Side that was an ethnically mixed slum back then. People getting killed by some form of violence was a daily, and I do mean daily, occurrence. Anestos found our dead janitor stuffed in a trash can, Gus's friend Sonny plunged to his death playing chicken jumping across rooftops, street gangs rumbled and blooded themselves using knives, chains, clubs, brass knuckles, zip guns, and Molotov cocktails.

I'll never forget one hot summer's eve leaning out our dining room window and seeing a gang from the East Side approach. Our neighborhood gang quickly assembled, and the gang leaders circled each other with stiletto knives just like Riff and Bernado. A gun was fired from a rooftop, a kid fell, and all hell broke loose. The screams were heard blocks away while chains flew, clubs swung, bodies fell— blood every where till the police siren was heard, and like the Jets and Sharks in "Rumble," all ran for their lives carrying their wounded. I went to The Winter Garden Theater everyday and I danced and pretended gang violence, then I went home and lived it. Yet for the entire run of the show, not once did it ever occur to me to connect the dots. It simply never entered my mind.

Now even though the show was running to packed houses, Jerry had us rehearse constantly. He had a reputation as a tyrant, which he was, but I found that he was not without a wicked sense of humor and that he laughed easily and often. Some of us affectionately called him "Big Daddy." After one truly grueling "clean-up rehearsal," my brother Gus, who as I mentioned played Action in the show and who is a wonderful artist, drew a caricature of Jerry with a demonic smile, smoke rising from the signature cigarette clenched between his teeth, holding a whip that circled his legs. He titled it "Big Daddy" and posted it on the backstage bulletin board. We didn't know how Jerry would react—well he loved the art and the likeness made him laugh, so it remained on the board.

Jerry was difficult and demanding, and when he became fixated on someone, his cruelty was unmatched. He was a master at aiming his crossbow at their weak spot and he never missed his mark. From then on nothing they did was right or good enough. Jerry ruthlessly dug deeper until the mere mention of Jerry's name made the poor soul panic and fall to pieces. The effect it had was to make us all work harder to be perfect. No one ever wanted to be on the receiving end of his wrath. Why or how one became "the chosen one" I couldn't begin to tell you. What I can say is, for reasons known only to him, he liked Gus and I, so we never had a problem. Maybe we reminded him of his sister, who was a dancer, and himself, or maybe because Gus was so intense then, he sensed Gus would deck him if he tried anything like that with either one of us. I do know those that stood up to him, he respected and left alone.

While *West Side* still played to full houses, Jerry asked me to audition for his touring company of Ballets USA. At Jerry's request, his assistant Tommy Abbot rented a rehearsal hall and I spent hours with Tommy learning much of the choreography.

"I changed my mind," said Jerry when I arrived at the audition. "I need you in the show. Besides, I want you for the movie," he said.

So I stayed in the show and screen tested for the movie, though I have no memory of the test. For film publicity, on the rubble where New York's Lincoln Center now stands, he had two female dancers and myself dance one of the "Cool" variations while a photographer snapped away. I wore the green homemade jumper, which Jerry later asked me to bring to LA. The classic black-and-white photo of the girls' "Conversation Variation" appeared in the *New York Times*.

I continued dancing in the show through the end of its run. Months went by with no word on the movie. I thought Jerry had changed his mind; now here I was on my way to fulfill a childhood fantasy. I went with no thought, expectation, or desire for a role. I was going to be a dancer in a movie, and it was thrilling. Never in my wildest dreams did I ever imagine I would end up as Riff's girlfriend Graziella. My welcoming committee at LAX was my brother Gus and my Performing Arts High School classmates, Tony Mordente (Action) and Jaime Rogers (Shark). Our beloved Suzie Kaye (Shark) was a PA drama student. I felt comforted being in the company of so many familiar faces on my first job away from home. It was night when we landed so I couldn't see much, but as I inhaled, my nostrils and lungs filled with a sweet, heady scent I later found out to be night-blooming jasmine. I had never smelled anything so deliciously intoxicating in my life.

Eight AM the following morning, with my dance bag slung over my shoulder, the boys took me to Samuel Goldwyn Studios, on Formosa and Santa Monica Blvd. When I crossed the guard gate and stepped onto the lot, I felt like Dorothy entering the Land of Oz. I felt as if in a dream, a wonderful, surreal childhood dream. Was it real, was I actually there, was this happening to me, Gina, a poor kid born to immigrant parents and raised in the New York slums? Deep gratitude for my good fortune overwhelmed me, and tears of joy and disbelief filled my throat. I gulped and swallowed, squeezing them down while my heart fluttered and trembled and dashed about in my chest, and the boys led the way down the main street lined with enormous sound stages. I couldn't believe how clean and manicured everything looked. I was used to streets littered with trash and newspapers, but these streets, as my mama would say, were clean enough to eat off of!

We finally walked through a set of open elephant doors onto a sound stage that was turned into a rehearsal hall. Where I learned, to my surprise, I was to be part of a skeleton crew, a handful of dancers Jerry had picked to help set the musical numbers. It was a huge space with dance barres built along the length of one wall and a wall of mirrors on the opposite side. A baby grand piano sat in the right-hand corner next to the mirrors. Standing by the piano was our pianist from the Broadway show, Betty Walberg, wearing her signature black-rimmed glasses and her silver hair pulled back in a low bun. Betty was the pianist I heard but couldn't see when I first met Jerry. Tommy Abbott, Howard Jeffrey, and Maggie Banks, Jerry's assistants, were milling about, and a few Hollywood dancers I didn't know.

One in particular caught my eye. He was stretching and warming up when I walked in. He was built compact, not especially tall, with a full mouth, cheekbones you could slice bread with, and straight, sandy-colored hair that fell over his slanted, Asian-shaped blue eyes. His body was muscular and beautifully formed, as only a male dancer's body develops from use; he reminded me of a large jungle cat. Now I have to confess, as a dancer, I love beautifully formed male thighs. My eyes zeroed in on his as I watched him bend his knees and they groaned through his tight-fitting blue jeans. Much to my surprise, my heart fluttered for a different and most unexpected reason.

"Everyone to the barre, second position!" yelled Tommy.

And that's how every day began—with an hour-and-a-half class starting at the barre with pliés and a forty-five-minute ballet barre to warm us up and keep us in dance shape. The hotty dancer with the great thighs just happened to be standing in back of me at the barre that first day. When we turned to do pliés on the other side, there were those thighs and, I might add, the best pair of buns, next to Mordente's right in my face. And when we moved to the floor and he began to dance, he took my breath away!

"Who is that and where is he from?" I asked Maggie.

"Oh, that's Bobby, Bobby Banas and he's from here. He's a Hollywood dancer."

"Damn he's good."

"Yes he is," said Maggie. "He's kind of cute, don't you think?"

"I'll say!"

Well, it seems hotty thought I was pretty cute too because he asked me out, and of course I said yes. We dated for about two years, but life had other plans for us and so we went our separate ways, though we remained life long friends.

My first week of rehearsal, I had a hard time processing that I was actually there. Meanwhile, Jerry used me as his dance-in for Anita and Maria. He had me dance and sing Maria in "I Feel Pretty," Anita in "America" and "Dance Hall," while he and his co-director Robert Wise staged the numbers and figured out camera angles.

When it came time to set the alley scene, where the Jets gather before going inside the parking structure for "Cool," Jerry looked at me and said, "You sit there and be Graziella for now." It was the scene where she cries when Riff's name is mentioned. I did the scene and I cried. Jerry looked at me, stunned.

"Can you do that again?" he asked.

"Yes," I said. We did the scene and I cried real tears again.

"Can you do it again?"

"I think so," I said, and every time we ran the scene I cried. The following day, Jerry pulled me aside. "Bob and I want you to test for the tomboy Anybodys," he said. After the test, he told me they felt I wasn't boyish enough to be a tomboy and that I was their Graziella.

"You want me for Graziella?"

"Yes." I was so stunned I was speechless. I came expecting to be a dancer and was thrilled with that. Now I was given the role of Riff's girlfriend and lead dancer of the Jets! Knowing Jerry's propensity to change his mind, I didn't allow myself to get too excited until I was asked to bring my green jumper to my first costume fitting at Western Costumes, with the film's brilliant costume designer, Irene Sharaff.

Ms. Sharaff was soft-spoken and so cool. She was tiny and was always very pulled together, very chic. She had silver hair and only wore black and white, black dresses, suits, or skirts with white blouses and black heels. Her clothes were understated, beautifully made, and expensive. I don't recall ever seeing her in slacks, but I never ever saw her without some sort of black hat and lots of eye make-up. Irene dressed her part, meaning she dressed like she knew what she was doing and could be trusted to make you look good. I envied her long, candy apple red nails and wished they were mine. Try as I might, I could never grow mine. Irene smoked lots of cigarettes, as most people did then, but hers sat on the end of a short, black, shiny holder. Her use of color to differentiate the two gangs was like eye candy. I loved looking at the intense reds, purples, magentas, oranges, and blacks for the Sharks and the cool blues, yellows, and grays for the Jets. I adored Irene. I remember her arriving on the lot with sketches and fabric swatches to show Jerry, and not just once but many, many, many times. Like every thing else with Jerry, the colors had to be just the right shade of purple or blue, and he wouldn't settle till he got what he saw in his mind's eye. Irene was fond of Carole and I, and we sought her out whenever we saw her on the lot. I loved looking at her sketches and asked lots of questions about her process, and she was always very gracious and generous. I sensed her sometime frustration with Jerry, but she never seemed to lose it with him. She might have screamed in her car with her windows rolled up all the way back to Western Costumes for all I know—I sure as hell would have—but on the lot she was always contained.

"Jerry likes this on you and he wants me to copy it for 'Dance Hall,'" said Ms. Sharaff. "Can you move in it?"

"No. Not really."

"Can you leave it?"

"Yes, of course."

Genius that she was, she took the silhouette and designed a dress with a front slit over my right leg and one in the back of my left, dropped an accordion-pleated, silk chiffon slip into it, and voila—the memorable orange dress from "Dance at the Gym" that I could move and freely kick my legs in.

Meanwhile, Jerry auditioned and auditioned and auditioned every dancer in town and then auditioned some more, while we rehearsed and rehearsed and rehearsed from morning 'til night and then rehearsed some more. Jerry replaced dancers as quickly as his cigarettes, making it clear that each and every one of us was replaceable if he found someone he liked better.

When I first arrived, a very pretty, tall, young Hollywood dancer named Taffy Paul befriended me. Taffy was set to play Velma. She was really sweet and an excellent dancer. Then one day she was gone. Just like that. It had nothing to do with her dance ability. She wasn't "street" enough for Jerry, too sweet. He did her the favor of her life. Within weeks of being let go, she got a movie, was signed to a major studio, her name was changed from Taffy Paul to Stefanie Powers, and a star was born!

Back at the rehearsal hall, every day began at the barre. Sometimes Jerry gave the barre; sometimes he just stood with arms crossed, a lit cigarette hanging from his lips, smoke spiraling around his face, watching with those intense eyes. The energy shifted when he came in—it prickled. There was no faking anything, not even a plié. Barre became an audition. Sometimes it was just that—he invited dancers to take barre, then we never saw them again.

"Get your ass into ballet class," he sometimes said, pointing a finger at me with fire in his eyes.

"Yes sir," I replied.

Though I was a strong musical and visceral dancer, my ballet technique needed help. A strong ballet technique is a dancer's foundation, and if I were to reach the potential Jerry saw in me, a potential I was clueless I possessed, I needed to get my ass into class and not just twice or three times a week, but every single day. Ballet class gave me the strength and technical freedom I needed to move through space with joy and ease I never dreamt possible.

For me, dance is and will always be about the music. I feel a good dancer is first and foremost a musician, and the body is the finely tuned instrument through which the music finds expression. One can be a great technical dancer, but if they are not musical the dance is lifeless. I happened to be a very musical dancer. It was not something I worked at, but a gift I was born with, only I didn't know it. It was just how I danced, and I think that's what Jerry saw in me.

A shift happened when I placed my hand on the barre, the music began, and I took that first plié. It was as if one part of my brain shut down, another part of me awakened, and the outside world disappeared. From then on, there was only the music finding breath and life through me. It was delicious feeling my muscles awaken inside the music—feel them work and slowly warm down to the bone while my mind automatically checked my turnout, my feet, my center and placement. I loved sensing the layer of sweat begin to cover my skin, collect under my breasts, drip and pool on my belly and trickle down my back, my neck, as my body warmed with each tendu and jeté and my lungs deeply inhaled, exhaled. My body automatically adjusted finding its balance, kicking my legs as high as possible in grand battement. My heart beat in my ears and pounded in my chest as my feet sunk into the floor and I jumped in changement, and sweat flew off of my red face with each snap of my head in pirouette. I loved sweating! Sweating and being in my body so completely was, is, and will always be, thrilling! And then there was the music—always the music filling my heart, whispering to every muscle, humming in every cell.

"Once more from the top!" shouted Tommy.

Or was it Howard—did it matter? I was filled and transported to that place where everything but the music disappeared and the borders where I began and it ended blurred.

"Take five!" I heard, and collapsed in a heap on the floor. But no matter how exhausted I was, when the music began, my body responded.

Rehearsing "Cool" was a trip. You see, Jerry had many versions of "Cool," and we were supposed to be able to pull out of our heads the one he wanted to see in an instant—be it version one or twelve, or any in between. For the life of me, I don't know how we kept them all separate in our heads and bodies and then gave him what he wanted on demand.

Soundstages are built on cement, which has no give and is brutal on the body, especially when spending hours doing the kind of intense dancing we were doing. There were days when my legs hurt so badly, I didn't know what to do with them—even soaking in a hot tub with bath salts didn't help. Rehearsals felt as if I was in some sort of time warp, my existence surreal. One day fell into the next, becoming one extended ballet barre, like a dream that repeats and repeats. I was always starting in second position, warming my muscles.

And there was Jerry yelling, "Again from the top!"

And I was drenched, trying to catch my breath thinking, *I can't do it one more time.* But I did, day after day after day, and relishing every deliciously achy second.

Jerry wanted tension between the Sharks and the Jets. "You're members of opposite gangs," he said. "No mingling."

So the Sharks went off to one stage to rehearse "America" and "Shark Mambo," while we rehearsed "Cool" and "Dance Hall" on another. Meanwhile, the boys dreamt up all sorts of pranks to play on each other. Like the Jets rigging pails of water on top of the Sharks' dressing room door, drenching whoever opened it, the Sharks grabbing Eliot Feld (Baby John) and smearing his face with red lipstick.

Gaffer's carts are used to load cables and lights on and off soundstages. I vaguely remember the guys found a cart sitting about and I think either Eddie Verso or Tucker Smith mounted it, pretending it was his chariot and yelling, "I'm Spartacus! I'm Spartacus!"

Then my brother Gus jumped on yelling, "No, I'm Spartacus!"

The guys joined in and had a great time pushing and pulling the cart around the lot, causing a ruckus and disrupting filming of other productions. Our frustrated first AD Bob Reylea had to give them another "talking to"—the guys were always getting into mischief of one kind or another.

Off the lot and on weekends, we became a family. George, Russ, and Rita became part of it. We had parties, saw Ray Charles at the Palladium, built bonfires at the beach, rode horses, went to the movies, went bowling, and celebrated the holidays together. But not once did it ever occur to me that we were creating cinematic history. We were just making a movie. It was a job, a fun dance job with wonderful people, and I was making SAG minimum—a small fortune coming from $75.00 a week on Broadway!

Carole D'Andrea originated the role of Velma on Broadway and was now doing it in the movie. We became good friends while sharing the same long communal mirror of the girls' dressing room at the Winter Garden Theater. Now we were roommates living at the Green Briar, a furnished apartment complex with a crystal clear swimming pool just outside our door. My brother Gus and several of our cast lived there as well.

We had all come from New York, a city known for its diversity. Race and color were a non-issue for us being in "the business." We sat around the pool one afternoon. Jaime Rogers and Jay Norman, both Puerto Ricans who could have easily been mistaken as fair-skinned blacks, were there as our guests. Someone from management came over and told them they could not use the pool, saying the pool was reserved for tenants only. Bobby Banas, however, with his blue eyes, sandy-colored hair, and fair skin was able to use the pool as much as he liked, even though he didn't live there. Only then did it dawn on me. I was born and raised in the tenements with Puerto Ricans, blacks, and every skin color in between. It was the sixties, this wasn't the South; it was the West but the only difference was down South prejudice was in the open.

I didn't think I would stay on the West Coast when I first got there, so I didn't bother learning to drive. Rapid transit was so great in New York, I didn't need to. Maria Jimenez (Teresita), however, did live there and did drive, so she became the girls' designated driver. I will never forget her car. It was a yellow and white Chevy with yellow and white leather interior. It's considered a classic and worth a small fortune today, but for us it was a cool yellow and white car we piled into to go to work during the week and go play on weekends and days off. I love to cook and many a weekend, if we were not at the beach or out dancing at some club, the girls were at Carole's and my place laughing and bonding over huge home-cooked meals.

During rehearsal, many stellar personalities stopped by to watch, but Charles Laughton is the one I remember. It was a hot day and the elephant doors were open. He sauntered in, blue shirttails hanging out, hands behind his back, cigarette in his mouth. In my eyes, this medium-sized man was a bigger-than-life legend, a true movie star! He was Quasimodo in *The Hunchback of Notre Dame* from my childhood, who tore my heart when he was flogged, yelled "Sanctuary!" swinging on a rope while saving the beautiful gypsy girl, named his bells, and rode Big Marie. He watched us rehearse "Dance Hall," smiled and nodded approvingly as he walked out, his hands never leaving his back and his cigarette never leaving his mouth.

When the the actual filming commenced, the "Prologue," which is the opening sequence of the movie, was filmed first. Jerry, Bob, the boys, and the crew went off to New York to film on the streets of the city, leaving us girls behind with time off. Every morning I woke to LA's breathtaking white light and stillness—a quiet that made my ears ring, a stillness that made my body hum down to the marrow of my bones and deep inside my soul, a quiet that never existed in the city where I woke to horns honking, taxi drivers yelling, brakes screeching, and the subway ceaselessly rumbling and shaking our building to its core.

It was confusing at first. I woke asking, *Where am I?* Then remembering, *Oh right, I'm in LA.* It was disorienting looking out my window expecting to see fire escapes, industrial buildings, and gray shadows and instead seeing white sunlight, blue skies, palm trees, flowers, and green everywhere. Stepping out my door I gasped, constantly greeted by open space and mountains, periwinkle skies, and air saturated with the sweet scent of orange and lemon blossoms, instead of gridlock, trash, and the sour stench of decaying garbage. It was delicious being daily immersed in such natural beauty, especially being a city kid and having been denied it most of my young life. And though I soon got used to it, I could not imagine the time when I would have to leave it all behind.

The spectacular sunsets I witnessed were part of daily life and taken for granted by native Angelinos. In my New York world of shadows and cement canyons, the horizon was something I saw only in movies. But here the sun shimmered on the horizon, painting skies blush magentas and peach, bruised reds and purples, leaving me breathless. And on top of all this natural beauty it was clean, no litter, not even a gum wrapper or cigarette butt on the streets. When I first arrived, making California my home never entered my mind. But now I had stillness, nature's beauty, space, breathtaking sunsets on one hand, and fire escapes, cement canyons, roaches and rats on the other. Do I stay or do I go? Which do I choose?

The New York shoot took longer than expected partly due to rain. We were told the guys did a rain dance to the rain gods daily asking for rain so they could play instead of work. It started as a joke, but when the rain came on cue day after day, as if the gods heard and sent endless downpours, Jerry forbade the guys from doing their daily rain dance.

Robert Wise was co-director. Bob and Jerry couldn't have been more opposite. Bob was a lovely, mild-mannered man, with kind, gentle eyes, and a sweet face. He was tall, had a full head of light hair, and two prominent front teeth. He made me feel safe, and there was something about him that reminded me of a white bunny rabbit. His presence helped calm the stage by off setting Jerry's tightly wound intensity. Bob was a seasoned filmmaker who came with a litany of film credits, including editing the classic *Citizen Kane*. The only direction I remember him ever giving however was:

"More salt and pepper. Give me more salt and pepper, kids."

My sense is that along with his extensive film experience and Jerry's lack of, the studio hired him not only to help Jerry with the technical aspects of movie making, but to also rein Jerry in. Time is money, big money when filming. Jerry was a perfectionist and it didn't take long for the production to fall behind. We were behind when the boys returned from filming "Prologue" in New York. Originally scheduled for three weeks, it took almost two months.

So when my heel snapped right off my shoe while shooting the big push-jump towards camera in "Cool" for the umpteenth time and the wardrobe department didn't have a replacement and the camera was held for hours till they located another pair, Carole D'Andrea looked at me and said, "Oh boy," under her breath. We knew what was coming; we dropped our eyes, but not before we saw him turn scarlet and his eyes got that look—that red, wide-eyed, glazed, non-blinking, lethal, all-hell-is-about-to-break-loose look so familiar to us. His head began to shake like a snake's right before it's about to strike, and the energy surrounding him crackled. He was deadly. Need I say the poor wardrobe person lost her job?

The "Cool" set was a garage with a low ceiling that pressed down on us. It was not a small set, but it felt confined. With bodies heating up—dancing, sweating, breathing, and arc lights lighting the set—it was like being in a sauna. I remember sweating and gasping for air while doing each section over and over and over, 'til Jerry got something he felt was good enough to print.

I personally feel that "Cool" is one of the most dynamic pieces of dance ever captured on film. In "Cool," every snap, every flick of a hand or point of a finger has purpose and is motivated from an inner life. It's acted, not merely danced. There are no wasted movements and if the dancer's inner life is not present, the choreography doesn't work. So in order for us to reach the needed emotional pitch for a particular section, Jerry had us dance it from the top every time—even if the shot was in the middle, near the end, or the end. The girls did everything the boys did with the exception of the knee work.

Filming "Cool" was so intense that I managed to injure my lower back. To arch or bend or lift a leg was excruciating. Jerry immediately called for ice, and a doctor who examined me gave me a shot in the injured area and taped me up. When Jerry asked if I was able to dance, I said yes. To stop filming was unthinkable. I was irreplaceable in "Cool." I had no choice but to keep going, and they were so behind they could not afford to stop filming. Fortunately for me, the "Girls Conversation" variation was already in the can. That particular piece of choreography is really hard on the back, and I wouldn't have been able to do it—drugs, tape, ice, and all. Every morning, the doctor gave me a shot and redid my tape, but by the end of the day when the drugs wore off and I came down from my dancer's mind set that blocks out pain, my back throbbed with excruciating pain. But I was used to pain. I was a dancer and pain came with the territory.

Jerry kept expanding Velma and Graziella's roles, adding them to "Officer Krupke," which they were not in on Broadway. Here's some trivia for you. By the time we got to "Krupke," I was so physically exhausted and my body so wrecked, I ended up in the hospital with mononucleosis. Time is money, and they were not about to hold camera until I was well enough to return to work. So they hired a body double, put her in my orange dress, and slapped a red wig on her. Now if you look carefully when the boys begin singing, Velma and Graziella move to the fire hydrant and Graziella sits on it with her back to the camera. Well, that's not me. It's my body double. Check it out. If you take a peek at Anita's rape scene in Doc's Drugstore, there is a shot of Anita's legs being pulled by her shawl. Well that was an insert shot they needed and Rita was not available that day, so they brought me in, darkened my arms and legs, and got their shot.

All the major dance sequences, with the exception of "Dance Hall," were in the can. It was scheduled to begin shooting in a couple of days. We had just finished running it for the umpteenth time, in a sweltering-hot rehearsal space, when Jerry stormed in, and I mean STORMED IN—his face red, his head pulsating, his mouth held tight, his eyes deadly. He felt like an out-of-control abusive parent who was about to land his blows. My heart started to pound and I thought, *What have we done?* We all looked down.

"I want to see 'Dance Hall'!" he said.

We were dripping wet, barely had time to catch our breath, and looked like drowned rats. But Jerry wanted to see it, so dance we did—full out from beginning to end. He asked to see it again, barely allowing us time to breathe. Finally he exploded, telling us we couldn't dance. He diminished us with each viperous word escaping his lips, not addressing his tirade to anyone in particular, but to all of us as a whole.

"You call yourselves dancers! None of you can dance!" he yelled. "None of you!"

And then—and I will never forget this—we had formed a circle around him, and he was in the center like the eye of a tornado, pointing his finger:

"Each and every one of you can be replaced! Each and every one of you right now!" he shouted, pointing to each of us, his neck and head shaking, eyes glaring, face red hot.

The whole time I was thinking, *What's he saying? They can't, we've been established. Are they going to re-shoot everything we've done so far? I don't think so.*

Then, as if reading my mind, he said, "Don't think because you're on some film you're not replaceable, because you are!" he yelled, and stormed out.

There was dead silence. No one moved; we just stood looking at each other.

Finally, Howard said, "Take a break."

"What the hell was that all about?" asked one of the guys. "Hey Howard, what's his problem?"

"We're behind, so the studio is pressuring him," said Howard.

"Yeah, well that don't mean he has to take it out on us. It's not like we sit around playing cards all day and doing nothing!"

Little did we know it was foreshadowing for what was to come.

The following day, a Friday, we rehearsed "Dance Hall" on set without Jerry. I didn't think anything of it. Monday morning, the set was lit, we were in make-up and costume, ready for our first shot.

A murmur went through the cast. "Where's Jerry?" we whispered to one another.

"Where's Jerry? Is he all right?" went the rumblings. The only one behind the camera was Bob Wise. And instead of Jerry conferring with Bob, it was his assistant Tommy Abbott, and Tony Mordente.

"Did you hear? They fired Jerry," said one of the dancers. "They fired him 'cause he was costing them too much money," he said.

"No! That can't be true," I said.

"What can't be true?" asked Carole D'Andrea (Velma).

"I just heard Jerry got fired. Do you know anything about this?" I asked.

"Tony just told me," she said. "I'm stunned! They can't do this without him," she said. "There's no way they can do this without him!"

We all felt the same. There was no way they could do this without "Big Daddy." But they did do it without him. Whatever else was left to shoot was done without him. Jerry would not compromise his artistic vision, how ever long it took, but the studio heads felt otherwise.

For me, "Dance Hall" suffered without his eye and artistic sensibilities. "Dance Hall" is more than a dance at a school gym. It's about two gangs taking the floor from one another and establishing their superiority. Without Jerry's presence and direction, the necessary tension needed within dance movement to tell the story just wasn't there.

The dream sequence, known as the dream ballet, was cut because it could not be done without him. The press release stated "creative differences." The irony of it all was that just a few days before we were on the receiving end of his venom, his finger jabbing the air in front of each and every one of us, telling us we were worthless as dancers and could all be replaced. So in essence, he was blaming us, saying it was our fault we were behind, we were the ones costing the studio money because we weren't good enough. But each and every one of us went on to finish the movie—he did not. Some might think that poetic justice.

I'd like to take a moment to share my personal thoughts about Jerry. I feel nothing but love, gratitude, and admiration for the man. I've had an amazing life because of him. As I look back, I see that part of Jerry's genius was in knowing his raw material, his dancers, and what they were capable of bringing to his work. None of us were cookie-cutter dancers. Jerry knew exactly what he was looking for, and each and every one of us was hand picked because of our uniqueness. He saw our potential and lifted us to a level of excellence that we didn't even know existed in us. It was frustrating at times because Jerry demanded the same level of excellence from us that he demanded of himself, and nothing less would do. Being in his sphere of influence got me out of my self-imposed limits and allowed me to dance with unimaginable depth and abandonment.

Jerry's *West Side* choreography was danced organically from the inside out. There wasn't a single snap that wasn't internally motivated. We weren't just dancers; we were characters with a back-story that was brought to every step. That's what made it so dynamic. What wasn't being said with dialogue was said with our bodies, and the seamless blending of the two was part of Jerry's genius.

I went back to see him the year before he died. I had not seen him since the movie some thirty-seven years earlier. My inner voice kept saying, *Call Jerry. Call Jerry, you have to see Jerry.* So when I was in New York visiting my family for Christmas, I called and we met for tea at his lovely brownstone. I brought my daughter Christina to meet him; she was eighteen at the time. I felt I had to honor him, I had to say thank you. Thank you for choosing me, thank you for recognizing my talent, and thank you for giving me the life I now own.

"You look exactly the same," he said as we settled in his drawing room. "You haven't changed a bit. I'd recognize you anywhere," he said, hugging me.

The man who greeted me was not the bigger-than-life god who made us tremble that we once called "Big Daddy." His eyes still sparkled with life and vitality, but the intensity I so vividly remembered was gone. The tiger leaning in ready to pounce was now a frail, vulnerable, smaller-than-I-remembered granddaddy. But when our eyes met, that unspoken connection and recognition I sensed as a young girl was still there.

"I'm shrinking," he said, bursting into peals of laughter. "And I don't hear so well," he said, putting his hand to his ear. "So you're gonna have to speak up."

He told me that since his open-heart surgery, his legs weren't that good either.

"But I'll keep on working as long as they hire me," he said as we moved to the dining room.

The table was elegantly set with white linen, sterling silver, and fine bone china. The spread of tea sandwiches, scones, jams, double cream, lox, cream cheese, bagels, and petite cakes was beautifully prepared and served. As we sat eating and sipping tea, I asked him about his crop of dancers at The New York City Ballet.

"I have one new young girl that shows promise," he said.

I mentioned that one of my favorite ballets that he had choreographed was *Dances at a Gathering*. It's an exquisite lyric piece danced on a bare stage to Chopin's piano music. Chopin is one of my favorite composers, and *Dances* is one of the most musical pieces I'd ever seen. It's the only ballet that makes me yearn to be young again so I could dance it, and I wondered why it wasn't being done anymore.

"It brought tears to my eyes and took my breath away when I saw it way back when, and I've been wanting to see it ever since. Why isn't it done?" I asked.

He paused a moment, then said, "Because I don't have the dancers."

"What?" I said. "Jerry, the kids today are brilliant! They can do things we never even dreamed of! They are so far better than we ever were technically."

"Yes, I know," he said, tilting his head and setting his cup into its saucer. "Technically they are brilliant. But I don't have the dancers."

That's when I got it. Technical brilliance was not what he looked for in his dancers. Yes, one had to be strong technically, but for Jerry, a dancer's musicality and passion were far more important. I understood then what it was he saw in me.

"I needed to see your face," I said. "I felt I had to see you and say thank you. I wanted you to meet my daughter Christina. She and her brother Nick wouldn't be here if it wasn't for you. I never would have left New York, never would have met their dad, and she wouldn't be sitting at this table right now if not for you," I said.

I likened him to a stone dropped in the middle of a pond and the far-reaching ripple effect created, the circles ever-expanding outward. How many lives had he touched and altered? The urge to see him was so strong, I felt as if I was a messenger—that I was saying thank you not just for me but for all of us and he needed to hear that, he needed to know.

I also got to meet his dog, a mutt who was lost and wandering about on the steps of The Metropolitan Museum of Art. It followed Jerry all the way home and decided to stay—decided that Jerry was his dad and his alpha. When it came time to leave, we hugged and he told me to come back in the spring to see his garden.

"It's a small paradise when the roses and the flowers are in bloom," he said. "And bring Christina," he said, as he hugged her.

"I will," I said.

"You've lived a full and rewarding life," he said, smiling and holding me at arm's length as if a proud parent.

"Thanks, but my small life is nothing compared to yours," I said. "Look at all you have done, your accomplishments, your body of work; the beauty and the legacy you leave behind for all time is absolutely stunning!"

"No, no, no," he said, shaking his head. "Look at all *you* have done. Your life has been a complete circle," he said, tracing a circle in the air with his finger. "You didn't just dance, you went on and did so much more, so much more. Look at the beauty and legacy *you* leave behind," he said, indicating Christina. "I've only done the one thing, only the one thing," he said.

His sincerity shook me to my core. My heart wept for the man, and I could barely contain my tears as I looked at him standing smiling at me with arms crossed. He was once a stranger who opened the door to my future and invited me to walk through—I did and here we were, many lifetimes later, and he was telling me my life was more meaningful than his. Then from no where, an old forgotten memory flashed before my eyes of him smiling just as he was, and laughing during rehearsals, as he hunched over the piano reading Charles Schultz's *Peanuts*. He loved Charlie Brown, Lucy, Snoopy, and the gang and never missed a strip. Funny how the mind works, isn't it? A year later, he was gone and I never got to see his roses or garden he loved so much. It saddens me that just as we reconnected, he was taken. Yet a deeper part of me feels that he and I are complete. We met, recognized one another, and had come full circle, and if there is such a thing as karma, whatever karmic debt we might have owed has been paid.

An amazing extended family formed from *West Side*, friendships that have lasted a lifetime. We all have been there for one another through weddings, divorces, births, deaths, illnesses, good times, and hard times. The bonds that tie us together are as strong as, and in some cases stronger than, our biological families. Rita Heid, a stunningly beautiful Hollywood dancer who was a Jet in "Dance Hall," became part of this family. Rita was petite, with jet-black hair, enormous blue eyes, a light heart, and a great sense of humor. She was a true beauty, the kind of gal who turned men's heads everywhere we went. She had her pick and chose my handsome brother Gus, whom the ladies adored. They were a couple for several years. Rita and I became roomies for a while when Gus and I decided to stay in LA "just a bit longer." Fifty-plus years have come and gone, and we are still here.

Brother Gus went on to have a successful acting career, then transitioned behind the camera and had a very long and successful career as a TV and film director. He's been happily married to dancer Barbara Andrews, who is now a therapist specializing in child development, and they have a son, Nicholas, a professional photographer. As I mentioned earlier, Gus is a wonderful artist and now that he is retired, he has returned to his true love. Rita has remained a lifelong friend. I remember walking the Malibu beach with her when I was going through my difficult divorce, and she was assuring me there really was light at the end of this dark tunnel, having gone through a horrendous divorce some years before, and she was right.

Robert Wise was part of this family as well. He was our daddy. We met for lunch regularly, and we loved hearing the stories of his early life as a film editor and director. He told us *West Side* was the only film he had worked on that maintained such strong and lasting friendships. Perhaps because we were all so young and we genuinely liked each other, or maybe because it was a life-altering experience for so many of us.

Among the stories he shared was how Natalie Wood came to be Maria. They were testing every young ingénue on both coasts, but she wasn't even a consideration. They were thinking of Warren Beatty as a possible Tony and looked at a clip from *Splendor in the Grass*, and when they saw her they said, "She's our Maria."

Shortly after *West Side*, Andre Tayir, Maria Jimenez Henley (both Sharks), and I went to London to do the first, if not the one and only, *Beatles Television Special* for British producer Jack Goode. Our visa read "eccentric acrobatic act," which meant no one else was able to do what we did, and there was truth in that. No one across the pond danced as we did yet. The critics called us "savages." They had never seen anything like us. The boys were lovely. They were quiet and kept to themselves. Paul sat behind a piano writing most of the time, George was shy and said little, Ringo was the most out going, and John was, well, John.

When cameras started rolling, helmeted police formed a human wall, separating the screaming females from the boys on stage. But it didn't stop the frenzied mob from breaking through, grabbing at the boys' legs, and clamoring to get on stage. It was frightening! Not only were they a danger to the Fab Four, but to themselves and the poor English bobbies that were trying to contain them. Bodyguards put themselves between the girls and the guys, and they were quickly escorted off stage to safety. When order was restored, the girls were told if they tried that again, they would clear the space and do the show without them. Filming commenced and the girls screamed so loud, we could not hear the music, and the only way we could dance was by feeling the rhythms vibrating through the soles of our feet.

Andre went on to have a long and fruitful career as a choreographer, and he was always there to give me a dance job when I needed one. He married Sarah Reed, a beautiful ballerina who danced with American Ballet Theater. They had three children, a boy, Henner, and two girls, Fancy and Honnora. For those of us who made LA our new home, their home became the gathering place for holidays and get-togethers, their door always open. Andre became like a brother and Sarah a sister, as did Maria, Carole, and Rita Heid.

Andre gave himself the nickname "Beaky Buzzard" because his hair was black and he was tall and wiry. He was a Southern boy with a great sense of humor who always made me laugh. And whenever his memory arises, I always see him with his head thrown back laughing. Andre loved to laugh, and it didn't take much to get him going. Once started, he couldn't stop. Next thing I knew, I was laughing. Then we couldn't look at each other 'cause catching each other's eye brought on another bout of hysterics 'til our sides and stomachs and insides were aching and we were crying and begging each other to stop!

Andre had one of the most tender, generous, and compassionate hearts of anyone I knew. He was the sort that, if needed, would give you the shirt right off his back and take you in rather than let you sleep on the street or go hungry. He was an animal-lover and an avid gardener with a remarkable green thumb, who delighted in making things grow and making life beautiful. He was a man who loved babies; he loved everything about them—how they smelled and felt, the sounds they made, and he loved, loved, loved holding them. I miss him, I miss his tall "beaky buzzard" self, I miss his humor, and I miss his laughter. Andre was an extraordinary man for the simple reason that he truly was a *good* man.

After London and the Beatles, Andre, Maria, and I then did *Shindig* for Jack Goode. It was another first—a wild, groundbreaking, fast-paced, rock 'n' roll TV series for ABC. Andre choreographed and Maria and I were part of the Shindig Dancers, a line of eight girl dancers. Maria and I did the mash potatoes on Little Richard's piano while he sang, "Good Golly, Miss Molly." We did the swim, the hitch-hike, and the pony on Jerry Lee Lewis' piano while he pushed back his stool and sang "Great Balls of Fire," then proceeded to demolish the piano for his finale. Meanwhile, our hair had to be sprayed stiff as a helmet so not a single hair moved, because hair flying and being tossed about was considered too sexually provocative for TV. We shook our booties for The Righteous Brothers, Ike and Tina Turner, The Rolling Stones, The Supremes, James Brown, Johnny Cash, and other greats of that time. Our fantastic house band featured Glen Campbell as our lead guitarist, Billy Preston on piano, and Leon Russell before he became "The Leon Russell" on piano as well.

Now here's a bit of history for you. We had many black performers on *Shindig*. Andre had choreographed a number for James Brown in which we danced with him and around him and partnered him. After our dress rehearsal, Andre came into our dressing room quite upset. He had gotten a note from the censors, otherwise known as Standards and Practices. He said we were not allowed to touch James Brown's *skin*. We were all flummoxed. What did he mean not touch his skin? He said we could touch his shirt, his sleeve, his jacket, any part of his clothing, but *not his skin!* If we did, the number could not air. What was not spelled out was clearly understood. We were eight white girls, he was a black man, and we were not allowed to touch his skin on National Television. Meanwhile, when Johnny Cash was on and we danced with him—pushing and pulling him, grabbing his hands and touching his skin, no such note came to us from the powers that be.

Here's another *Shindig* side note of interest: the pilot and the first few episodes were directed by a British woman director, another first for that time. She established the innovative look of the show—nothing else on TV looked like it. Lots of tight close-ups, fast cuts, different angles, and shots from a crane. She had the guys moving those cameras all over the floor, and they were not happy. They were not used to working that hard, for starters, and they were being told what to do by a woman! A woman! So they sat on their hands, said she was difficult to work with, and what she was asking was impossible. Sad to say, she was replaced by a male director. At the producer's request, he studied and mimicked her style and somehow with the orders coming from a guy, the gents on the floor had no problem whipping those cameras about. The male director replicating her work went on to win several Emmys as director of the show, and the female originator couldn't get a job in this town. We have come a long way since then, I'm happy to say.

Shortly after *Shindig* finished, my then-*Shindig*-rhythm-guitarist boyfriend Russ Titelman and I hitchhiked through Europe—it's what students did back then; things were different and it was safe. We threw our backpacks over our shoulders, stuck out a thumb, and saw Europe, meeting lots of interesting and generous people on the way. Our first day on the road out of Paris, we were picked up by a French farmer. What took me by complete surprise, looking out the window on this country road, were the abandoned bombed-out villages and ruins left as a result of WW II. My mind's eye automatically saw the trenches, the explosions and smoke of artillery, and heard the rat-tat-tat of gunfire. I asked the farmer why.

"Monuments to the war," he said. "So people don't forget."

He took us to his home that resembled a postcard of French country life, introduced us to his family, fed us, and gave us a place to sleep, asking nothing in return except to send him a letter and a postcard. He was a stamp collector and loved collecting American stamps. When we returned, we sent him not just one of each, but as many as we could find to repay his kindness.

We were working our way to Greece when this crazy Arab guy (who had already been driving nonstop for some twelve hours) picked us up in his VW bug. We lacked this piece of information when we got into the car. There we were, all three scrunched in the front seat, and he tells us he picked us up to keep him company and keep him awake by talking to him. In the course of conversation, Russ mentioned that I was Graziella in *West Side* and the guy went nuts.

"Really? Really? Graziella...*West Side Story* movie... Really? The best movie…the best. My favorite movie…*West Side Story*… Girl in orange dress…you?"

"Girl in orange dress, me, yes."

"Sing to me 'America.'"

"I wasn't a Shark," I said. "I was a Jet, I did 'Cool.'"

"No matter," he said. "Sing to me 'America,' I love… I want to be in America," he sang.

And so I began… "I want to be in America, everything free in America…." Luckily I knew the entire song since I sang it often enough while setting "America" as Anita's dance-in, and hearing it sung a gazillion times on stage. I secretly wanted to be a Shark just to sing and dance that number (which was choreographed by Peter Gennaro, by the way). Peter choreographed the "Shark Mambo" and "America" on Broadway. In case you didn't know, "America" was Anita's number and done only by the girls in the Broadway version. Jerry expanded it by adding the boys for the film, which for me gave it power and a whole other dimension. But now, here I was on a country road in Europe, heading for the Greek border singing "I want to be in America" as if on a loop to keep a crazy man from falling asleep at the wheel and killing us all!

At one point, I looked over and said to Russ, "I think he's asleep with his eyes open."

"No," said Russ, "he's awake."

"Look at him, he's asleep with his eyes open, do something."

The car started to pick up speed as his foot slumped on the pedal and I smacked him on his arm.

"Hey! Wake up," I said.

"I fall asleep, sorry," he said, jerking awake and laughing.

He did stay awake after that, and we did arrive at the Greek border in one piece. He thanked us for helping him stay awake and said he was happy meeting Graziella from *West Side Story* and couldn't wait to tell his friends.

"I hope he makes it," I said to Russ as he drove off.

"I do too," he replied.

The sixties in California were a wild and wonderful time to be young. It was the time of love-ins, flower children, and the Monterey Pop Festival. The Monterey Jazz Festival was well known, but the Monterey Pop Festival was something entirely new. It was a first, a festival of rock bands like The Mama's and the Papa's, Jefferson Airplane, Buffalo Springfield, and musicians like the legendary Ravi Shankar. The Monterey Pop Festival started it all (Woodstock later copied it) and there I was, right smack in the middle of this historical event with Russ.

Long-haired men and women with flowers in their hair dressed in bright-colored flowing tunics, beads, and bell-bottoms smoked pot and dropped acid in the open with the Park Rangers standing right in front of them, and no one got arrested. People walked around smiling and handing each other flowers. It was a peaceful gathering of thousands.

I stood out like an apparition in my baby-blue-and-white-polka-dot Alice shirtdress, white tights, and white patent-leather Mary Jane's. And like Alice, I had fallen down a rabbit hole, finding myself in the most fantastical of places. I was probably one of the only, if not *the* only, sober person there. I didn't do drugs. Dance was my drug of choice, and being sober in the midst of all this was a hallucinogenic trip in itself. So, when Timothy Leary, a WASP in white guru robes, stood on a stage telling a crowd of thousands to "turn on, tune in, and drop out," I didn't get it. But the sea of thousands stoned on acid nodded in agreement.

I watched in utter disbelief a group called Big Brother and the Holding Company, whose female lead singer was none other than Janis Joplin. Russ and I had somehow stumbled upon them on a lesser stage, not the main stage. They were relatively unknown at the time and not a main attraction. Well, I'd never seen a female performer so raw, so visceral in my life. She was absolutely mind-blowing! I was used to Ronnie and the Ronettes and The Supremes in their coiffed hair, high heels, and smart clothes, who sang songs like "Be My Baby" and "Baby Love," with smooth, controlled voices while smiling the entire time.

But here was this braless young woman with masses of untamed, red, curly hair, dressed in antique velvets, her neck draped in bead necklaces, bangles to her elbows, rings on every finger, holding a bottle of Jack Daniels and swigging it down like water while singing "Piece of My Heart." Her husky, howling voice was racked with such deeply felt emotion, her face so distorted with pain, and her body language so spastic, I felt as if I was looking at an exposed nerve gone mad! I could barely watch from feeling her pain and yet, I couldn't look away—my eyes were glued on her like iron shavings to a magnet. She was electrifying! I managed to look around at my longhaired contemporaries, some with painted faces, most with drug-glazed eyes and smiles on their faces; their bodies swayed and heads nodded with the music. I looked back at Joplin and as I stood watching, it felt as if she was expressing the pain and frustration of an entire generation. A generation that was struggling to free itself from the suffocating binds of convention.

Earlier, Russ and I had seen Buffalo Springfield on the main stage performing "Something's Happening Here." And something was happening, for it wasn't a guy that looked and sang like that. It was a woman! And a white woman to boot! As a white female, I was not allowed to touch a black man's skin on national television, and I had to spray my hair until it was as stiff as a helmet so not a strand moved. Yet here this wild slip of a girl was howling and publicly guzzling Jack Daniels! Unbeknownst to me, Joplin and this festival of rock performers were harbingers of things to come; the seams of our staid society were beginning to come undone, and our *Donna Reed* and *Father Knows Best* role-playing way of life was about to change drastically.

That same evening Jimi Hendrix strutted onto the main stage with a magenta feather boa wrapped around his neck, looking stoned out of his mind. He played the meanest, sexiest guitar of anyone I had ever heard while he sang Hendrix classics like "Foxy Lady," "Hey Joe," and "Purple Haze." At the end of his set, he put his guitar on auto play, drenched it in lighter fluid, and with great flourish, set it on fire. He walked off stage, head held high, boa trailing behind, the flaming guitar wailing on its own, and us going wild!

After *Shindig*, I worked on the *Hollywood Palace*, a very popular weekly variety TV show where I danced with Fred Astaire. Fred Astaire! Talk about a childhood dream come true! He was my idol and was hosting the show. The opening number was from *Cabaret*. I was on his left, another dancer on his right. I was dancing with the God of Dance, our arms linked, and if I never danced another step again, it would have been OK by me.

It was a great time to be a dancer. There was so much work for dancers, I was doubling up on jobs and having to turn work down. I did a movie called *Good Times*, starring Sonny and Cher. Andre Tayir choreographed a western saloon sequence in which the dance hall girls and cowboys were paired, dancing on the bar. Maria Jimenez was in a swing swinging over us. The back of the bar had mirrors, glasses, bottles, etc. Andre had us doing an airplane lift where the guy holds one wrist and ankle and twirls the girl around while she arches her back and extends her free limbs. After the umpteenth take, my hands and my partner's were sweating and I heard him say, "I can't hold onto you. I'm going to lose you, I'm going to lose you!"

Next thing I knew, I went flying across into the back of the bar, smashing the mirror, glasses, bottles, everything while Maria continued swinging overhead. Now you'd think I must have gotten cut up pretty bad with all that glass shattering over me, but I managed to come out of that without one cut or scratch. It was a brutal shoot and many dancers got hurt; several ended up in emergency, one with a concussion.

I was also one of Tiny Tim's dancing ladies at the then-brand-new Caesars Palace in Las Vegas, choreographed by Andre—another first. We didn't think we'd last a week. Tiny Tim was such a novelty with his long stringy hair, pear-shaped body, strumming his ukulele and singing, "Nymphs and shepherds come away, Flora 's on a holiday," in a high, trembling falsetto. But the crowds loved him and we were held over for six weeks.

I continued to dance in many movies and television shows, but sooner than later it was time to hang up my dance shoes. All the head rolls and neck snaps and a neck injury incurred during the filming of *Shindig* had finally taken their toll.

"But I'm a dancer," I told the doctor. "I don't know how to do anything else."

"Well you better learn. If you keep doing this, you will damage the nerves and end up in surgery," he said.

I was devastated. I had no idea what I was going to do with the rest of my life.

As I look back I see that my life was, and is, touched by grace. That God and the Universe, in their infinite wisdom, knew far better than I what was best for me, placing me where I needed to be for the next phase of my life to begin.

As a child my favorite pass time was designing clothes for my dolls and paper cutouts. As I grew, so did my interest in costumes and clothes. When I went to the movies, my eye was naturally drawn to the smallest details of what people wore. Their clothes and shoes said so much to me about who they were—hence my interest in Ms. Sharaff's sketches and swatches, which foreshadowed my future, only I didn't know it then.

As luck would have it, while assisting Andre on the *Oral Roberts Show* at NBC Studios, the costume designer casually asked, "Have you ever considered doing wardrobe? You'd be very good at it."

It was as if he read my mind. "Funny you should ask," I replied. "I have, but I don't know how to go about it."

"Let me set up an interview with the head of the department."

So he did and thanks to him, my transition from in front of the camera to in back was effortless, beginning a long and very successful career as a costume supervisor. I learned my craft hands on by assisting the very best in the business. Gradually, I took on my own shows. My credits are too numerous to include all, but some of them were *Facts of Life, The Hogan Family, Full House, Family Matters, Perfect Strangers*.

Costuming was not my passion, it was something I did; it was my job, a fun creative job I was good at and enjoyed doing, but in my soul I was still a dancer. And in the midst of all this, I managed to get married, give birth to my son Nick and daughter Christina, get divorced, and raise my family as a single mom, with my *West Side Story* familia emotionally supporting me when needed. I would like to add, with all that I've done, giving birth to my children was one the most exhilarating experiences of my life. Seeing them for the first time is an image I will take with me to my grave.

When Nick was just a little tike, not even walking yet, he crawled to a cupboard holding a wooden spoon in his hand. He pulled out some pots and began beating on them. That cupboard, spoon, and pots were his favorite toy. He grew to be an amazing drummer, as steady as a heartbeat, and is now a professional musician and composer.

Christina thought she was Sarah Bernhard. She was always putting on productions. She climbed up on a chair and said, "Hi, my name is Christina and I'm going to put on a show for you." She put on shows, which she wrote, produced, directed, costumed, did the sets, starred in, and charged the neighbors twenty-five cents admission. She is now a professional actress/writer/producer.

When Christina was ten, she fell off her bike and tore her anterior cruciate ligament in her knee with a chunk of bone. She was rushed to Children's Hospital of Los Angeles for surgery. While in recovery, a woman came in and read to her. I saw the healing effect that stories had on her, and I vowed to become a bedside reader when I retired. I made good on my word. One day a week, for two years, I read to sick kids. Kids hooked to IV's and beeping monitors and tubes attached to them everywhere. The calming effect of a story never ceased to amaze me. Watching tense little bodies and pained faces relax, frowns turn to smiles; being able to give that to a child, if only for a few minutes— well, there was nothing quite like it in the world.

Though retired now, my life is so full I ask myself, *How did I ever work and do life at the same time?* I continue to take my ballet classes. I have to for my body, but more importantly for my soul. Placing my hand on the barre and taking that first plié still centers me; the outside world disappears and yes, sweating and feeling my muscles work down to the bone is still thrilling! And then of course there is the music, always the music humming in my cells.

I believe much of how our lives turn out has to do with timing and luck—being born at the right time, being at the right place, and paying attention to that faint whisper that nudges at your heart. I was born to dance. I knew from a very early age, this was what I was made for and meant to do. For me, to dance is to express God's joy. I am happiest when I am dancing.

But alas, a dancer's life is too short-lived and the body is unforgiving. It takes longer for my body to warm up now. I feel every injury I've ever inflicted on it. My legs don't kick as high, my endless stamina is now limited, I don't stretch as easily, my balance is not what it was, and there is much I can no longer do; still, I don't regret my aches and pains, for they remind me my body has been well used. At least when I meet my maker, I can say I didn't waste it. So I will take class for as long as my legs and body will allow. It's too painful remembering and comparing, so I try not to. I'm grateful instead for what I am still able to do. Class is my drug of choice. I get "a little nuts" without it.

"Mom, you need to go take ballet class like, now!" says my daughter Christina.

"Get your ass into class," Jerry said, pointing a finger at me time and again. Well, if he were still alive, he would be pleased to know my ass is still in class and all because of him. I have had an extraordinary life, a blessed life, and I owe it to Mr. Robbins. Had *West Side* not happened, had our paths not crossed, had he not hired me, I would have had a life, but not this delicious one. I would have had children, but not my Nick and Christina, the true jewels in my life.

I feel honored to have worked with Mr. Robbins and honored to be part of this cinematic masterpiece. When I likened Jerry to a stone in a pond and the ripple effect put into motion, I can say the same for *West Side*. Its effects are as far-reaching. I cannot begin to tell you how many young dancers have said to me, "I became a dancer because of you." "When I saw you in *West Side Story*, I wanted to dance just like you."

And these are the ones who have crossed my path. What of all those I will never meet, or those inspired by others in *West Side*? *West Side Story* will continue to influence and inspire young dancers because it is timeless, and we have its creator to thank for that. So I'd like to end by saying thank you, "Big Daddy," for giving us *West Side Story*. I thank you, those of us whose lives you've touched thank you, and all the young dancers that have yet to be born say thank you, Mr. Robbins, where ever you are. – Graziella

Gina Trikonis

"Velma"/Jet — Carole D'Andrea

I WAS VERY fortunate in that I didn't have to audition for the film…I was the original Velma on Broadway. I grew up in Altoona, Pennsylvania, and I started dancing at the age of four. I come from a very large Italian family on my father's side, and a large Welsh family on my mother's. I had two older brothers, Ronnie and Terry. We didn't have a lot of money, but my parents worked very hard to send me to dance school. I was so fortunate to have had a great ballet teacher, Miss Ruth Barnes, who gave me a foundation that prepared me, when the time came, to compete in the dance world in New York.

In 1955, three weeks before I was about to graduate from high school, my parents were killed in a car accident. They were very young, in their early forties. My mother died that night, and my father ten days later. After two very sad funerals and my last dance recital (I couldn't let the other teenage dancers down who had rehearsed for months), I graduated from high school. Two months later, I got on the train to New York, knowing no one, and with $500 in my pocket. I checked into a hotel, got two jobs, one at Macy's, running the elevator, and one taking tickets at a movie theatre. I took ballet classes at Ballet Theatre. I found a few jazz classes, but my favorite was taught by Peter Gennaro, who ended up choreographing all of the Shark dances in *West Side Story*.

Six months later and I'm dancing in Peter Gennaro's jazz class next to Chita Rivera and every other Broadway gypsy. I knew no one in class, yet the miracle to me is how right and effortless it all felt. I also auditioned and got a scholarship to the American Academy of Dramatic Arts. It's incredible to look back and see how the choices I made determined my life. I was scared but also filled with faith, wonder, and excitement.

I had heard about the Girls Rehearsal Club on 53rd Street. That was the basis for the famous film *Stage Door*. I was running out of money. A roommate from Pennsylvania, who had joined me in New York, went home, and I had heard about this haven for young female artists that provided a bed and three meals a day. I told them my story about how I came to New York and they decided to take me on. I found out later there was a long waiting list. They put me in a room on a cot with three other girls. What great luck! If I hadn't moved in there, *West Side Story* may never have happened, but that's for later.

I got my first job through one of the girls at the club. She told me of an audition for the world famous *Copacabana*. It seems every dancer and model in New York tried out. The requirements were not "Dance 10, Looks 3," but "Looks 10, Dance 3." Glamour was top priority. Only eight dancers were needed from hundreds of hopefuls.

Well, Jimmy Durante, who was headlining, sat in on the audition and insisted they hire me, despite my 5'4" frame.

"Put her on the end, but hire her," he said.

You just never know when or where you are going to make an impression. They changed the line every 6 months, but I was there a year and worked with all of the greats: Frank Sinatra, Tony Bennett, Sammy Davis Jr., and Jerry Lewis. It was a great job. Two shows a night, good money, and time to study during the day. The world of night clubs was enticing, but certainly not where I was headed. I was taking three to four dance classes a day, one singing lesson a week, and acting classes at night. Everyone knew you had to be a triple threat to be on Broadway, and I was preparing.

I was so very fortunate, my first audition in New York for the

Copacabana and I was chosen. My second audition was a year later. I went for my first summer stock call. I had planned on audition-ing for all the top summer stock theaters to get my Equity card, but once again was stunned when I was offered a job at the prestigious Lambertville on my first outing. I was told I would also be under-studying one of the leads in *Pajama Game*—Gladys, a role I had been dreaming of doing ever since seeing Carole Haney in between Peter Gennaro and Bob Fosse doing "Steam Heat." It was the first Broadway show I saw when I arrived in 1955, and it left a passionate mark on me. My thoughts echoed that of that wonderful line from *A Chorus Line*: "I can do that!" A little voice inside said, *"Carole, just keep studying..."* and I listened, and most importantly, believed. I knew summer stock was a great training ground, and I was looking forward to Lambertville.

One week after signing my summer stock contract, one of the most monumental moments of my life took place. I often wonder what would have happened if one young woman at the rehearsal club hadn't come into my room and asked me a very important question....

"Carole, do you have an extra pair of black dance tights I might borrow for this very exciting dance audition at the St. James Theater tomorrow morning?"

"Of course, what's the audition?" I asked.

"West Side Story," she said.

The very first time I ever heard the name, and it gives me chills now that the next question I asked was critical for the direction my life took.

I said, "Isn't that the musical about gangs in New York, don't you have to be Puerto Rican to audition?"

She was also fair like me.

"No, it's about rival gangs," she said.

"One Puerto Rican and one American. Why don't you audition?"

I said, "Well that's great, but I'm not Equity yet, I will be after I do Lambertville this summer."

She again had the right answer that would start me on my way.

She said, "They've already had the Equity call, and the union requires an open call to give everyone a fair chance. It's already 98% cast, but you never know."

My plan had been, after summer stock and an Equity card in hand, to start auditioning for Broadway in the fall. Here was a great opportunity to see what it would be like. I knew open calls were referred to as "cattle calls," with hundreds of girls auditioning, and that I could assess the process with no pressure, and enjoy every moment, completely anonymous.

What I awoke to the next beautiful April—I am an acting teacher now, and one of the truths I teach is that the mind takes pictures of every important moment of our lives, and in a second, the memory will recall all of our five senses and every detail that occurred. There are a number of moments in our lives that are truly life-changing, and here I was about to have my first. I will treasure it forever.

I remember the impact of the image I saw: a line four blocks deep, stretching from the St. James Theater all the way to 8th Avenue, around the block, and beyond. At least one thousand hopefuls. The line moved surprisingly quickly. I later was to learn why. Jerry Robbins knew exactly what he wanted and what you had to offer and was very quick to eliminate. I couldn't wait to get inside, get on stage, and be a part of it all. By now, I was aware of what a major audition this was, and also the odds of anyone actually being chosen from this open call. A million to one, at least! So oddly enough, it only relaxed me more. I had nothing to lose, and in my mind, actually standing on a Broadway stage to show them what I could do was a dream in and of itself. I had been preparing since I was four years old.

Inside finally. Yeah! Down the stairs to the dressing rooms…so many bodies…we were told to change quickly and form another line to go back up to the backstage. Once backstage, all I could see were dancers all over the stage in groups being given ballet combinations. When finished, they were told to go to stage left if you passed, and stage right if you were eliminated.

I was suddenly on stage with at least 50 dancers, being taught a ballet combination...only a few moments to regroup...then in groups of eight told to perform "Full out, please, no marking!" It was so exciting...a blur...so many faces...bodies...music...voices from across the orchestra pit, in the dark...yelling instructions. I couldn't believe it! I'm told to go to stage left and wait! Then another combination... many regroupings...many "stage left please, and the rest, thank you."

By then, I had come down from the fantasy of anonymity. Someone was noticing me! I now had a chance to really look around and see the competition. I had already been told by other dancers that everyone from the New York City Ballet Theater and Ballet Russe, every Broadway gypsy in every show on Broadway, had already auditioned at the Equity call, and all he needed was one American Jet girl to be cast. Can you imagine the odds of being chosen? The dancers I was auditioning with were outstanding. I could only imagine the quality of the Equity call. I passed all of the ballet cuts and now I could breathe. It's a miracle I'm still here, and now my favorite—jazz!

Something amazing is starting to happen. There is a man who keeps coming up to me backstage while I am learning yet another combination, asking me to tell him my name and a little bit about myself. After hours of finding him very distracting, I finally said, "Listen, do you mind?"

I was trying this new combination—a mambo. It's the afternoon now; "Stage left, please." This man was persistent. He kept asking me questions. Everyone was looking at him and his relentless pursuit of me.

He finally confessed his intentions. He said, "I am writing a film called *Bonjour Tristesse*. Otto Preminger and I have been looking for the right girl for the starring role, and we haven't found anyone that interests us. I've been watching you since this morning, and you are that girl. You are perfect for the role. You have all of the qualities we have been searching for."

Well, my response was, "That's lovely, thank you, but I really need to focus right now on yet another combination, knee pads and all, so just leave your name and number, I will give you a call tomorrow."

I will never forget his smile after I said those words to him.

He continued, "Let me introduce myself properly. I am Arthur Lawrence, and I am the author of *West Side Story*, and you needn't worry about this show—you've already got it, but I want you to do my movie."

In hindsight, it was the true definition of a dream. No part of me could absorb what he was saying. What was he talking about? I already had it?

Suddenly, I'm back on stage...the dream continues...I am now dancing between Peter Generro and an assistant—just like *Pajama Game* only it's me, not Carol Haney. Jerry Robbins is right in front of me, watching my every move...seven hours later, few dancers left. It's like something unfolding out of an MGM movie fantasy I had as a child. Decisions are being made, and my life is about to change forever.

Jerry stops everything and asks everyone to take a break. He then takes me by the hand and leads me to the side of the stage. I will never forget his remarks.

He said, "You have an amazing sense of dance...where did all of this intensity, anger, and passion come from in someone who looks like you? How old are you? Why weren't you at the Equity call?"

I replied, trying to find my voice, "I am not Equity, but I will be this summer when I do Lambertville."

"Oh, you aren't doing Lambertville. We'll get you out of your contract. I really want to work with you. You are doing my show," he said.

At that very moment, Arthur Lawrence came over and said, "She's not doing this show, I want Otto to meet her. I want her for my movie."

They proceeded to argue until Jerry finally said, "We'll discuss this later."

Shock! I was experiencing utter shock! I remember turning my back to see an empty stage. Where did they all go, all of those fellow hopefuls? I was the only one left and I was told that I would be called. Did I hear him right? Did he say I had the show? Nothing official, only those quiet words from Jerry to me. What exactly did it mean? I didn't question any more of it. I just floated, truly, back to the girls' Rehearsal Club. I remember the euphoria. The disbelief and the belief that, yes, miracles do happen. I remember the excitement and the noise as I entered the downstairs dining room. They had already heard; the girls were cheering and asking a million questions.

During the next week, I heard "Congratulations!" from everyone in my dance classes. They were so thrilled for me, but I knew I was still waiting for that phone call. The phone call came. It wasn't, "Carole, you have the show"; it was, "The final call back will be this Monday."

Déjà vu the lines, the dancers, the excitement—the shock; whatever made me think I had this show? Did I hear him right? Was I even in the running?…auditioning again…same combinations…"stage left, thank you and rest"…not one look from Jerry Robbins…does he even remember me? All I could do was be the best I could be and leave the results up to God. I had nothing to lose and was having an incredible adventure. I remember how high the stakes were at that point. There were new faces in the audience now, new opinions of our talent. I suddenly felt anything but anonymous. I was starting to get nervous—so few of us left. The division had begun. The Jets to one side, the Sharks to another. We were all told to get ready for the singing audition. I did "Steam Heat" and threw in everything in me. I can imagine Leonard Bernstein's face…and ears. By now, we all knew he was out there listening.

More dismissals…script is thrust in my hand…"Read Velma and read Anybodys." A brief description of both…Arthur Lawrence suddenly on stage, with an encouraging smile. These are, after all, his words. He told me Otto Preminger had already decided on a new actress called Jean Seaberg and that he was the director, but for now, we would be together on *West Side*.

Quiet in the theater now…"step forward, step back, stand with him, step back"…"thank you, you're excused…you, wait"…quiet, hushed voices from the dark…breathing on stage. Finally, Jerry is on stage, shaking my hand, and moving right down the line.

First day of rehearsal, "Dance Hall," Jerry is demonstrating and trying out new choreography on Tony Mordente and me. We have to remember the A, B, and C version of every combination. No time for fear, just do it and it better be perfect, so he knows what to keep. Tony Mordente kept quietly patting the small of my back for reassurance. My fellow Italian, he was the best dancer and dance partner ever.

Jerry took me aside and said, "I want you to understand, if I ever come down hard on you, it's not personal."

My reply was, "Don't worry, I can take care of myself."

I didn't realize that at that moment, I had gained his respect for all time, and unlike a great number of the cast, I was spared his wrath and devastating comments...a few have yet to recover.

4:00 p.m. Friday afternoon we had our first preview. Every dancer/actor/singer on Broadway was out front, along with every choreographer/director/producer. There is a quiet stillness in the theater. Is anybody even breathing? Then the first snap and the curtain goes up on the "Prologue"; a powerful experience has taken hold of everyone on both sides of the footlights. It doesn't let go for two and a half hours. The hush as the curtain goes down. Silence. Then a united crescendo of sounds, as we step forward. Bravos and cheers, a standing ovation that went on forever. We all knew that we had just made history and that musical theater would never be the same.

We opened in Washington, then Philadelphia—amazing reviews, but it's not New York. It's not Broadway. The word is out...the critics were waiting.

1957, Winter Garden Theater, New York City. Opening night. It is 10am, our last day of rehearsing. We were all seated in the back of the house. Jerome Robbins was speaking: "What we are doing here this evening is unprecedented in Musical Theater. There is a very good chance that we will not be well-received, and the critics will say this is a dance piece and should be presented uptown at New York City Ballet. I want you to be prepared."

8:00 p.m. A highly charged audience...curtain up...curtain

down…a stunned silence…then, a roar. *West Side Story* explodes and takes theater by storm, indeed, making history.

After a year and a half, I left *West Side* to do *Gypsy* and then went on an amazing Far East dance concert tour for The State Department. It was 1959, when *Ballet USA* went to Europe for the first cultural exchange that we had with other countries. The Russian Bolshoi Ballet Company came to the New York City Ballet, and I went with Rod Alexander's "Dance Jubilee" to the Near, Middle, and Far East.

It was a highlight of my life, and I was completely out of touch for nearly nine months. After growing up in a small mountain railroad town in Pennsylvania, it was an awesome experience to be exposed to other countries and cultures. In every country, we were met by heads of state, kings and queens, and we danced in palaces and at the State Royal Theatre. We were asked to learn the dance of each country and region we were in and perform it at the end of our concert. Then the next day their most brilliant dancers would do a special concert for us. I can still smell the smells of each country, especially India, where we stayed for two months, and I can still see the brilliant colors and landscape. I had nine months to explore the cultures of all of these countries.

On my first day back in New York, in 1960, I went to take a dance class, and I heard that a film of *West Side Story* was going to be made. While I was out of the country, every dancer across the country had auditioned over the past year. I had completely missed out on this casting and was deeply saddened. At the same time, I had met the well-known, two-time Tony award-winning actor, Robert Morse, right before I left. He kept asking me out after we first met in Luigi's jazz class. I said, "No," as I was about to go on this Eastern tour, but he was tenacious. Nine months later, I walked back into Luigi's class, and there he was. Our first date was on the back of his motor scooter, with me holding this huge Ravi Shankar sitar from India. I was moving into a new apartment with some roommates.

"Next time you move, it's going to be with me. I am going to marry you some day," he said in the elevator.

I was only back for two weeks when Bob's agent called him and told him that Carole had a call from Jerome Robbins' office. They had been looking everywhere for her over the past year. They just heard that she was back in NY, and that you were dating. Could you give her this number, and have her call Jerry in California immediately?

I remember calling the number sitting on a stool, in this little empty hallway, at my new unfurnished apartment. I got Howard Jeffrey on the line and he then got Jerry, after what seemed like an eternity.

Jerry said, "It's about time, Carole, where in the world have you been this past year? We were asking everyone and no one knew where you had disappeared to. I want you to come out to play Anybodys in the film." I understudied Lee Becker on Broadway, and he had seen me go on for her many times. "If I can't convince Robert Wise that you are right for the tomboy, you will do your original role as Velma." I was stunned and beyond thrilled.

He then said, "Mr. Wise wants to meet you at his office, which is on 57th Street. Whatever you do...

WHATEVER you do, DO NOT tell him your age! He has this idea that only teenagers will be convincing on film."

I had a wonderful meeting with Mr. Wise. He asked me many questions about my training, where I was from, and how I got the role of Velma on Broadway. I felt it was a done deal.

As I was leaving Mr. Wise's office he said, "Oh, by the way, how old are you, Carole?"

Without thinking, I said, "Twenty-one."

He said, "Oh, you would have been perfect for the film. That's disappointing."

I was stunned. I would have been perfect for the film? I already created and played Velma. During my subway ride home, I felt numb. Shocked at how, with one wrong answer, I just lost my role in the film. When I got home, the phone was ringing.

Jerry was yelling, at the top of his lungs, "I thought I told you whatever you do, you were not going to tell him your age!!!! It's OK, I told him I am making this decision, and you are doing the film! I want you to book a plane out to Hollywood ASAP!"

After five months of filming, Mr. Wise didn't feel as though I was enough of a tomboy.

"Too pretty for Anybodys," he said.

"Don't wear any make-up to rehearsals," said Jerry.

"I am not wearing any," I said.

Finally, Mr. Wise won out and hired a 14-year-old, and Jerry cut the role considerably. I took over my original role as Velma. The role, along with Graziella, was enlarged, and we were added to "Officer Krupke," so all worked out perfectly. There was, however, one sad note. The dancer who had been playing Velma was a young girl named Taffy Paul. She was never told or never realized that if I didn't do Anybodys, I would then resume my role as Velma. She was hired to do Velma while I was on the dance tour and Jerry couldn't find me.

It was heartbreaking for her, and we all felt so badly. The good news is that she changed her name to Stefanie Powers and then went on to have a wonderful career as a film and TV actress. We had a lovely, tender reunion when she later starred in a Disney film, with my husband Robert Morse, called *The Love Boat*.

Jerry was in such a hurry to have me pack and get to California in a few days. When I got there, I found out that I was the only girl from the original cast to have gotten the film. A few of the guys, including my partner Tony Mordente, were also cast, which I was thrilled about. Gina Trikonis came into the Broadway show as one of the first replacements the second year, a few months before I left, and was cast as Graziella. We ended up rooming together. I adored her, and somehow found it perfect that Velma and Graziella ended up roommates. The guys' scheduled two weeks of filming on the streets of NY turned into two months, so Gina and I had a great time getting full pay, and getting to know Hollywood until they all came back.

Jerry auditioned and hired new dancers for "Dance Hall" on Monday, watched them take class with us every morning, watched them learn the choreography, and by Friday, he fired all of them. Then he would start the process all over again the following week. He wanted his dancers to be PERFECT.

They were having a very difficult time casting the role of Maria, and one day Jerry and Robert Wise came to me and said, "Carole, we want you to look over these sides. It's the balcony scene, and I know you are surprised, this is a long shot (stunned was more like it)...but we want to audition you for Maria. You will come in Monday, and we will have a dark wig for you, make-up, and an actor for you to read with. It's important that you don't say anything to any of the cast members."

"We know you don't look Spanish, but it is a fresh, passionate young spirit we are looking for, and you have that," they then said.

I am still amazed that Jerry saw me as Anybodys, Velma, and now, possibly, Maria. I had my screen test a few days later with the assistant director. I felt so strange doing the "Balcony Scene" in a black wig, costume, and darker make-up. They gave me a few notes, and we were finished. I never saw the actor who played Tony again. I had my first experience of kissing a complete stranger on film. It was all surreal, and I never told anyone. A few days later, we heard that they had decided to cast Natalie Wood. Honestly, I was relieved. I was completely wrong for the part, but flattered Jerry had so much belief in me. To have been in the original cast on Broadway, and then to have had the opportunity to recreate Velma for the screen, was one of the biggest blessings of my life.

During the filming of *West Side*, we woke up around 5 am so we could be at the Samuel Goldwyn Lot by 6 am. We had an hour and a half class each day to prepare us for the challenging day ahead, then into make-up and costume. Jerry and Robert Wise were co-directing. We were all new to film, and the biggest challenge for all of us was to keep our dancer bodies warm and ready with energy, through many takes and many hours of waiting, while the set was relit, camera angles discussed and changed, and our costumes and make-up checked. It was all very exciting and new. There were no complaints. We were thrilled to be there.

Everyone loved one another. We all had so much respect for each other's individual talents and the road that got us here. As I said, Jerry would hire new dancers for "Dance Hall" every week; by Friday, after watching them take class every day and learn the routine, he would fire most of them. His standards were very high.

We rehearsed for three months before filming began. "Cool" took us three weeks to shoot on a soundstage built as an underground garage. We filmed in August, so the heat was intense. I remember how exhausted we were from so very many takes. Jerry was learning about film and trying every possible angle, much to Mr. Wise's and the studio's dismay. Thank heavens he took the time; the result was incredibly effective. I loved the whole experience, and the challenge for us was to keep up the moves full out and the acting intense.

I never did know why they changed the script from the original one on Broadway. In the Broadway script, "Cool" is about keeping our cool before the rumble. Riff, gang leader, sings it in the drugstore before the "Rumble." In the film, the rumble is before "Cool." Riff has been killed, and they created a new character called Ice, who takes over the Jets and makes Velma his girlfriend. Tucker Smith was excellent, and he sings "Cool" for us to calm down after Riff's death. Tucker died, much too young, from cancer in his fifties.

One morning, we were all asked to come to one of the sets and were all shocked when they told us that Jerry had been taken off of the film. This was his creation, he was a god, how could anyone fire God? Jerry was let go a month or so before we finished shooting. The "Dance Hall," "Officer Krupke," and the last, very important scene on the playground had yet to be shot. We were all in shock. The studio said he was taking too much time and spending too much money. We eventually learned that he was allowed to come to the studio, at the end of each day, to watch the dailies that Robert Wise shot and Tony Mordente staged. I am sure he was allowed input on the editing.

Robert Wise asked Tony to help him stage the "Dance Hall." This was a huge task with so many dances and dancers to oversee. I think if they thought Jerry took three weeks to shoot "Cool," it would or could take him months to film all of the "Dance Hall." Tony did a wonderful job. He was Jerry's favorite dancer on Broadway and film, and I was so fortunate to have been partnered by him. On Broadway, Jerry used to try out many versions of every number on the both of us. Tony was a seasoned Broadway and Ballet Theatre dancer, and it was my very first show. I still remember Tony's hand on my back, patting me not to worry, I could do it. He literally had my back day in and out, as I tried to look cool.

We started work on the Dance Hall.... I remember their patience with Natalie Wood with the "Cha-Cha." We spent three days filming that one important moment when Tony and Maria come together, and right behind them, four Sharks and four Jets dancing the "Cha-Cha." She was having trouble with the simple choreography where she had to do turns and end up on half point. After three days, she was finally able to do it. It was excruciating for everyone, and she was very embarrassed and angry. She was so very guarded with us that I felt for her. She never ever made eye contact with any of us. If, just once, she had been able to turn to us and say, "I am not a dancer," or "Lord, this is hard for me," with sensitivity and even some humor, we would have given her so much love, help, and reassurance, but she never gave us the chance. Fear of not looking perfect or having to live up to her movie star image robbed her of so much support.

Then the unthinkable happened. She watched the dailies and said, "I am sorry, but this just won't do. All you see is Carole's face and blonde hair instead of me."

Well, the next day, we started the "Cha-Cha" all over again, with my back to the camera now. Actually, I thought she was completely right. The focus should be on them, not me.

I look back now, and I so wish that I was able, somehow, to swallow my pride and tell her what a hard worker she was and how much I admired her effort, but she felt unapproachable. After all these years I still feel badly that I never took the time to introduce myself and speak to Natalie. I had always thought she was a wonderful talent, but she was having a lot of problems with her marriage to Robert Wagner and was in a very fragile frame of mind. I don't remember one time that she ever looked at any of us or spoke to us. We were also told she was very intimidated by us and our dance ability. She became very close to Jerry, his two assistants, and Tony Mordente. She felt safe with them. It must have been a blow to her safety when Jerry was taken off the film, and she hadn't yet done her very important "Dance Hall" scenes or the last 20 minutes of the film.

Very few people know that it took two Jet girls to teach Rita Moreno her big dance number "America." Jerry didn't choreograph it originally; Peter Gennaro did. So, he asked Gina and I, since we both had been on Broadway, to work with her. I loved Rita. She was warm, funny, and scared of this big challenge.

She kept saying, "I am not a dancer like Chita Rivera. I am doing the best I can."

What a trouper, and she ended up with an Academy Award for Best Supporting Actress, which was very well deserved.

Gina and I also were asked to sing on the film cast album not only for our Jet numbers, but also with all of the Shark girls on America and "I Feel Pretty" with Spanish accents. They needed more young voices. Lucky us. We had a great time.

It is a well-known fact that Marni Nixon was brought in to dub Natalie's voice. It was, however, a big secret at the time. Natalie did not have a trained singing voice but insisted on singing her songs. We all knew she was being dubbed, but she did not. She was not told until the film was completely in the can. They were afraid she would leave the film in protest. I never felt it was handled honestly with her, but when time and money are involved, there is no arguing with the studio heads.

The last scene we shot was the last scene in the film. It took nearly a week or more. Richard Beymer (Tony) kept running around the studio to get into the mood and Natalie was not happy waiting for him, since she also was getting into the mood of deep grief. He never was her choice for Tony. I remember Mr. Wise telling us she was way over her contract and it was costing a lot of money to keep her, so we all had to give it everything we had in each shot.

When we were in the last weeks of filming, Robert Wise called me up to his office one day to meet the famous casting director Lynn Stalmaster. Mr. Wise had chosen three of us from the film to show Lynn film on us and to get us work when the film was done. I was just so surprised and moved by his belief in me. Lynn said he already had an offer for me from 20th Century for a seven-year contract.

I will never forget their faces when I said, "Thank you so very much, but I left Pennsylvania when I was seventeen (knowing no one) to go to New York to do theatre, not Hollywood to do films, and I will be going back to New York when we finish."

I still remember both of them staring at me in disbelief for what seemed like forever. In actuality, it was just a few moments that turned their disbelief into respect for my sticking to my goals. How I loved Mr. Wise for his care and belief in me, and I had plenty of time, over the years, to thank him.

When the film opened in New York, a year and a half later in October, I had married Robert Morse. He was, thankfully, persistent. He used to fly out to Hollywood every Saturday night and leave the following Monday morning to go back to *Take Me Along*, the Broadway show he was starring in with Jackie Gleason.

I was seven months pregnant with my first of three daughters to come. *Time* and *Newsweek* magazine did a photo cover story on my husband Robert Morse for *How To Succeed in Business*, saying that the Morse family were having three openings that year, and they printed many pages of photos of us at both theatres, as well as our apartment on the Upper West Side. His Broadway show and my film both opened in October, and the arrival of our first child was due in December.

It was a glorious night, and the pride I felt for all of my fellow dancers and friends remains a memory that I will always cherish. I have, to this day, two *West Side Story* families: The Broadway cast and The Academy Award-winning cast of the film.

After

IT WAS SUCH an honor to be in a classic that touched so many people's hearts and inspired them to also study, create, and contribute to theatre and film in their very own original way. Filming ended in February of 1960, and I went back to New York. Gina, the guys, and some of the new friends that I had made in the film stayed in California. That was hard, as we became so close, and I missed them all.

After flying out to Hollywood for eight months every weekend, Bob gave me an ultimatum. He said, "I don't want to date you anymore. I love you and want to marry you, so if you are not sure, then we have to end this."

The light came on in my heart, and I couldn't imagine not seeing him anymore.

I took him back to Pennsylvania to meet my brother and realized later that I was testing him. He was so great with my nieces and nephews.

"OK, do you still want to marry me?" I said on the six-hour train ride back to New York.

He said, "Yes," but he didn't trust me. "OK," he said. "Name a date next month." He was about to go into rehearsals for a show that was written for him: *How to Succeed in Business without Really Trying*. I just picked the first weekend date of the following month, Saturday, April 8, 1960. We had a lovely small ceremony in New Jersey, where his parents lived, for our friends and family. I remember my brother Terry gave me away. He, my other brother Ronnie, and I were going to be strong. Since my parents had died in that tragic car accident back home just a few years prior, we never mentioned how emotional it was for us not to have them there.

Right before the music began, and just as I started down the aisle, Terry said, "I can't believe Mom and Dad are not here."

Well, I will never forget those words and my reaction, which was to cry all through the wedding. Tragically, a few months later, at the age of 27, with three small children at home, Terry died. He had four wisdom teeth pulled, and they gave him too much sodium pentothal at the hospital, and his heart stopped. I came home once again to Altoona, and my brother Ronnie and I had our third funeral to attend. I treasure my brother Ronnie and want him to live forever.

Bob and I had three daughters in the first five years of our marriage. During those years, I always took classes. Dance, acting, and singing. Bob was having huge success with many films, so we were flying back and forth to California. At that time, I also worked on a lot of sitcoms and did many commercials.

I want to share an amazing experience I had in 1975. I had some friends who were doing a new musical down at the Public Theater, and they urged me to come see the first preview in the smallest theatre, upstairs, on a very cold winter's night. I was sitting with my three young daughters, and the name of the musical was *A Chorus Line,* and I was crying. I was instantly transported back to the small town I grew up in in Altoona, Pennsylvania.

It is 1941, and my mother is calling me to get ready for dancing school. I am four years old and would rather play out in the yard with my brothers. Thank God she was adamant that I clean up, put on the pink tights and tutu, and climb that "steep and narrow staircase" to my first ballet class, and my destiny.

It is 1949 and "I Can Do That." I am twelve years old, and my dance teacher has added magic to my life: tap shoes and tap classes. I feel a new freedom and rhythm with my body, and the music is so natural and freeing to me that I feel transformed. As the song "I Felt Nothing" begins, I am reliving fear. I feel cold and numb.

I am remembering my first acting class in New York, age eighteen, when an acting teacher said, "Carole, you are going to have to touch the feelings that are full of vulnerability and need, if you want to be a well-rounded actress."

I felt nothing. To feel any emotions meant I was going to have to re-experience the loss of my parents. In dance I could rage, feel, and cry in silence. I felt safe. The structure and warmth of my dance classes were very familiar to me.

As they sang "Everything is Beautiful at the Ballet," I was, once again, comforted and reassured. "The Music and the Mirror" was a perfect metaphor for my life. All I ever needed was "The Music and The Mirror"! It took me back to my roots when my whole family was still alive, watching my every move. All the dance recitals from age four to seventeen. I loved the line, "All I ever needed was the chance to dance for you." I believe in my heart they have seen it all.

As my daughters were growing up, I began to choreograph and direct some musicals in New York and the surrounding area. Then, twenty-seven years ago, I was asked to fill in for a teacher with her singing performance class. I found to my surprise that I just loved teaching, so I began my own classes, teaching, acting, and singing performance classes, in the very prestigious Carnegie Hall.

My daughters were all grown up and on their own. Andrea had gone to work for Tom Cruise, as his assistant, and ended up traveling the world with him. She then became the executive director of his company for the next eighteen years. She hired her husband as an assistant director, and he, ultimately, became an associate producer with Tom a few years later. He produced with Tom the first few *Mission Impossible* films, among others. They have a beautiful little son, Lance.

Robin was having success as an actress in New York on Broadway. Her first show, at seventeen, was playing Chita Rivera's daughter in *Bring Back Birdie*. How amazing that we both worked with Chita on our first Broadway show in our teens. She did other Broadway shows and is now a very respected acting and singing performance teacher in New York (www.robinmorse.net). She has two cherished children, Lucy and Frankie.

Hilary headed for California to live with her father at twenty-one. She did a few films and television spots and went on to originate the role of Sally Simpson in the musical *The Who's Tommy.* She is married with two great little boys, Jagger and Marlon.

I decided after living in New York for 36 years that it was time for a major life change. I moved out to Los Angeles and began the search for a theatre where I could start all over again. I was 53 and it was quite a challenge, but I had so much faith if I had success in New York, I could do it again in Hollywood. I started the search for the right theatre and location. In the heart of theatre row on Santa Monica Boulevard in Hollywood, I was fortunate to find two theaters under the same roof. I started a singing performance class at the Complex Theatre Tuesday mornings and acting classes, at the Flight Theatre next door, on Wednesdays. It is now 20 years later, and I continue to teach classes as well as privately coach many illustrious artists in film, TV, the music industry, and theatre. One day, I looked west on Santa Monica Blvd. and realized I was exactly half a mile away from the Samuel Goldwyn Studios, where we filmed *West Side Story,* on Formosa and Santa Monica Blvd.

I think I could actually see the twenty-one-year-old Carole looking up the street saying, "Welcome back to Hollywood...so glad you gave it another chance."

I want to share a speech I made, as I was recently inducted into the Hall of Fame for Performing Arts in Pennsylvania. I was so very honored. I had come full circle, and to know that I was making my family happy and proud meant the world to me. I have always loved the quote, "If it's meant to be, it's up to me," and Nelson Mandela quoted in his inaugural speech, "My playing small does not serve the world...I am so proud I did not play small."

PENNSYLVANIA HALL OF FAME SPEECH
"Get on the Train"

I FEEL SO BLESSED TO BE HERE TONIGHT...THE TITLE OF THIS SPEECH IS "GET ON THE TRAIN"...BECAUSE IF I

HADN'T FOLLOWED MY DREAM AT SEVENTEEN, GOTTEN ON THE TRAIN, AND GONE TO NEW YORK KNOWING NO ONE AND WITH MY BROTHERS' BRAVE ENCOURAGEMENT, I WOULDN'T BE HERE TONIGHT.

THE FIRST TIME I MADE AN APPEARANCE ON THIS MAGNIFICENT MISHLER STAGE WAS WHEN I WAS FOUR YEARS OLD. I WAS A STUDENT OF THE VERY LOVED DANCE TEACHER RUTH BARNES. EVERY JUNE, WE HAD OUR DANCE RECITALS HERE.

I WILL BE FOREVER INDEBTED TO HER FOR INSTILLING IN ME THE LOVE OF DANCE AND A SOLID FOUNDATION AND TECHNIQUE THAT ALLOWED ME TO COMPETE IN NEW YORK WHEN THE TIME CAME.

MY LAST APPEARANCE ON THIS STAGE WAS IN 1955 WHEN I WAS SEVENTEEN YEARS OLD FIFTY-FIVE YEARS AGO...TODAY I AM SEVENTY-TWO, AND TO BE GIVEN THIS HONOR IS SO DEEPLY MOVING.

MY PARENTS AND MY FAMILY NEVER MISSED AN APPEARANCE OF MINE IN ALL THOSE YEARS. I AM SO VERY FORTUNATE TO HAVE FAMILY ONCE AGAIN HERE; THIS MEANS EVERYTHING TO ME THAT RONNIE IS HERE THIS EVENING. HE AND MY SISTER-IN-LAW, JOANNE, BECAME MY WHOLE FAMILY AND MADE SURE I ALWAYS HAD A HOME FOR MY DAUGHTERS TO COME BACK TO, SO THEY COULD KNOW THEIR AUNTS, UNCLES, AND COUSINS. WE BOTH KNOW THAT I WOULDN'T BE GETTING THIS HONOR THIS EVE IF NOT FOR ALL THE YEARS OF OUR PARENTS', JESSIE AND PATRICK D'ANDREA'S, HARD WORK IN PAYING FOR MY LESSONS AND THEIR LOVE AND SUPPORT.

I KNOW MY PARENTS AND MY BROTHER TERRY ARE HERE THIS EVE WATCHING OVER BOTH RONNIE AND I. I AM A GREAT BELIEVER IN THE WONDERFUL QUOTE, "DON'T GIVE UP FIVE MINUTES BEFORE THE MIRACLE." BECAUSE I DID FOLLOW MY DREAM AT SEVENTEEN AND GOT ON THAT TRAIN TO NEW YORK…I ENDED UP WITH THREE AMAZING DAUGHTERS, FIVE GRANDCHILDREN, AND A CAREER THAT IS STILL IN FULL BLOOM AFTER ALL THESE YEARS. I AM DEEPLY GRATEFUL FOR THIS HONOR THIS EVENING, AND I WOULD LIKE TO END WITH WHAT THE WORD "GRATITUDE" MEANS TO ME.

"GRATITUDE UNLOCKS THE FULLNESS OF LIFE. IT TURNS WHAT WE HAVE INTO ENOUGH AND MORE. IT TURNS CHAOS TO ORDER. GRATITUDE MAKES SENSE OF OUR PAST, AND BRINGS PEACE FOR TODAY."

Carole D'Andrea's 50-year career has spanned all phases of the entertainment industry. She began dancing at the age of four, and was a seasoned Broadway performer by the age of nineteen, having been cast as the original Velma in both the Broadway and film productions of *West Side Story*, as well as in *Gypsy*.

As a performing artist, Ms. D'Andrea has appeared before many heads of state, and has been featured on many television specials and sitcoms. She has directed several plays and musicals off-Broadway, as well as many regional theaters throughout the United States. Directing credits include *Company, Guys and Dolls,* and *Damn Yankees*.

Sharing her vast experiences through teaching is merely a natural step in this far-reaching career. She has taught thousands of serious performers for stage and film at New York City's illustrious Carnegie Hall. Ms. D'Andrea has also emerged as a highly sought international coach for actors in England, Ireland, Germany, Japan, and Australia.

Ms D'Andrea currently offers Acting and Singing Performance

classes, as well as private coaching sessions, at Hollywood's Flight Theatre in the Complex.

The prestigious book _The Actor's Guide to Qualified Coaches: Los Angeles_ names Carole D'Andrea among LA's top 30 most-qualified acting coaches.

Ms. D'Andrea's life and body of work were recently preserved in a BBC documentary production.

Carole D'Andrea – Velma

Sharks

"Juano"/Shark — Eddie Verso

I WAS FIFTEEN when I first met Jerome Robbins. I had auditioned for *Bells are Ringing*, a show directed by Jerry and choreographed by Bob Fosse, which was slated to open on Broadway. They kept me till the end of the audition. It was obvious I had caught Bob and Jerry's eye. But after a great deal of discussion, they explained to me that they just could not use me because I was too young. A couple of months later, I attended an open audition for another Broadway-bound musical, *Oh Captain!* They offered me the job, but when I went to sign my contract it seemed my age, again, was going to be an obstacle. In the end, however, I was hired, and performed in my first Broadway show. As exciting as this was, it was not an easy time for me. I struggled to keep up with my schoolwork and my duties as a performer.

At the time, I was a student at The High School of Performing. PA, as we called it, is the high school that later acquired notoriety from the movie *Fame*. PA was a wonderful experience and much like the movie, our lives really centered around dance. I entered the modern dance department as a freshman and I had a terrible crush on my modern dance teacher, Nancy Lang. So when she left the school, I transferred to the ballet department, and at the same time my friend Elliot Feld transferred from the ballet department to modern dance. I studied with some really wonderful teachers at PA, the most memorable being Norman Walker, Harry Asmus, Nina Popova, and Bella Malenka. Many of my schoolmates and other alumni went on to have successful careers in the entertainment industry, and several went on to become cast members in different productions of *West Side Story*—these classmates included Jaime Rogers, Jay Norman, Tony Mordente, and Elliot Feld.

Of course, when I found out about an open call for the London production of *West Side Story*, I cut school and went to the audition. At sixteen I was a young hotshot having already performed on Broadway. Needless to say, I was a little cocky when I walked into that audition. I didn't know a soul but I was secure in my abilities, and like most teenagers, I was ready to take on the world.

It is now clear to me this was exactly what Jerry was looking for—young strong personalities with that unmistakable teenage mentality, plenty of attitude and no concerns about consequences. Life was black and white to me just as it was for the characters in *West Side*. In retrospect, the ability to dance was only one element of what Jerry sought in his cast. Ultimately the group he chose were tough guys, funny guys, but all strong personalities—Jaime Rogers, Jay Norman, George Chakaris, Tony Mordente, Eliot Feld. Many of us, myself included, were street savvy and reflected the world he was trying to capture on film.

You see, I was born on the lower east side of Manhattan. I lived in an ethnically mixed neighborhood so my friends were a variety of nationalities. Even though we were tough little street rats, my friends knew and accepted the fact that I took dance lessons. I guess I was confident because at age nine or so I began giving lessons to my big brother's friends and charging them a nickel a class. I started dancing at the age of eight. My first classes were in acrobatics and flamenco, but at my teacher's suggestion, I quickly added ballet and tap. I took ballet class at a Lithuanian Church in Brooklyn, and tap with Ernest Carlos in New York City. My mom and dad were my most avid fans. My mom took a job to pay for my lessons. I was frequently the only boy in class, so my teachers paid a great deal of attention to me and that was OK by me. My family moved to Queens when I was around ten.

By age eleven I was sent to study ballet with Nickolias at Carnegie Hall, but after a year or two, Nickolias told me there was nothing more he could teach me and sent me to study with Vincenzo Celli. Celli was an amazing ballet master who was born in Chicago, but had traveled to Europe to study with Enrico Cecchetti—arguably the most prominent and well-respected ballet teacher in the world in the early 1900s. Cecchetti taught in Europe and Russia and was the legendary prima ballerina Anna Pavlova's private teacher.

Enrico Cecchetti codified a method of teaching known as *The Cecchetti Method*, which I studied with Celli from the time I was twelve till I was sixteen. *The Cecchetti Method* encourages natural turnout as opposed to fabricated, that is, the normal range of motion without forcing. Fast footwork, bodyline and smooth transitions are most important in the Cecchetti Method. Cecchetti believed that one exercise done correctly was the equivalent of twelve sloppy repetitions; his method gave me a strong technical base by working every part of my body evenly, but only in my adult years was I able to appreciate how fortunate I was to have had Celli as my teacher. His studio was at the old CBS building on 53rd Street and Broadway now known as the Ed Sullivan Theater.

Interestingly enough, shortly before the movie, Jerry choreographed *Opus Jazz* for his company, Jerome Robbins: Ballets USA, which had the same feel as *West Side Story*. He seemed to be attracted to that strong, defiant, unapologetic attitude that young people possess—a take-it-or-leave-it kind of demeanor contrasting the tension of a world with expectations and rules.

As I look back over my dance career, I have to say that the *WSS* audition was the hardest I had ever attended. We danced for hours and hours, watching each other, waiting to see who was cut and who was kept. The call back was held a few days later, and the wait was agonizing. Upon my return to school, I was dutifully reprimanded for cutting school, but it was short-lived when they found out I had received a call back—an opportunity to be seen one more time with the remaining candidates.

Well I got it. I was cast in the role of Baby John and was also asked to understudy the role of Action. My dream of dancing for a living was becoming a reality, and I was elated. My parents were also excited but more than a little anxious. At seventeen, I was one of the youngest dancers accepted into the cast, and my parents felt I was too young to go to London on my own. As far as they were concerned, it was completely out of the question. I, on the other hand, was determined to take this job. I told them I would run away if they did not let me go. So after a great deal of bargaining, they relented.

I performed in London for sixteen months. Though London was an exciting place to be, I was still a youngster and over time I became homesick and decided it was time to return home. But before I left, I couldn't resist the urge to see Europe. David Bean, Diesel in the London production, decided to join me. We jumped in his car and fled to the continent.

As luck would have it, while passing through Germany, I bumped into my former modern dance teacher from The High School of Performing Arts, Norman Walker. He was in the army stationed overseas. After a couple of weeks on the road, we arrived back in jolly old England, where a message from Jerry was waiting for me. It was a personal invitation to audition for the *West Side Story* film! Talk about a thrill—not only was I auditioning for a movie, but the choreographer *asked* me to be there! I was on cloud nine!

Back in the US, several of my friends from PA had been involved in different productions of *WSS* and/or had auditioned for Mr. Robbins, hoping to have the opportunity to work with this choreographic genius. So on the day of the audition, I was not really surprised by the astounding number of dancers and actors that showed up. Everyone was there, school-friends, studio acquaintances, and lots of familiar faces—the best dancer/singer/actors that New York had to offer. Though I can't remember where the auditions were held, I do remember it was some sort of vacant lot; walking onto that lot was like a homecoming reunion. I expected a lot of jitters, considering this audition was for a major film production, and I'm sure there was some nervousness, but mainly, the atmosphere was charged with excitement; I felt it in the air. Then the word came and a few weeks later, those that made the cut were whisked off to Hollywood, first-class seats, not something lowly dancers often enjoy. We were so excited we drove the stewardesses crazy.

Hollywood was just as I had pictured it. I remember seeing a palm tree for the first time and immediately thought, I don't think Christmas will be the same. Upon arriving in Los Angeles, we all set out in search of housing. Cast members found roommates and somehow, I found myself rooming with David Winters (A-Rab). He got an apartment that was only two blocks from the studio.

David was a great guy but very unusual. He decided he wanted a pet but he didn't get a dog or a cat. He got a monkey. Why he chose a monkey as a pet I have no idea. I knew nothing about monkeys but thought, *Hey, that's a cool pet*, so I went along with it. While we were on set during the day, the monkey had the run of the house. I soon discovered the challenges of living with an untrained, undomesticated animal. Every evening we came home to a new disaster. The monkey got into everything, and he was not housebroken.

One day we came home and discovered the monkey missing. We set out to find him. We looked all over the neighborhood, up and down the streets, asked around in local stores, and asked passersby. Finally someone told us the monkey was seen running into the nearby synagogue. David recovered the monkey, but not before the little beast had wreaked havoc in the house of worship. David had to give it up after that incident, so that was the end of the monkey.

Though some of us had worked in movies, we had never held a significant acting role, but that was about to change. Each of us was given a screen test—the dreaded process of auditioning in front of the cameras. Bob Wise, Jerome Robbins, and everyone else that would be on the other side of the camera was there. I remember being very nervous; having the camera come in close was more than a little nerve-racking.

We shot at Samuel Goldwyn Studios, which was located on Santa Monica Blvd. and Formosa Avenue. Even before the parts were cast, we rehearsed for Robbins on a soundstage turned into a makeshift rehearsal hall. After the casting was posted, we had the option of staying or leaving. If my memory serves me correctly, I think we all stayed. What a great decision.

As already mentioned, Jaime Rodgers, Eliot Feld, and I went to The High School of Performing Arts together. We were friends and certainly got to know each other even better when we did the film. Jaime knew my brother before he knew me. Jaime and I had a knack for instigating trouble. Looking back, I have sympathy for Assistant Director, Jerry Siegel, who had to keep a bunch of cocky, mischievous youngsters from New York in line. In truth, even though we were dancers, we were not that far removed from the juvenile delinquents we played. Bob's *sit-downs* with the cast became a near daily event. He often threatened us with, "You'll never work in this town again if you get fired from this film."

For many of us Hollywood, though wonderful, was not our dream as much as the New York stage. Consequently, his "sit-downs" had little impact on curbing our antics. One day we found lighting carts that were left on the back lot. I don't remember who started it, but before long, we were pushing each other around the lot in the carts as if they were chariots. Well we were having so much fun and making so much noise that Donna Reed came out to see what the commotion was all about, and she was not very happy having to stop production on her shoot. She scolded us just like she did Bud on *Father Knows Best*. The only problem was, we weren't Bud and we weren't listening, and of course that led to one of the famous *sit-downs*.

Spending many hours waiting for the next shot can be very boring, but as youngsters, we made the best of the situation using the time to conjure up tricks to play on our on-screen rivals—the Jets. Jaime Rodgers and Jay Norman were some of the biggest pranksters, and as one of the youngest cast members, I tagged along learning from these pros. Jerry enjoyed this and even encouraged it. One day we found a water hose just sitting around the lot. All I can tell you is the Jets had a lot of costume changes that day.

Our crazy antics were not limited to the set. We often spent our days off together and played games in public like jumping in our cars and traveling in a caravan, each car packed with cast members. When we stopped at a red light we all jumped out of the car, demonstrated a rather realistic fight scene with the cast members in the car in front of us, then jumped back in the cars and drove away, causing a stir on the street and leaving many dumfounded pedestrians wondering what just took place.

My brother and I often went to the desert to hunt jackrabbits. One day, as we were loading the car, some kids across the street started harassing us. Fellow Sharks Jay Norman, Andre Tayir, and Jaime Rodgers lived in my building. I went in to the courtyard, and summoned my gang with the *West Side Story* whistle, and in a heartbeat my fellow Sharks came to our aid.

While in Hollywood, Robbins rented a two-seater Ford Thunderbird. One day he asked if I could take the car to be washed. I had just gotten my license and wanted to practice driving so, of course, I happily complied. The idea of cruising down the Boulevard in his T-Bird was any young man's dream come true. My sidekick, Jaime Rogers, of course, accompanied me on this important errand. Not surprisingly, he asked to drive the car. The thought of him behind the wheel of Jerry's rented T-bird scared even me! Against my better judgment, I could not say no to him. From then on, I made it my business to ask Jerry every day if his car needed a wash. I think we drove his car more than Jerry did. Thankfully, Jaime is a much better driver today.

We all had a good time on and off the set and even when filming. John Astin, of *The Adams Family* fame, played the social worker Glad Hands. He was a very funny guy, and though we didn't know him well, we did spend a little bit of time with him during the shoot. In the "Dance at the Gym," his role was to integrate the two gangs—get the guys and gals to dance with the other side and to "'make a new friend." Our role was to show little or no interest or respect to him in his attempts to bring us together socially. We took it upon ourselves to go off script a bit and did a little ad-libbing. We had him laughing through the whole scene. I know that even in the final cut, John was choking down his laughter amid the side cracks thrown his way by these wise-ass street kids.

It's a given that the actors and dancers say their lines and hit their marks with impeccable proficiency and artistry, but there are many other elements that come into play during the filming process, not the least being lighting. It takes time to light a set, and whenever the camera is moved to cover a different angle, the set has to be relit. It is also important to note that Jerry Robbins was a perfectionist. He had a vision in his head, and he would not quit till his vision was captured on film. So sometimes the wait on the set between shots was rather substantial.

To keep ourselves occupied and out of trouble, we found a reasonably quiet pastime. We gambled. Cards and craps were our favorite way to handle the delays. Nearly the whole cast and crew played at one time or another. In fact, we had visitors from other films being shot on the lot coming to sit in on our game. One day while we shot craps for big stakes, I turned and noticed the person standing next to me was Mickey Rooney! He was filming on a nearby soundstage, heard our game going on, and wanted in. He was not one of the winners that day, but it was a lot of fun and thrilling to be playing craps with this bigger-than-life movie legend!

While on location in New York, we all stayed at the same hotel. A group of Sharks acquired the key to Ice's room. We snuck in with the intention of short-sheeting his bed, but to our surprise, he was in the room taking a shower. Spontaneity prevailed. We grabbed him as he came out of the shower with the intention of shaving his private area. But during the tussle, his face got scratched. The next day, Ice was scheduled to finish a close-up shot started on the previous day but as he got on his mark to match the shot, the director noticed that his face was scratched, and the shot had to be postponed till it healed. The delay cost the studio money and they were not happy.

Bob Relyea gathered the Sharks off set. Much like the scene in the movie, where Detective Shrank tries to identify the culprit who pierced Baby John's ear, Bob tried to identify who was responsible for the scratch. Of course no one owned up to it. He threatened to fire us all as he frequently did, including his famous last words, "You will never work in Hollywood again."

Now Jerry was emphatic about avoiding injury, so at 8 AM after make-up and costumes, we prepared to dance by doing a ballet barre to warm our muscles. What a sight it must have been to people walking up and down 67th Street between Broadway and 9th Avenue, seeing what appeared to be gang members doing ballet in the middle of the street!

Most of the film's New York exteriors were shot where Lincoln Center now stands. We could only shoot when the weather was clear. As luck would have it, there were several days we were sent home early due to rain. Of course, we were still paid for a full day's work. This little fact did not go unnoticed by the cast. For a group of young creative minds, it was an opportunity waiting to be exploited. I can't remember who started what; someone says something that causes a reaction by someone else, and things happen.

Well, this was the case with our now famous "rain dance." Each day while waiting around on set, one of the guys would start singing and dancing to the rain god, asking him to look kindly on us and send some rain, and the rain god granted us our wish. Of course, this was not funny to Bob Relyea, especially when each day of rain cost the production thousands of dollars. Still, we persisted with our dance and the rain came day after day. Though the production staff knew we could not actually control the weather, their patience had worn thin. They actually forbade us to perform our "rain dance" on the set!

Though it was hard work, filming West Side was a lot of fun. I think the only sad day on set was the day we found out Mr. Robbins had been terminated from the movie. I remember him giving a speech to the cast. In essence he told us that no one was irreplaceable. It was a Friday, and by Monday Jerry was gone.

People often ask me if Jerry was difficult to work with. I had no problems with Jerry. He had high expectations but rightly so. He was a choreographic genius and a perfectionist. *West Side Story* has stood the test of time. Yes it was a great story, but it was the characters, the intensity and the timeliness of the era that has captivated audiences for so many years.

After the movie finished, I came back to New York and joined Jerome Robbins: Ballets U.S.A. at Jerry's invitation. It was a wonderful experience. We danced all over the world. I went on to become a principal dancer with American Ballet Theater and Joffrey, where I continued to dance in Robbins' works.

With my wife Karen, I now own and run The Dance Center of New Jersey in Bernardsville. Together we direct The Repertory Dancers, a pre-professional dance company. I am the father of three wonderful children and two beautiful grandchildren.

Dance has given me a wonderful life. I can't imagine doing anything else. I am privileged to act as repetiteur for the Jerome Robbins Foundation/Robbins Rights Trust, to restage some of Mr. Robbins' ballets on dance companies such as New York City Ballet, Alvin Ailey, and Joffrey. I recently restaged *Moves* on Kansas City Ballet. Restaging his works has been a joy and a privilege.

Eddie Verso

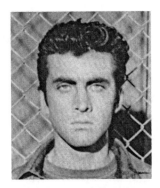

"Toro"/Shark — Nick Covacevich

The Audition

IT WAS LIKE any other day. I was lounging around wondering what my next dance job would be when I get this call from Samuel Goldwyn Studios in Hollywood, letting me know about an audition for the forth-coming movie, *West Side Story*.

"You would be a good type for the film," said the voice, but didn't tell me what that type would be.

So I went to the audition, which turned into many grueling auditions, held week after week, with many cuts, as the group got smaller and smaller. One of the worst things that can happen, is to go all the way to that final audition, thinking this is it, "I've made it!" then be told, "Thank you very much." But as fate would have it, this was my lucky day! Six long months followed with challenging hard work and friends that I will never forget.

But if I may, I'd like to tell you what set this all in motion, tell you how I got to this point in my career. I came into this world south of the border in Monterey, Mexico on January 11, 1938, the youngest of three boys. My father worked on the railroad for many years and my mother was a farm girl who was the youngest of eighteen children. In 1946, looking for the 'American Dream,' we packed up and moved to Houston, Texas. I was eight years old, and longing for a change.

My father was hard to get along with. He consumed much too much booze. By today's standards he would be classified an alcoholic, but in those days he was a drunk that couldn't hold his liquor. He flew off the handle at the least little thing, becoming physically violent and verbally abusive and I could not coupe with it any more. So while in the sixth grade, I decided it was time to strike out on my own. I was only fourteen when I hitched hiked from Texas to Los Angeles, California, with no money in my pocket and no clue as to what lay ahead. When I arrived, I had to sleep in parks and scavenge for food and water.

I managed to get part-time jobs such as dishwasher, busboy, and janitor mopping floors—anything to support myself. I finally got a steady nine-to-five job as a busboy, with a nice salary and generous tips at the famous Ambassador Hotel on Wilshire Blvd. I fell in with some new friends I met at the hotel, and we hit the local nightclubs, dancing, drinking beer, and smoking weed. It was so easy to get sucked in with this fast crowd and things were happening so quickly, I couldn't catch my breath.

I was invited to a party in Compton—not your average neighborhood. Never having been there before, it was a pretty scary place and an eye opener. When the door opened, I stepped into an unbelievable nightmare. It was a dark world of gang members, drug dealers, and LA low life. Guys and gals were shooting up drugs and doors left ajar exposed unusual sexual activities. The air was filled with smoke from weed, and everyone was walking around with glazed eyes.

Sitting in a dark corner of the room was this beat-up looking character with a deep fleshy scar running down the right side of his face. He must have forgotten to duck in a gang fight and got sliced, not shot with an automatic weapon like the way it's done today. He was smiling, showing his pearly whites, and he had a laugh that would send the Pilgrims back to England.

A month later I was invited to yet another party, but this time in East LA, with a lot of Latin music blasting all through the house, and it just so happened I was a pretty good mambo, cha-cha dancer. Everyone was churning, bumping, and throwing his or her pelvis to and fro when suddenly, the floor cleared. A young slender black kid, with strong Asian features, started to let loose to a very popular tune at that time, "Caballo Negro," by Perez Prado. He performed all the wild mambo moves, but incorporated Afro-Cuban and Modern Jazz Dance. I was completely blown away! I'd never seen anything like it.

My eyes were glued watching him move as he did and still keep the mambo rhythm going. When he finished to thunderous applause and screams of appreciation, I approached him and asked where he learned to dance like that? I said I would like to learn that style of dance, and he was kind enough to write down the address of a dance studio in Hollywood where I could study.

"Check it out," he invited.

"Are you working as a dancer somewhere?" I asked as he started to move away.

"No, not at this time."

Some time later I found out that he was supporting himself as a waiter. It was a time when African-American dancers were not hired for regular shows, only specialty dance jobs that called for black dancers, such as the movie *Carmen Jones*. So jobs were far and few between.

The following week I went to check out the studio in Hollywood. The studio was called Dance Theatre—Lester Horton Modern Dance School. I heard the pounding drums and felt their pulsing rhythms before I even entered the studio. I loved walking into a new and exciting world and anticipating the hot rush that would ultimately take over my whole body; so when I opened the door to a dance floor filled with barefooted dancers, all shapes and sizes, moving to infectious primitive rhythms, it made my internal juices flow with an intense desire to join in. I was completely turned on by the class and signed up on the spot. After taking classes for around four months, I was told

I had potential and was offered a scholarship. I couldn't be happier.

Lester's was a first-rate school and theatre combined, and it gave the students the opportunity to perform on stage. The protocol was that everyone, regardless of race or gender, was treated as equal and with respect.

Studying dance certainly turned my life around. My passion and love for dance grabbed my heart and soul. All my time was consumed in fine-tuning my craft, leaving no time to be a JD. My experience has been that the arts, be it singing, dancing, playing an instrument, or acting, can be a powerful driving force that can guide you in a positive direction and keep you out of trouble.

Being at the Horton School was the beginning of my dance career, and I was lucky to have been a student there. The dedicated and talented teachers personally worked with me to bring out my best, mentally and physically. I knew dancing was considered feminine by a lot of young men, so they simply stayed away from doing it as a profession. They thought of it as being for girls and gay guys, but I didn't feel that way and I wasn't a gay guy. Then when John Travolta and Michael Jackson came on the scene with their smart moves, that all changed.

After about a year, I started to perform with the Lester Horton Dance Group, not because I was so good, but because there weren't a lot of male dancers—as I said, dancing, and I don't mean social dancing, was considered taboo for straight guys.

In 1958, our dance group got an offer to perform at The El Cortez Hotel downtown Las Vegas. There were six of us, a mixture of Afro-American, Caucasian, and one Asian girl. We were confined to living in the black area of town because of our multi-ethnicity. We lost many offers to perform because we were interracial. Prejudice and ignorance was a way of life at that time. Even though we have come a long way, we still have a very long way to go.

When we returned to Hollywood, four of us, two male and two female, were hired to do a dance number for the movie *Calypso Joe*, with three of the dancers being black and myself white. We rehearsed on set but when it came time to shoot the dance number, the director decided that I was too white and had the make-up department put this very dark make-up on me, so that I would blend in with the other dancers. Unfortunately, I still looked like a white boy with a dark tan. C'est la vie! I continued to work with the group for another two years, but then decided to branch out on my own.

The year was 1959, and Hollywood's Moulin Rouge Theater on Sunset Blvd. was having an open dance call. Not only did I get the job when I auditioned, I was given a featured part and I was making $120 a week, which was considered pretty good money at that time. The show was loaded with these luscious showgirls, all beauty contest winners. Being a straight guy with this bevy of leggy beauties, well I just couldn't resist, I felt like a kid in a candy store. I had one affair after another. The show ran for about a year, and I started to go steady with one of the beauties and wound up marrying her. After a year, I'm sorry to say, it turned into a disaster. We got divorced, end of story.

When the show closed, I was able to find work dancing on television. There were a lot of television variety shows being produced at that time that needed background dancers, and dance jobs were plentiful. I happened to meet this very attractive girl while working on one of those TV shows, and we connected right away. It started as a friendly relationship, but turned into a very passionate love affair. We both were hot all the time and would have sex four or five times a day. Little did I know, as the body changes, with that kind of heavy performance I wasn't going to last very long. But when she came to me and told me she was pregnant, the shit hit the fan. I hadn't a clue what to do. She told me not to worry and took complete responsibility and had an abortion.

Looking back, I was such an immature adolescent with no scruples. I was a handsome dude with a taste for beautiful women. It became very dangerous, went out of control, as I found out in later years, when loads of trouble came my way. What is that famous saying, "Live and learn"?

It's funny how fate works. I finished one dance job and then waited for the next. Sometimes I was able to go from one job to another with no down time, but sometimes I sat on my ass and waited and waited. Then all of a sudden the word was out—open dance call for a Marilyn Monroe movie, *Let's Make Love*, at 20th Century Fox Studio, 10am Friday.

The choreographer was the brilliant Jack Cole, one of the great dance masters of that time. Watching him was like watching perfection in motion. His moves were strong, sharp, quick, and precise. After being hired, I found out what made his choreography so difficult. It was his timing and his precise movement that lent itself to every beat of the music. He rehearsed us over and over until it was perfect, but no one could come close to the way he did it. He would execute a very powerful movement with a full open chest, and then work his hands in such a fluid, graceful way in complete harmony. I was always amazed, never knowing where he was coming from, but somehow interpreting the music perfectly. I remember that some of the music we worked with wasn't very exciting, but he made it work. Sometimes I wonder what he would have done with today's music. I loved working with Cole and loved his style of dance. That experience certainly made me a better dancer and prepared me for what was to come.

Now back to *West Side Story*. The Goldwyn Studios, as I mentioned, had called about the up and coming audition and said I was a good type! The day I arrived at the studio for the audition, there was hardly any parking on the street. I eyed a spot a few blocks away and managed to squeeze into it.

At first I thought I was late, 'cause I didn't see anybody arriving at the same time I did. But as soon as I entered the front gate, it was like Saturday Night Football. Hundreds of dudes, all sizes and shapes, were waiting to enter the rehearsal hall to try out. They were already warming up, stretching, throwing high kicks and lunges; some were showing off by doing jump splits, tumbling, and jump turns in the air. It felt like a circus.

Then Mister Robbins, shadowed by two assistants, Howard Jeffrey, and Tommy Abbott—oh yeah! There was a gal, Maggie Banks, helping out also. The room was packed like a can of sardines, and the audition lasted two to three hours—line after line with people getting cut or asked to stay, till we were a handful and asked to come back. I was pretty confident about the dance combinations; however, the way we were shown the dance steps demanded more acting than straight dancing, making it much more challenging. I understood what Jerry wanted, but I was not used to working in this way. As I said, the training I received working with Jack Cole, who I think was among the very best, definitely helped me get the job.

The Filming

I REMEMBER JERRY saying in rehearsal on more than one occasion that the dancing was an extension of the character that you were playing, and it was not just about the dancing. Most of the New York dancers had done the Broadway show and were on top of the game. It was quite an experience watching them work. They pretty much knew what Jerry wanted and they already knew the choreography, even though Jerry reversed the steps to keep them and us on our toes. It was new to me, and too much to comprehend all at once. But I finally caught on and managed to bring it up to Jerry's liking. He emphasized details in the hands and emotions that he wanted to see expressed through the dance movement. He made us do it over and over till he felt it was exactly what he wanted. He caught each and everyone, as we struggled to do our best, with his arms folded and a cigarette dangling from his mouth.

Then he commanded, "One more time. Full out!"

The New York dancers were inspiring to me, like Jaime Rogers. He was fast, had tremendous energy and great dance skills. David Winters and Tucker Smith excelled in both acting and dance. Not great technicians, but very focused and professional.

The East Coast dancers were not humble in asserting that New

York dancers were superior to West Coast dancers, and that sometimes rubbed me the wrong way. It's not that we were less talented,
but they were more exposed and better trained. Plus there are so
many dancers in New York and so much heavy competition, it moti-
vates you to keep improving yourself.

In Hollywood in the '50s and '60s, we were laid back and did a
lot of step-touch-type dancing. I used to get bored on a lot of jobs.
But that's what was available, especially TV dance shows. We were
hired for our looks and personality first, and our dance ability second.
However, in the '70s things began to change, when the East and West
became intergraded.

I auditioned for Bernardo but I didn't screen test. I didn't get that
far. Some LA dancers tested for different roles, but most parts went
to the dancers that did the Broadway show. Bobby Banas and Bob
Thompson were two LA dancers I had worked with before. Bobby
Banas was a great dancer and all-around talent.

Filming the "Prologue" in New York was quite an experience for
me. I'd never been to the Big Apple, and it was a whole different
world! Everyone in the city seemed to be in a rush to go somewhere,
traffic was mind-boggling, but there was lots to see and great eating
places and, of course, Broadway, with all those fabulous musicals.

During the filming of the New York street scenes, many people
came to watch us rehearse and film. The streets had barricades at
both ends, and gang members were hired by the studio to keep the
peace. Many of the curious onlookers asked questions about the
movie, some asked for our autographs, and some became friends. I
felt like a celebrity!

After *WSS*

AFTER *WSS*, I became a regular "Gypsy Dancer" on many TV shows
and several movies. "Gypsies" is what dancers were called because
we went from job to job, worked the hardest, got paid the least, yet
managed to have the most fun. I was Audrey Hepburn's dance partner

in the ballroom scene in *My Fair Lady*. Then in the movie *Take Her She's Mine*, I was a French Apache dancer partnering Sandra Dee in a dream sequence.

I even tried out for the Cuban Ballet Company, run by the famous ballerina Alicia Alonso. I must admit, I was not much of a ballet dancer and found that her choreography leaned more towards character instead of classical. The moves were very strong, open, and free. She liked the way I moved and hired me. But a few days later, I got a job for a big TV show and had to turn down joining the company. Then I heard through the grapevine that the Cuban Ballet Company had played in several Havana nightclubs as part of their tour and got caught up in the Cuban Revolution. They were confined to their hotel rooms for a week, as bullets were flying everywhere. I realized how lucky I was not taking that job—who knows what might have happened? Then for no reason, I decided to change my name to Nick Navarro. To this day I really don't know why I did that.

I think it's great how dancing has evolved today, especially technically. During my years as a dancer I specialized primarily as a jazz dancer. I could do some modern and some ballet, and I knew some ballet dancers that could do some jazz, etc. But today's dancers can pretty much do it all and I must say, I admire them for their abilities. Yet, on the not-so-positive side, I have also noticed that porn has slipped into the mainstream including the dance world, and pretty much "anything goes," while sultry and class are lost. "Cheap" is in and all else is considered "old-fashioned." But I do believe dance will continue to evolve, and I hope I'm around twenty years from now to see where it goes.

During my time as a dancer and later as a choreographer, when working with a celebrity singer or star, my job was to make them shine as the main focal point. They were "the money," what the audience was there to see, and it was my job to make them look their very best at all times and never distract from them. I devised ways to make it seem as if they were doing much more than they actually were, and never ever allowed my dancers to upstage the star. I staged it to look as if the star was controlling the number with simple but direct movements. But when the dancers took center stage, they became the focal point with a knockout explosive number.

I've seen many celebrities on stage and television with over-choreographed backup dancers doing distracting moves for every count of eight. It begins to look like a bunch of wild cheerleaders, rather than complementing movement to the star. In my time, that definitely would have been unacceptable and you would be labeled a very bad choreographer. It would be hard to get back in the game after you did a show that turned out not to be a winner.

Now back in the early 1970s, some Las Vegas producers hired me to do small lounge production shows for different hotels. I would cast and choreograph the shows and put myself in as lead dancer. I did quite a few shows like that and it was a great experience.

Then my big break came when Don Arden hired me to do the famous *Lido de Paris*. This was considered "The Show" in Vegas at the time, and was the most spectacular production show on the strip. The cast included the *Blue Bell Girls* from Paris and a huge ensemble of dancers, singers, and specialty acts. Don Arden was to stage and direct the show, and I was to choreograph the dance numbers. I was always amazed at how he moved traffic on stage. Working with him was a hands-on course on everything you need to know about staging huge productions 101—like moving large numbers of people while coordinating lighting, music, scenery changes, etc. It helped me tremendously when I did some large productions in South Africa, Japan, and other countries. Whether you liked a Don Arden show or not, he always managed to create his trademark beauty and glamour on stage.

After *Lido* opened, two producers from Spain, who had seen the show, hired me to do their production called *La Scala*. So I went off to Spain for three months and loved the culture, food, and lifestyle. The director was a German from the 1930s. Needless to say, the show moved at a very slow pace. It was hard for me, as I wanted to get it moving. But I was professional and followed the direction of the show.

After that a Hollywood star named Juliet Prowse hired me to do her new nightclub act. I had worked with her as one of her dancers when the well-known choreographer Tony Charmoli did her act and did a brilliant job. I was very excited and very nervous. To follow Tony was not an easy thing to do, especially when his show-stopping number *Bolero* blew everyone away. Fortunately we came up with a very good concept and the new act was a big success. I won an award that year, 1976, for "Best Choreography," and my career as choreographer took off. I continued to do many shows, and by then I got married to a very nice girl. We started a family, and the success with Juliet's act got me a contract to do three shows in Sun City, South Africa. Juliet had appeared there and again the producers saw the show and had contacted me.

Although I was a married man with a family, my addiction to be with many women was still a big problem for me. I started to sleep around with some of the girls in the show during rehearsals, and this created some difficult situations, which continued for the next 20 years. I finally got divorced in 1999, not knowing that all those years, I had an unmanageable sexual addiction. I just assumed that was just the way the creator made me and there was nothing I could do about it. I had one affair after another, and in every show there was some cute girl that was ripe for the picking. It became a repeated pattern that I couldn't break. My wife was very tolerant, but neither of us realized that I had a medical problem and needed counseling. When you're in the spotlight and everyone wants to be with you, it's easy to find someone to sleep with. Being immature, as I happened to be, the temptation was overpowering. I also obtained some pills from Peru that made me perform like a young stud, and that became another bump in the road for me. In abusing my sexual drive, I developed prostate problems, making me feel confused and afraid. But the illness made me take a good look at myself, addressing this addiction and what it was doing to my health. My prostate problem continued for two or three years. When I was finally cured, I started my same pattern again, but this time I became a little more selective and cautious. I could hear a voice say, "Old habits die hard!"

In 1984, a Canadian ice-skater who had worked in one of my shows in Spain contacted me to do something very different. Workout gyms were starting to become very popular all over, and Canada was kind of the frontrunner in promoting it. This individual had an idea to combine fitness bodybuilding with dance, to create an out-of-the-ordinary stage show. He engaged me to do the show and hired the top champion bodybuilders from all over the world. I was to stage and choreograph the show to be done in Vancouver, Canada, with local dancers. I decided to go to Vancouver a month ahead to do some research. I joined a gym and learned everything I could about fitness to incorporate it in dance form for the show. The show never really got off the ground. It performed a few months and went on a couple of tours, but it was too expensive and ahead of its time. Ten years later it might have worked. Who knows? Look what Cirque du Soleil has done.

I am now seventy-one years old, retired, and happily married to a Japanese woman from Okinawa. Occasionally something will pop up that will bring the taste of performing back. As recent as three years ago, I was asked to be a substitute dancer for Agie and Margo, a famous dance team from the past, for the Cirque du Soleil's *Zumanity*. My partner and I were the understudies and performed once a week. We were called the Senior Dancers. This job lasted eighteen months. Which just goes to show, you never know what will come up, so it's a good idea to be ready and stay in shape.

I think I've finally settled down and am more at peace and content for the first time in my life. I feel a sense of freedom and appreciation for myself and for life. I'm saddened when I get calls from many of my dancer friends who stopped dancing because of their age. As a result, they have developed health issues. Our bodies are machines that have had certain rhythm and circulation patterns for the majority of our lives, and when that machine starts to slow up, complications set in. I try to stay active and eat healthy, maintain a positive attitude, and exercise. Yoga has helped me to prolong my youth and energy in my senior years. If I had to do it all over again, I would train harder, refine my expression, and take my dancing to a much higher level. I would be less selfish, be more caring, and stay away from so much foolishness.

My sincere wish for whoever reads this book is to work hard in whatever you do, stay healthy, and be a caring person. Accept everyone for who they are and be there for those you care about.

Nick Covacevich

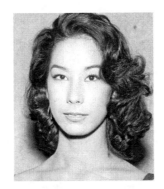

"Francisca"/Shark — Joanne Miya

The Audition — Passing for Puerto Rican

I HATE AUDITIONS. The director of our dance school used to encourage us to go for the "experience." For me, the "experience" always got my blood boiling. How many times after an audition that I knew I aced was I approached with apologies and words like, "You're a good dancer, but we just can't use you…you'd stick out."

I was used to sticking out. In the mid-fifties, Japanese-American dancers were a rare breed. After a while I'd go to auditions in sheer defiance, even if I knew I didn't want the job, or the call was for "blonds only." But this audition was different. It was more than a job. It was something I wanted to be a part of…*West Side Story*, the movie.

I first saw *West Side Story* at the Winter Garden Theater on Broadway in 1958. I was an LA dancer in my first Broadway show, Rodger's and Hammerstein's *Flower Drum Song*. It was a Sunday Benefit Night show. From the first note of Bernstein's overture, the music dragged me through a torrent of emotions beyond anything I'd experienced in a theater. Of course, I was crazy about the dancing.

The dancers were real characters, not just a moving backdrop, as in most musicals. The stage magic was like Kabuki con-Latino. I still remember the streamers unfurling from the top of the stage and dancers spinning in from left and right, and whoosh…Dance Hall. Amazing! But what I related to most was the story…*Romeo and Juliet* on a street level, singing and dancing the story of immigrants, gangs, racism, with lovers trying to bridge two different worlds. I felt like *West Side Story* was my story.

My father's parents came from two different worlds. Grandpa Tamajiro Miyamoto migrated from Japan to Idaho to work on the railroad. Grandma Lucy Harrison's English ancestors crossed the prairie with Mormon settlers, somehow ending up in Idaho. How Tamajiro and Lucy met, we don't know. Fortunately their love didn't cause a shootout like Tony and Maria's. Somehow, they found a way to marry. The price was Lucy's excommunication from the Mormon Church.

My mother was a child of pure blood Japanese immigrants. Like Maria's traditional Puerto Rican parents, my mother's father disapproved of her "marrying out" of her culture. It took my mother five years to stand up to him and tell him she was going to marry my half-breed father whether he liked it or not. Our family was riddled with race drama. Being mixed-blooded Japanese did not exempt us from a stint in U.S. concentration camps during WWII. As a one-year-old, possible spy, I became a child of Japanese Relocation. My family was moved, like 110,000 other Japanese Americans from our homes in Los Angeles and other coastal areas, to places like Santa Anita Racetrack, then to Montana, and finally we were released in Ogden, Utah, where my father got a job. In the midst of this chaos, my father, an ardent classical music buff, took me to my first concert. Sir Thomas Beecham was conducting Handel. The beauty of that music transformed my gray and uncertain world into Technicolor. I came home and played my father's classical records and danced, danced, danced! My mother somehow found a dance school in Ogden. So this dislocated child found a home in the world of dance. Little did I know where that would take me.

So I'm at the Samuel Goldwyn Studios in Hollywood for the audition. Will I really get a chance to be part of *West Side?* Oh my god! I'd never seen so many dancers packed into one place in my life. It was an assembly line of dancers squeezed into a sweltering rehearsal hall. They were dressed in their coolest, jazziest, sexiest dance outfits. I was in my basic blacks with long sleeves and turtle-neck. My ancient orange "good luck" security blanket sweatshirt was tied snugly around my waist. I felt invisible in the row after end-less row of wannabe Sharks and Jets. I was just one of them.

There he was, Jerome Robbins, his restless energy contained behind a long table at the front of the rehearsal hall, surveying the stampeding herd of Hollywood dancers passing before him. Would he remember me? I was just 15 when I first worked with him in the movie *King and I*. Robbins choreographed the ballet sequence of "Small House of Uncle Thomas," or "Uncle Tom's Cabin." I wore white face, and my forehead remembers the heavy sky-pointing hat that left a dent for months!

My creaky knees also remember the hours and days of floor work we did. Rita Moreno was in that film too, playing Tuptin, the slave that was a gift to the king. She was a Puerto Rican passing for a Siamese! Or was it Burmese, I can't remember. *King and I* was the first of many "yellow face" jobs I did in my short career. Then there was *Kismet*, playing an Arabian princess of Ababu, and *Flower Drum Song*, an entertainer in San Francisco's Chinatown. Now I'm a grown-up twen-ty and I'm looking to "cross the color line." My hair is black like a Puerto Rican, my skin is rather dark...could be Puerto Rican. My eyes,.....well.

Howard Jeffrey, one of Robbins' assistants, was giving us ballet combinations. One row would perform, followed by a quick "thank you" or "stay." Then there were jazz combinations, with more "thank you's" and a few "stays." The "god of dance" was determining our fate, and dancers reacted with sighs or smiles. This went on for hours, with hundreds of dancers waiting their turn outside. I had several "stays" that day. No "thank you's" or apologies. Wow! I made the first cut.

When I started dancing at the age of four, my mother used to show me pictures of the great ballerinas like Maria Tallchief, an American Indian, Sono Osato, who was Japanese and Irish, and Alicia Alonzo, a Cuban. They were like baseball's Jackie Robinson, trailblazers who opened the field of ballet for others to cross the color line. In 1960, when the movie was being made, our country was in the midst of the Civil Rights Movement. "Crossing the color line" in the South meant the struggle to sit at a lunch counter like white folks, or drinking from a common fountain, or sitting down in the front, rather than the back of a bus. For me, a Japanese American, "crossing the color line" meant a chance to dance with the Sharks.

In the auditions that followed the numbers dwindled, but the demands on us intensified—dancing, acting...even singing. Jerome Robbins was a perfectionist. We got down to what looked like the finals, and somehow I was still in the ring. But there was one more hoop. We all had to do a screen test! Just like they did for starlets in old Hollywood. Who would be Sharks? Who would be Jets? In some cases it was a matter of eye color—brown for Sharks, blue for Jets. They could put make-up on us, but in those days there were no colored contact lenses. In my case I'm sure what they wanted to see, with the help of Max Factor's Dark Egyptian Make-up (Lena Horne's skin color), was could I pass for Puerto Rican? I guess I did!

Rehearsals and Shooting

THE FIRST DAY on a film is sort of like the first day at a new school. I felt like a total outsider...and my shyness didn't help. Most of the dancers were New Yorkers who came out of the Broadway show. I did know the Los Angeles members. I'd danced in many a class with Maria Jimenez at American School of Dance. Jose De Vega and Bobby Banas also studied there. Robbins' assistant, Howard Jeffrey, was once a haloed scholarship student at American School we all looked up to. As it turned out, I wasn't the only Asian in the cast. Jose De Vega, who was in the original Broadway show, was playing

Chino. Or should I say, he was a "Chino." Yes, there were actually lots of Chinos in the Caribbean, Chinese, and even Japanese who migrated as farm workers to Puerto Rico, Cuba, and other islands of the Caribbean. These "Chinos" eventually intermarried and blended in like the other Spanish, indigenous, and African mulattos. So, Jose and I being part of the cast were not so far-fetched. Jose was actually Pilipino and Guatemalan. He was so cool looking I often wondered why Maria passed him up for Tony. Of course, then there would be no movie, but more about Jose later.

The New York dancers had a different vibe than the West Coasters. On top of their virtuosity and familiarity with the dances, they were very rowdy! They were already the Sharks and the Jets, and it seemed like they were checking us out to see if we were worthy to be part of their gang.

I was used to the rigors of dance, but nothing prepared me for the work that went into the rehearsing and preparations for shooting the movie. At the age of 12, I was given a scholarship at Eugene Loring's (choreographer of *Billy the Kid*) American School of Dance in Hollywood, taking twelve classes a week during the school year, and eighteen classes in summer. We took ballet, modern, jazz, choreography, and more. At fifteen, my first job was working for Jerome Robbins in the movie *King and I*, learning the intricate hand gestures and knee-killing style of Siamese dance.

I celebrated sixteen working for Jack Cole, in the movie *Les Girls*. Cole was the innovative creator of American jazz dance (he choreographed *Kismet*, *Man from La Mancha*, and Marilyn Monroe wouldn't do a movie without him). He was an infamous slave driver/perfectionist in his pace-setting style of movement, which often borrowed from Asian, African, and Latin forms. Legend had it that Jack Cole's dancer's feet were so tough they could put cigarettes out barefoot! Luckily, I wasn't a smoker.

But working for Robbins in *West Side* was another level. He was known to be meticulous, demanding, and sometimes, all right, a little cruel. But he also had an endearing sense of humor, making us willing subjects to endure his delicious torture for artistic excellence. Once, during *King and I*, I remember him spontaneously performing "Uncle Tom's Cabin" à la Siam, portraying all the characters in fast motion, like a Charlie Chaplin movie. He had us on the floor laughing, then snapped us back to work!

We were gang members, but we lived the life of a ballet company. Our day started with a one-hour ballet class at 8 or 9am (6am during shooting), followed by a half-hour jazz class. I had never experienced this level of training within a commercial job. Usually, doing a warm-up was your own responsibility. But like I said, it was like a ballet company, but with a lot of grit, rowdiness, and grease. I especially loved the guys' street style mixed with their balletic virtuosity. They were like bullfighters—doing something daring and dangerous, like vaulting that fence, but looking so cool and sexy at the same time. For this, they had extra training. Fences were built in the rehearsal hall to simulate the ones they were to climb in the playground scenes. Each morning after our one-and-a-half-hour class, they faced the fences, scaling, jumping, and vaulting like Olympic athletes!

After a couple of weeks of rehearsal, divisions started happening, not based on race, but on the numbers we rehearsed together. The Sharks bonded by rehearsing "America" and "Dance Hall." The Jets went underground rehearsing, and rehearsing and rehearsing "Cool." Also, the Shark girls were often separated from the guys. So Suzie Kaye, Maria Jimenez, and myself bonded in our clique… and we had our leader. The "Queen of the Sharks," I call her. She was a real Puerto Rican, an earthy dancer with rumba imbedded in her DNA. She was also a worldly-wise New Yorker, very intelligent and VERY funny. Yvonne Othon, who became Wilder (in more than name), was not only the leader of the girl Sharks, she had a viral sense of humor that spread her silliness throughout the entire company, even reaching the bosses, Jerry and Robert Wise. Her comic relief was often a welcomed stress buster on the set. Working 12-hour days during shooting, the cast was fighting fatigue, injury, and even mononucleosis. The bosses had time anxieties, money anxieties. So, around 4pm when Mr. Wise started self-medicating with his saltine crackers (natural ulcer medicine), Yvonne's crazy antics were right on time.

When the opening sequence was being shot in NY, the cast and crew went to NY leaving the girl Sharks and Jets behind. For weeks we went to work at Sam Goldwyn's Studio with Yvonne running rehearsals. She was a really hard taskmaster. We did our daily morning dance classes, and then she ran us through all the dance numbers. Sometimes she taught us some of her own jazz choreography. Occasionally, Natalie Wood would come and rehearse with us as well. All this usually happened before lunch. When our work was done, Yvonne had the authority to excuse us for the day. So while the guys were dancing in the sweltering streets of NY, we girls would beat the LA heat with a swim at Santa Monica Beach! Sometimes on weekends, Yvonne took us all mambo dancing at VIRGINIA'S, a Latin club near downtown LA. It was the place where Latinos went to dance, and they always had a hot "live" band. Of course, this was all "research," preparing us for "Dance Hall."

Yvonne and I were about as different as two people could be. She was outgoing, zany, and Puerto Rican. I was quiet, introspective, and Japanese. But somehow she turned out to be one of my closest friends. She was a frequent dinner guest at my family's home. When she went to London to play Anita in *West Side Story*, she entrusted my family with one of her most cherished belongings, her dog—an adorable Yorkshire terrier named Charlie Brown. Like Yvonne, Charlie made my family laugh, not an easy task for our normally quiet Japanese family.

The movie business is a caste system. One is very aware of your station within it, especially if you are a dancer. Dancers were usually anonymous blurs in movies. We train long, sweat a lot, and get paid little. Stars had names on their own chairs and had trailer dressing rooms. During rehearsals when Natalie floated in, she never seemed to sweat. She always looked…like a movie star. But Rita

Moreno was another story. She was a bona fide star in the film, but Rita sweated a lot. She showed up for ballet class and stayed the whole day. She was one of us. She dressed funky, sweat-ready, wore no make-up—no make-up! I couldn't believe how un-vain she was. I would never leave the house without some make-up, especially when on a Hollywood set! But Rita was totally unafraid to show up with her "real face" and just concentrate on the work. Of course, on shooting days, she knew how to look good. She was a real artist and continues to be. But this "un-star" attitude sometimes worked against Rita. I remember during "Dance Hall," she was suffering from a sprained ankle. They didn't postpone the shoot because of her pain, or shoot around her to give her a break. They strapped up her ankle and threw her up on the set. Somehow she made it through with colors!

The "Cha-Cha" take #23 was the moment I wanted to disappear. It was the magical moment when Tony and Maria meet in the dance hall for the first time. Everything slows and fades in the background but the lovers. The dance is simple, a delicate cha-cha à la Robbins. Three couples are the background. My partner Bob Thompson and I were among them. We started shooting the sequence around 9 am. Take #1: And one and two, three, four, "I just met a girl named," turn two, step together. Seemingly simple…to a dancer trained in years of ballet. Take #5: "Roll it." Always, in such a scene, there're close-ups, different angles. It's a lot of pressure for Natalie and Richard, two actors not exactly known for their dancing. Take #10: It's lunch-time and the simple dance is not wrapped yet. After lunch we start in again. Take #15: And one and two…more stumbles. The micro-scope of the camera is unforgiving. Take #19: Richard is unstable. Take #20: Natalie falters. Take #22! It's almost six now. It's got to be this shot or we go into overtime. Mr. Wise has long since been downing his crackers. We're all tired. The simple dance has become hard labor. In the background, our arms, once lovingly entangled over our heads, have become heavy as tree trunks. Take #23. We all do it somehow. Tony and Maria, all of us, it's perfect! But, my mistake is looking my partner in the eye. Our soft smile says "Shit! Finally!" And I lose it! My back to the camera, I start shuddering, then laughing uncontrollably. "Cut!" Suddenly I realize what's happening. Oh no, it's me! I've ruined the shot! No! I've ruined the whole day! I break down into tears, and then I hear:

"We finish tomorrow!"

None of the bosses said the usual friendly good night to me. I just did the laugh that cost $50,000!

"Or maybe it's fleas!" was an itch that became a turning point for me. Yes, that silly line I sang in "I Feel Pretty" was, in a strange way, a life-changing moment. I always loved singing…in a group or alone only in my car. So rehearsing the songs "America" and "I Feel Pretty" with Yvonne and Suzy was great fun. Yvonne's voice was chesty and Suzy's was a higher timber. I was comfortable right in the middle. Our daily vocal rehearsals with vocal director Bobby Tucker were a nice break from our day of hard physical labor. And I enjoyed singing. We were well prepared for the recording session, creating the tracks which we would lip-sync with during the shooting.

It was during the last few days on the job that they called me to come, by myself, to Studio 7. This was the huge studio they used to record the huge orchestra with Johnny Green conducting the score for the movie. Watching that was amazing! But now I was here… alone, by myself, an ant in this huge hall to sing for my image on the upper left side of the screen in "I Feel Pretty." All I had to do was sing those four silly words…"Or maybe it's fleas!" Simple? Not!

I had earphones on and heard us all singing, "It must be the heat, or some rare disease, la la la, or too much to eat," and I'm supposed to chime in. But somehow, each time they played it I freaked. Come on, I've done this a hundred times with Yvonne and Susie! But now I'm alone; where are they? Each time they played it, my anxiety was rising. My voice just didn't want to come out.

I was swearing to myself: "What's wrong with you? Are you scared to hear your OWN VOICE?! YES!"

I don't know how they did it, but somehow they squeezed it out of me. So, "Or maybe it's fleas," is there for eternity, in spite of myself. But I decided something that day. I decided I was going to really learn to sing and get over this fear of my voice.

One of the most heart-wrenching days of the shoot was the Monday we showed up to start "Dance Hall." There was a weird vibe around the set, which was usually pumping with energy at the start of a new scene, a new set. We looked around, expecting to see him stride in ready to work, but no Jerry. I can't remember how an announcement was finally made that Jerry was not going to be there. He was gone. He was fired. Fired? How could they fire the boss, the director, the creator of *West Side Story*? It was his baby. But they did. The producers fired him. The production was way behind schedule. Jerry's experimenting and innovating was just too time-consuming and therefore pushed them over budget. He'd set all the numbers, and probably all the shooting angles already. His assistants knew enough to help Mr. Wise, the co-director, finish. Jerry was gone.

I remember feeling confused. Should we refuse to work without him? Should we stand together in protest? Should we demand an explanation? I felt stunned, like the breath was knocked out of our collective body. How could we dance without him, the one who pushed us beyond our limits? How could we dance without him, the one we strived to please? But as Robbins' assistants, Tommy Abbot and Tony Mordente, moved us into our formations for "Dance Hall," our breath began to return. As we walked through the beginning of the dance, I think there was a sense that now we HAD to do it...for him. We had to deliver this baby for Jerry.

Post *West Side*

SO HOW DO you follow *West Side Story*? There was a rare sense of security one gets working with a genius like Jerry in a masterpiece musical. I think it left all of us with higher expectations for ourselves. It was an artistic experience that made one hungry for more. In retrospect, it was a milestone for me, a beginning. *West Side* gave me a kind of momentum. Especially that excruciating "Or maybe it's fleas" moment that sent me running for the hills! My *West Side* buddies, Susie and Yvonne, led me to a wonderful singing teacher, Dini Clarke, an African-American pianist and vocalist from Washington DC. Dini gently nudged me beyond my fear of singing alone. He opened up the world of song to me, and women singers like Billie Holiday, Nina Simone, Carmen McCray, and of course Aretha. I was moving on a whole new path. And I wasn't alone.

It was the sixties. Young people were making a noise, "finding voice" for their beliefs—blacks, Latinos, students, and women. I broke loose from my Hollywood dreams when my Italian filmmaker friend, Antonello Branca, asked me to help him make a documentary about the Black Panthers. It turned my life upside down. I got involved. I didn't know anything about politics, but I jumped in the water and it was deep! People didn't even know I was an artist. In NY I connected with other Asians like myself, who were searching for their voice. One was a soulful singer/guitar player, Chris Iijima, and the brother could write a song. Together our songs became "a voice" for the burgeoning Asian-American movement. We were troubadours touring the country, on what might be called the "rice circuit." We made what is touted to be the first album of Asian-American songs called A Grain of Sand. It's now part of the Smithsonian Collection. I guess that's another milestone in my life.

West Side Story was made real the years between '69 to '73 when I lived in NY as an activist and artist, exposing me to some interesting folks. One of them was a Puerto Rican named Henry who was a Black Panther. My brother and I used to hang out with him from time to time, and one day at lunch, he was looking at me from under his tilted black beret.

"You look so familiar," he said.

"We all look alike!" I laughed.

"No," he said, "I know your face."

Then he bolted! "Yes! *West Side Story*, I remember you!"

I'd never told him I was in it. Then he told me he'd seen *West Side* 18 times!!! Henry was a "real" Puerto Rican from East Harlem. *West Side* was the only show or film that remotely related to his cultural experience. *West Side* was his story…or close to it.

I lived on the Upper West Side in those days, 91st Street and Columbus, in a neighborhood of mostly Puerto Ricans and Dominicans who were getting displaced by Urban Renewal. They called it "Urban Removal"—moving out the poor to move in the rich. These folks started a Squatter's Movement, taking over empty buildings in the neighborhood and moving in people, rent-free. We Asians got involved too and got ourselves a storefront for a drop-in center. It was the first time I really felt like I was part of a community. We also started a coffee house called "The Dot," where singers and performers of Nueva Cancione from all over Latin America would come to perform. That's when Chris and I started to write and sing songs in Spanish. A couple of our songs were recorded with Latin musicians and played in jukeboxes in Puerto Rico. For me this experience felt like another *West Side Story*.

In 1973 I returned to my hometown, Los Angeles, to find a way to use my music and creative work in my own community. I found a spiritual home and rehearsal space at Senshin Buddhist Temple in South Central Los Angeles. In 1978 I established GREAT LEAP, a multicultural arts organization using ART as a way of creating social change. In 1980 I went to a *West Side Story* reunion party and reconnected with Chino, Jose De Vega. Jose became an integral creative force in Great Leap, as a choreographer and director. Jose died of AIDS in 1990. But, if I'm the mother of GREAT LEAP, Jose is definitely the father.

After a career of striving for artistic excellence in "show business," the focus for Jose and I became using excellence to tell our stories and create community, especially among people of color. We worked with artists as well as non-artists, giving them opportunities to participate and create. Perhaps it is restoring art as part of communal ritual, bringing it back to the village. I've composed songs/dances in the Buddhist Obon tradition, danced yearly by the hundreds in our festivals. Jose and I staged one of these dances for the finale scene of the film *Karate Kid II*. I directed *Laughter from the Children of War* with the Vietnamese group Club O'Noodles. I've also collaborated on Liz Lerman's Hallelujah Project engaging Japanese, Jewish, and African-American communities. When I created a harvest dance with Detroit's urban garden movement, I started thinking more about how to use art to educate about the environment.

After 9/11, it was important to connect Muslims, Jews, Buddhists, and Christians. They shared their stories in workshop and then on the stage. As I write this we're preparing to take our interfaith performance LEAPS OF FAITH to perform for the Parliament of World's Religions in Melbourne. So, this work has taken me quite a distance.

I remember thinking after *West Side* that I may not be able to dance my way into old age, but maybe I could sing my way into it. So I am still singing and writing music. I've made a few more in-dependently produced albums, among them To All Relations. This is starting to sound like a resume. If you want to find out more, go to www.greatleap.org.

In 2003, Japan came into my life for the first time. I was invited to go to rehearse for an international collaboration I was involved in with Yoko Fujimoto, singer with KODO, the famous Taiko group, PJ Hirabayashi of San Jose Taiko, and me from GREAT LEAP. We were creating a theater piece called *Journey of the Dandelion*. For me it became a pilgrimage, my first time to visit the place of my grandparent's birth, and meet my mother's family in Fukuoka, Japan. I felt like the "dandelion" returning.

In Tokyo I was invited to give a talk to a group of artists and scholars who were interested in my work as a Japanese-American artist. I spoke about creating a cultural voice for Asian Americans, and mentioned my background in dance and, of course, *West Side Story*. There was a gasp. *West Side Story! West Side Story!* Everything stopped. People later explained to me that each year they show the film in theaters around Japan. It's like a cult movie! Japanese people love *West Side Story*. And yes, they were aware that there was a Japanese in the film. I guess it made them feel more a part of it. And now Joanne Miya has claimed her Japanese name, Nobuko Miyamoto. In those long and hard-working days in the making of *West Side Story*, we knew we were making a great film, but had no idea how far and how long it would travel…sort of like a dandelion.

"Crossing the color line" also became a theme in my personal life. I'm married to a wonderful African-American writer, Tarabu Betserai Kirkland, who plays Afro-Cuban drums and taught me the Chinese art of Taichi. Our son, Kamau Ayubbi, is an artist and hospital chaplain, whose conversion to Islam and becoming an Imam in the Naqsbandi Sufi Order has been a source of more line crossing. We celebrate all holidays in our house…Christmas, Kwanza, Ramadan…and we dance the circle dances for the Buddhist holy day of Obon to remember all our ancestors. I have four beautiful grandchildren named Asiyah, Muhammad, Noora, and Ahmed, whose bloodlines have African, Asian, Caucasian, and Native American tributaries, and we are still flowing.

The haunting refrain in *West Side*'s finale, "There's a place for us, somewhere a place for us…," surely captures the hopes and desire for my family, my community and me. I'm proud to be a part of that song, that story, not just because I "passed for Puerto Rican" and got to dance with the crème de la crème, not just because I was a part of Robbins and Bernstein's artistic masterpiece. But because the communal effort so beautifully expressed through movement, song, word and passion, spoke a truth that needs to be heard. I believe that is why *West Side Story* is still relevant and still moves people of all ages and cultures. It's a hope, a prayer that "Somewhere, somehow, we'll find a way of forgiving, we'll find a new way of living—somewhere."

I hope it's here and everywhere.
In peace and gratitude,
Nobuko Miyamoto,
AKA "Joanne Miya,"
AKA "Francisca"

Nobuko Miyamoto

"Teresita"/Shark — Maria Henley

The Audition

WEST SIDE STORY had taken Broadway by storm in 1957, and a new art form was birthed. On July of 1959 I had no idea my life was about to change. There was a road company production of *West Side Story* at the Civic Light Opera Theater in Los Angeles with Larry Kert, Devra Korwin, Lee Becker, and Gus Trikonis heading the cast. That performance will be branded in my heart and soul forever. I had never seen dancing like that before. Not only did they dance brilliantly, they WERE those characters. I was approaching my sixteenth birthday and in my third year studying on a full scholarship at Eugene Loring's American School of Dance. Every day of those three years I focused on one goal—to become a great dancer. After seeing that production that night, I left the theater so inspired and full of hope that I yelled out loud, "THAT'S WHAT I WANT TO DO WITH MY LIFE!"

Now, a year later, this masterpiece was going to be made into a movie, and every dancer in the world was auditioning for it. I was nearing my seventeenth birthday and more than anything I had ever felt, sensed, or dreamed of, I knew I was destined to be a part of this movie. I begged Mr. Loring for guidance and help.

"Marie, all I can do is make the call, but it will be up to you to make them want you." I didn't say a word as he continued, "Do you believe you're ready?"

Without hesitation I answered, "Yes."

Mr. Loring called his agent, who then in turn called Stalmaster-Lister, who was doing the casting.

For the next six months Jerome Robbins auditioned dancers in London, Australia, New Zealand, Israel, New York, Hollywood, and every place where there had ever been a production of *West Side Story*. There were "open cattle calls" as well as Sag, Aftra, and Equity union calls for the more professional and experienced dancers. Robbins was not going to leave a stone unturned. I recall the hundreds of dancers identified only as a number, crammed together like cattle into the Sam Goldwyn soundstage.

Every audition was the same. The floor work required a ballet technique that separated the "trained" dancers from the "wannabe" dancers. If you made the first cut, you were asked to stay and learn all the combinations that were thrown at you. Howard Jeffrey and Tommy Abbott were Jerome Robbins' assistants, and they demonstrated each combination quickly and no more than twice. I never once stopped to think, "Can I do this? Will I make an impression?" There was never a doubt. The only thing I knew was to be the best that I could be at that given moment. To me, it was a matter of life or death. I gravitated to front row center, which was my comfortable and safe spot. Being small and ethnic, I always felt the need to prove my right to be there more than anyone else.

I discovered that Howard Jeffrey was also an American School alumnus, and I prayed that he would honor my being a Eugene Loring scholarship student. I never wanted anything more in my life. I was desperate for it. I was ready. During the six months of endless auditions, waiting for the "call backs," I never missed a class. When I got a call to do a screen test, not one but three in total, I started to believe maybe I did have a chance. I was paired off with a partner and asked to do a combination from "America" on a rooftop while they filmed us. They also filmed us in different wardrobes. It was like a dream that I was sleepwalking through.

I remember one special afternoon I decided to get in the car and drive to my parents' home in Temple City. I had just gotten my driver's license and wanted to drive home to celebrate. In truth, I needed some of my mother's home cooking and tender loving care. For months I had been consumed with nothing else but the auditions and taking classes every day. I was burnt out and tired both physically and emotionally. The newspapers had announced that Natalie Wood had been cast in the role of Maria and Rita Moreno in the role of Anita. More announcements were coming, but there were still some smaller parts not yet cast.

"Mama, I have done everything I know to do," I said, lying on the couch in the den.

"I believe that, mijita," she said softly, continuing, "Si Dios querer. It's in God's hands." I had heard that all of my life and had come to believe it completely.

Suddenly the phone rang and it was like a gunshot going off. I bolted off the couch and ran to answer it. Then I froze.

"Mama, this is it. THIS IS THE CALL! I know it! You have to answer it! I can't do it," I said, handing her the phone.

My mother took the phone and said, "Hello. Yes. This is Mrs. Jimenez, Maria Jimenez's mother. Yes. What? Are you sure?"

"What are they saying?" I whispered, yanking at my mother's sleeve, dying to know.

Holding her composure only made me crazier. "Yes, yes, I will tell her. And thank you." Then she hung up.

"Mama, WHAT DID THEY SAY?" I burst out.

Without changing her expression, looking straight at me, she said, "You are to report to the Samuel Goldwyn Studio Monday morning at 10:00 A.M. sharp, and congratulations!"

I was struck dumb. Was this just another fairy tale? Could it be that my dream was really coming true? Me! The little short

Mexican from Temple City chosen out of thousands of dancers from all over the world to dance in the movie *West Side Story*? I let out a scream.

I knew it was not a dream when my mother started to cry as she whispered, "Maria, you got your wish."

In a matter of minutes I was jumping and yelling all at the same time, "I GOT THE JOB!! I DON'T BELIEVE IT!! MAMA, IS IT REALLY TRUE?"

The whole neighborhood must have heard the news because I kept howling in disbelief. I couldn't wait for Daddy to get home from work so I could tell him. Nothing that enormous had ever happened to a Jimenez. I was to be the first.

Then the unthinkable happened. It came out of nowhere. I immediately doubled over in the worst pain I had ever felt. I fell to the floor. My mother quickly realized something was terribly wrong.

"My stomach, it hurts!" I cried. The next thing I remember was my mother carrying me out the front door grabbing her purse on the way.

"It's going to be all right," she said as she opened the car door and laid me in the backseat.

"Where are we going?" I asked, moaning and clutching my stomach.

"To the hospital."

The doctors said my appendix was about to burst and I had gotten to the hospital just in time. They did an appendectomy, stitched me up, and sent me home the next day, which was a Saturday. My body was hurting and the medication they gave me didn't help. My mother had called Howard Jeffrey the night before the surgery to tell him about my appendicitis attack. Now he was calling because Jerome Robbins needed to know if I was going to be able to report to work Monday morning or would he have to replace me?

"REPLACE ME? NO! MAMA, DON'T LET THEM DO THAT!" I cried out in desperation.

Covering up the phone with her hand my mother said firmly, "Maria, you can barely walk."

"YOU TELL THEM I WILL BE THERE!" I cried out. "TELL THEM **YES**, MAMA, PLEASE!"

I will never forget the look on my mother's face. It was as if I had suddenly grown up right before her very eyes and she was seeing me for the first time. There was a respect for me in those eyes that told me, "If you say you can do it, then you will." We both knew I wasn't her baby girl anymore.

She kept looking at me as she resumed talking into the phone, "She will be there, Mr. Jeffrey. I will have her there at 10:00 A.M. sharp."

When she hung up the phone, I started to cry.

"Thank you, Mama, thank you."

Filming

IT HAD TO have been God who got me through that first day. I didn't sleep at all the night before and my incision burned and I ached terribly. Morning came and Mama was so quiet as she put fresh bandages on me and taped me up with strong white adhesive tape. If she was as frightened as I was, she never showed it. I just kept telling myself I was going to make it, bandages and all. What usually took ten minutes to get ready, took me forty-five minutes this time. When I went to put on my favorite leotard and tights, the pain hit me like a hot branding iron. Every time I turned my body, it felt like a knife cutting into me.

"Mijita, let me help you," my mother said.

"No Mama, I can dress myself," I shot back, continuing, "I can do this! Really, Mama, I'll be all right."

Then she said what I needed to hear: "Oue' milagrao! Of course you will."

I checked my dance bag five times to make sure I had my ballet slippers, my point shoes (just in case), my jazz shoes, my character shoes, an extra sweat towel, and my favorite good luck cardigan sweater. It was an old worn-out black sweater washed so many times, making it thin in texture and soft to the touch. Somehow, when I wore it, I felt older, more mature and confident.

The drive from Temple City to the Samuel Goldwyn Studios in Hollywood was a somber one. As we turned onto Formosa Street off of Santa Monica Blvd. and drove up to the side entrance gate, I began to get nervous. My mother must have sensed my fear because she reached over and tapped me on the leg. She didn't have to say a word. That simple gesture told me she believed in me.

As I got out of the car my mother said, "Maria, I'll be back here at 5:30 to pick you up."

I said good-bye quickly because I knew if I looked at her a moment longer, I wouldn't have the guts to get out of the car. The guard at the gate stopped me and asked for my name. When he found it on his list, he pointed me in the right direction and I walked especially tall because I didn't want him to suspect that I was all taped up. As I got closer to the big soundstage, it looked familiar. Of course, how could I forget? It was the same stage I had auditioned on all those months.

"God, is this really happening to me?" I asked myself out loud as I walked through the big elephant doors and onto the soundstage. They called them elephant doors because they were so big. When they were closed, all the sound from the outside was shut out.

As I entered, I looked around and saw other dancers gathering. That's when it really sank in. I was going to be a Shark girl in the film *West Side Story*. Most of the dancers seemed to know each other. The only persons I knew were Bobby Banas, who had gotten the role of Joyboy, a Jet, and an American School of Dance alumni named Patti Tribble, also cast as a Jet. Patti was a wonderful ballet dancer with a perfect turnout and long legs. When I saw her in class, I always felt she should have been in Balanchine's ballet company. The majority of these dancers were from New York. Some had even been in the original Broadway production. I knew I was in the midst of giants, and they didn't even know I was there.

"Tell me, Mama, tell me I belong here," I whispered to myself.

I recognized George Chakiris, who had just returned from the London production of *West Side Story*, where he played Riff. He now was cast as Bernardo. He looked Puerto Rican to me and I was surprised when I found out he was Greek. I noticed Russ Tamblyn, who was playing Riff, laughing and joking around with some of the guys. He looked so confident and at ease. Then there was Rita Moreno.

I immediately recalled all those previous months of auditioning, when she would come and take classes at The American School Of Dance. It could have been my imagination but I swear I would catch her looking at me, studying me, while I did a combination across the floor. It was probably wishful thinking.

Then one day she walked up to me and asked, "Have you auditioned for *West Side Story*?"

I told her I had auditioned a hundred times and even got called back for some screen tests but had not gotten the call that I was picked. I really believe Rita put in a good word for me to Jerome Robbins and it helped get me the job.

That first day she came in strutting and ready to work. She radiated sensuality and a boldness that I wished was mine. When I saw her, I smiled and she acknowledged me. Did she remember me? Maybe I wasn't so alone after all. My head began spinning as I tried to keep all my emotions under control. It made me forget about my stitches.

A beautiful Japanese girl with straight jet-black hair and light skin walked past me, not saying a word. Was she feeling out of place like me? I had never seen her in class or at the auditions and wondered who she was. I later found out that she too had been a scholarship student of Eugene Loring, but she had already left the American School by the time I was put on scholarship. Her name was Joanne Miya (short for Miyamoto) and she was hired to play a Shark girl. I didn't understand why a Japanese girl was picked to portray a Puerto Rican.

A man with a clipboard came up to me and asked, "Marie Jimenez?"

"That's me," I answered as he checked my name off.

I recognized Howard Jeffrey and Tommy Abbott from all the auditions. They were talking to an older woman with a blonde ponytail. I was later told her name was Maggie Banks, Jerry's third assistant. Another woman with beautiful white hair was sitting at the piano talking to some of the other dancers. Jerry had brought her from New York and her name was Betty Walberg. She was to be the musical assistant and pianist. More dancers started to gather inside the soundstage.

Suddenly, I heard a low languid voice announce, "Find a place at the barre. Yes, we're going to have class every morning before rehearsal." It was Howard's voice.

There was a wall of mirrors that were mounted on rollers. I quickly found a place at the barre where I couldn't see myself because it broke my concentration if I saw my reflection.

"All right, everyone! Now that you have marked your place," Howard yelled out, continuing, "come back out on the floor and let's warm up first."

There were about thirty of us who sauntered back onto the center of the floor and took our positions. We did the usual head, neck, and shoulder rotations. This warm-up was familiar to me and it made me feel more at ease. Inhale, exhale. Breathe. Just then I felt the first twinge of pain coming from the middle of my stomach where my stitches were. I quickly tuned it out.

"Everybody, back to the barre," Howard ordered.

As I walked back to my place at the barre and did my first port de bras, I was hit again with another sharp pain. Every time I moved, my torso felt like it was on fire.

Two New York dancers, Gina Trikonis and Carole D'Andrea, who were playing Graziella and Velma, were in my direct eye line. Their whole attitude intimidated me. They had done the New York production and knew they belonged here. The two-hour ballet class had begun, and I soon discovered that the girls from New York were not great ballet dancers. Suzie Kaye, a Jewish girl who was cast as Rosalia, had the least training, I thought, because her feet never looked like they were pointing at all. Yvonne Othon, a real Puerto Rican in the role of Consuelo, was strong and had everybody's respect. I was told she was a Jack Cole dancer, whom I had heard of but never studied under. She laughed and joked a lot and the dancers gravitated to her. She had an identity about her. It was a confidence that spoke volumes. She knew who she was and was proud of it. Just watching her the first few minutes doing some mambo moves made me feel so "white," like such a gringa. Thank goodness ballet wasn't her strong point. I immediately decided that these New York dancers weren't such a threat. Joanne Miya, on the other hand, was the one I had to watch out for. She was an exquisite dancer AND she was so beautiful. She definitely was the one I had to keep up with.

The throbbing pain in my lower right side was now becoming constant, but I told myself not to give in to it. Even though this was the first day of rehearsal and our first class, it was about being the best. I would gain or lose respect from these dancers by the way I performed in this one class. I began to feel overconfident. I told myself that this was just another dance class to be the best at. I had no idea what was about to be revealed.

All of a sudden, the energy changed. Jerome Robbins suddenly appeared and I started to see people standing straighter and taller and dancing full out. I thought they HAD been dancing full out because what other way is there to dance? It was as if a bolt of electricity shot through the class. Some of the men, like Tony Mordente, Tommy Abbott, Bobby Thompson, Eddie Verso, and Howard Jeffrey, who were all strong ballet dancers, took the lead. David Winters, Eliot Feld, Gus Trikonis, Jay Norman, Jaime Rogers, and even the girls became brutally competitive. A revelation hit me smack in my face. Jerome Robbins handpicked every single person here to play a specific role, and it wasn't just about dancing technically perfect. It was about stepping into the shoes of the character Jerry had cast you in. Each dancer was special, hired for a specific reason, destined to be here. Their intensity obliterated all the confidence I had mustered up. In Jerome Robbins' presence, every dancer here became territorial and ruthless. Was it just because they wanted to please their leader? I was glad that they didn't talk to me. I needed that distance to face the battle. I now had to prove to all of them that I had a right to be here just like them. All my pain, physical and mental, blended together like an absent thought. I only focused on dancing harder. It seemed very simple. It was a matter of do or die. I jumped higher, did triple pirouettes instead of double, and did the double cabrioles across the floor as high as some of the male dancers.

Mr. Robbins watched us all like a hawk, searching, waiting to find the weak link. It was NOT going to be me! Eugene Loring and his American School of Dance, my mother's love and support and the hours of her driving me to classes, and all the blisters, torn ligaments, and muscle spasms I'd ever had prepared me for this very moment. God brought me here and now He would give me wings to soar like an eagle. I danced and danced and danced, transporting myself mentally into that magical arena that held perfect harmony of mind, body, and soul. Everything around me faded as I was enveloped in a euphoric veil of pure joy. I had so succeeded in transcending myself out of my natural pain that I didn't realize what was taking place. Blood began seeping through my leotard. My stitches had opened up. Jolted back into reality, my first thought was, "I am so glad I wore black." Then under my breath I said, "Oh, God, did Mr. Robbins notice?" I quickly went to my dance bag and pulled out my lucky black sweater, tied it around my waist in hopes that it would soak up the excess blood, and went back onto the floor.

How I got through the rest of the day is a blur. I vaguely remember Howard sending me to the studio medic and being told I would have to have new stitches because I had ripped open the original ones. When my mother picked me up at the end of the day, there was so much to tell her about my first day, but instead we argued about my stitches all the way home.

"Maria, you have to get new stitches, otherwise you won't heal properly."

"Mama, don't worry. I got through today, didn't I? Just put extra gauze and tape around me and I'll be okay. You'll see, tomorrow will be even better."

Just in that one day, I had been sent to the front line of battle and returned older and wiser. I had changed. I didn't get new stitches and my mother was right. It didn't heal properly and I still have the scar to prove it.

My memory of the first two weeks of rehearsals, the pain of my appendectomy behind me, I remember feeling alone and apart from the other dancers. If you call "hi, good-bye" a conversation, that's what I had. Then one day, something happened that I'll never forget. Always during our breaks, they would open the elephant doors and five or six dancers would rush outside to have their much-needed cigarette. Being closed off in a soundstage was like being inside a tomb. I too, followed them out and embraced the fresh air. The California sun was warm as I shut my eyes, inhaled deep, and soaked it up.

"Hello," someone said.

I quickly opened my eyes to see who it was. A tall lanky male dancer with straight jet-black hair, a cigarette dangling from his mouth, was standing directly in front of me.

"I'm Andre Tayir," he said, extending his hand for a handshake.

I wondered who shakes hands except my parents and grown-ups.

"Do you want a cup of coffee?" he asked as I timidly shook hands with him.

"Sure, why not," I mumbled, as we walked over to the crafts service table. I didn't even drink coffee but was so grateful to this person for even speaking to me that I would have gladly consumed a gallon of the stuff. His kindness to me that day I will carry to my grave. I had no idea our friendship would last beyond four decades.

The second person to speak to me or acknowledge that I existed was Suzie Kaye. She generally remained inside, always whipping out a deck of cards and gathering together two or three people around her for a quick card game. One day I walked over to watch them play.

Without looking up at me, she said, "Do you want in?"

I didn't know she was talking to me so I didn't respond.

She then looked up at me and said very succinctly in her New York accent, "Do you want to play some gin?"

I quickly nodded my head no and said, "I only know how to play Go Fish."

"Well, sit down and I'll teach you," she said. That was it. She had accepted me and I began to feel that I really was part of this elite, chosen family. Who knew that a few years later, Suzie and I would become roommates. Like Andre, she and I remained friends for over forty years.

As the rehearsals continued, I learned I had become a member of Jerry's "skeleton group." This skeleton group rehearsed all the staging and choreography before it went on camera. We learned each other's choreography, and if Jerry wanted you to step in for someone, even if you were a Shark and now you had to be a Jet in "Cool," you were expected to know every step perfectly. It seemed as if we learned a dozen versions of "America," "Dance Hall," and "Cool." I loved rehearsing the vocals and the dialogue in "America" up in Jerry's apartment that he had on the lot, where he gathered us all together to rehearse the songs with Betty Walberg and Bobby Tucker, the vocal coach. In high school I was in the glee club and knew I could carry a tune, but working with Bobby Tucker, I discovered I had a strong voice and excellent pitch. I learned to love the singing almost as much as the dancing. A couple of times Gina and Carole stood in for Rita and Yvonne. Jerry would just watch and listen to the vocals and the reading of the dialogue. I loved the intimacy of those rehearsals. What was it about wanting to be accepted by the Teacher, the Choreographer, the Mentor? Did I just have a big ego, or was it about needing to be accepted by the world? I always knew that I would fight anyone to the death for center stage, but was that because deep down in my soul I still didn't think I was worthy? How could that be? I loved the challenge and the field of battle. No. Insecurity had no place in my wardrobe. I gave it no place.

As the weeks turned into months, the *West Side Story* family got tighter. I was the only one that had a car, a 1956 Chevy Belaire, and

I gladly became the girls' chauffeur. I had moved into Hollywood and my apartment was about ten minutes from The Green Brier Apartments, which was on Fountain and Crescent Heights, where most of the New York dancers were staying. Every morning I picked up Gina, Carole, and Suzie and drove to the studio. All of my spare time was taken with this new "familia." At the end of the day I dropped the girls back at the Green Brier and sometimes stayed and smoozed. The place was always so busy with bodies and people jumping in and out of the pool. Gina and Carole were rooming together, and since Gina was such a great cook, everyone always ended up at their apartment. Carole barely knew how to boil an egg, so she really lucked out rooming with Gina. David Winters, Jay Norman, Eddie Verso, and some other regulars parlayed their weekly paychecks playing poker every weekend. Sometimes they'd start playing on Friday night and finish Sunday morning. Rumor had it that David usually won.

All through high school, my hair was long enough for me to sit on. Unfortunately all of my hair tests proved to be unsatisfactory. My ponytail didn't work because every time I swung my head around, my partner got slapped in the face. The hair department tried putting it all up in a bun on top of my head, but Jerry didn't like that. He said it made me look too old and he wanted me to look like the teenager I was. No one seemed to know what to do with this mane of mine.

One Friday night up at one girl's apartment, Rita Moreno and Yvonne Othon sat me in a chair and said, "We have to do something about your hair."

The first thing that popped into my head was, "Mama is going to be horrified if they cut an inch of it." As soon as I sat in the chair, I had already decided there wasn't anything I wouldn't do for the sake of the film. I closed my eyes and the sound of the scissors making that first cut blasted in my ears. Did I make a mistake? I wondered. I opened my eyes to check the damage. They had cut about a foot, making the length come to about my waist. That didn't seem so bad, but they didn't stop there. I shut my eyes again as they continued cutting away.

When they finished, I heard, "Okay, open your eyes. You're going to love this."

I slowly opened my eyes and looked in the mirror. I couldn't believe what I saw. I had a short pageboy-length hairdo.

Then I heard different voices saying, "Isn't it cute!" "Doesn't she look better?"

I don't recall who said what because I was in a state of paralysis. To me, I looked like a cartoon. All I needed was fat little curls and I could pass for Little Lulu in the comic books. I didn't have the nerve to tell my mother what had happened. The following Monday morning my hair was pulled back into a ponytail, which was now the length of maybe two inches. Jerry kept looking at me trying to figure out what was different. Could he not see that I had been scalped? I never found out if he liked my new haircut or hated it. The hair stylists turned my hair into the Minnie Mouse hairdo that I had to live with for the rest of the entire shoot. I hated that hairdo, but I don't regret sacrificing my hair for my art.

Jerry started instilling in us his philosophy that the Sharks and the Jets had to stay away from each other. He wanted to maintain the tension. As a diversion, Andre, Jaime, Jay Norman, Larry Rockmore, Eddie Verso, and myself—all of us Sharks—would sneak away to go horseback riding at the Pickwick Stables in Griffith Park. It's odd that I really don't recall any of the girls joining us. These New York City boys loved pretending they were cowboys in the Old West. I loved to ride, and sitting in a saddle came natural to me. Why, I don't know, because horseback riding was an expensive luxury that I couldn't afford nor had the time for. Perhaps it was because I also had Uto-Aztecan Tarahumara Indian blood mixed in my veins, and that made it familiar to me. Before setting out for the stables, I would play the soundtrack of the movie *The Big Country*. I loved that music, and it always put me in the right mindset for riding. They nicknamed me Bell Starr and I admit, I felt special. I cherished those times.

We also knew that if Jerry found out about our riding escapades, he would be furious. Should anything happen, or if an accident occurred to cause a delay in the schedule, it would cost the studio a lot of money. The guys were more indispensable than me, but it didn't stop them from riding. On one particular day, the guys were acting really crazy and riding the horses hard and fast. One of them got thrown and hit his head. We all panicked and everyone was talking at the same time.

"Don't tell Jerry!"

"He'll fire us all!"

"No he won't!"

"Yes he will!"

"Don't anyone say anything and he'll never know!"

Our cowboy days ended that late afternoon. Did Jerry ever find out? I'll never know.

August 10, 1960, the guys took off for New York to start shooting the "Prologue." It was supposed to take two weeks to shoot but it took four. For those of us who were in Los Angeles, the studio still expected us to show up every day since we were on salary. Yvonne, Gina, Joanne, Carole, Suzie, Rita sometimes, some other dancers, and myself would give each other ballet classes. The rest of the morning was spent with Gina teaching us how to knit, while Suzie played cards. Gina was a fabulous knitter, so we quickly started coming to work with knitting needles and yarn as well as ballet shoes and sweat towels. I found out later that Jose De Vega was also a knitter, and he later taught me another way to cast on stitches. That year I made ten sweaters. Getting paid for knitting sweaters and taking class was the greatest.

When the crew and the guys returned from New York, everything accelerated. The studio lot was buzzing again, and we wanted to hear all the stories and the gossip. How Jerry was like a driven machine, always demanding retakes, adding another version. He was such a perfectionist, looking to always make it better. The guys said the heat was stifling and it was a miracle that no one had heat stroke. I had heard that Jerry made Eliot run for hours doing the chase scene over and over again, take after take. It never seemed good enough for Jerry.

Which was funny because Andre, the fastest runner of them all, had to constantly put on the breaks and slow down, pretending not to outrun George and catch up with Eliot. Every morning the guys took a ballet barre, and I remember Tony saying that on the first day of shooting, real New York gang members were out front and center watching from behind the barriers as our guys leaped through the air doing tour en l'airs and snapping their fingers. Our guys felt so ridiculous.

One of my favorite stories was when the movie *Psycho* came out and everyone was talking about the scary shower scene and how no one wanted to take a shower alone. This was what I remember hearing. Jose De Vega was rooming with Nick Covachevich at the time and he had just returned from seeing the movie. As a joke, the next day after rehearsal Nick was showering and getting ready to go out that night. Jose dressed up as the Norman Bates character, knife and all, and lunged at Nick as he got out of the shower. Poor Nick, macho as he was, fainted dead away. I don't know why that cracks me up to this day. I think it is because I have always loved scaring people.

We began final rehearsals of "America," which I think was the next thing to be shot. I'll never forget one special afternoon in the rehearsal soundstage when Jerry had to decide who would be the fourth female singer in "America." Pre recording was scheduled in two weeks, and it was between Joanne and me. We did "America" over and over again. Jerry made changes and moved us around in different positions like pawns on a chessboard. Everyone stood watching, making mental notes as to who they thought was the best choice. First Joanne did the number with Rita, Yvonne, and Suzie, then I would do it. Each time we did the dance, I kicked my leg higher and threw my head back further than before as Howard and Jerry looked on. I knew my voice was stronger than Joanne's, and I really believed I danced like a Shark with more Latin juts than Joanne, but I also knew Joanne was a favorite of Jerry's. We both wanted the part, but I think in my desperation I wanted it more. Finally Jerry made his choice. When he called out my name as the fourth girl, everyone clapped and I jumped up and yelled, "YES!"

This also meant that they were going to upgrade my contract from SEG (Screen Extras Guild) to SAG (Screen Actors Guild). I couldn't wait to call my parents. I learned that Jaime Rogers was to be my dance partner. He was about my size and we fit each other like a glove. He was (and still is) a brilliant dancer who still has the intensity and energy of a thousand-watt voltage.

We also started rehearsing "Dance Hall." They brought in about fifty or sixty more dancers for "Dance Hall" alone. Jerry never let us forget the line separating the Jets from the Sharks, even though people inevitably crossed it. It was one big party with everybody dating and pairing off. With all the new additional faces and "competition," I noticed there was one dancer that everyone seem to eyeball.

"Who is that girl?" I asked someone, pointing to a gorgeous brunette who looked like Elizabeth Taylor and Ava Gardner all in one. I hadn't seen anyone that beautiful since the movies. She had the biggest blue eyes and a mouth full of long white perfect teeth that were constantly being exposed because she was always laughing. Why is it that all the beautiful people have perfect teeth? Her skin was white as alabaster, and her thick head of hair as black as a raven.

"Her name is Rita D'Amico. She's a Hollywood dancer," someone said.

"What is a Hollywood dancer?" I asked.

I was told, "A Hollywood dancer means she's not a 'serious dancer.' She danced at the Moulin Rouge and travels in the Hollywood scene."

I honestly didn't know what that meant. I thought if she got this far, she had to have some training. Later I found out she married very young and already had two kids. Now she was divorced. She was a woman of the world. That I understood. Who could compete with that? She was Scooter Teague's partner in "Dance Hall," and they made a great-looking couple. She had learned "Cool" with Francesca Bellini and Patti Tribble in hopes of being cast as the third girl in "Cool." This pretty face proved to be a better dancer than I'd thought, but going against Francesca and Patti, both technically strong ballet dancers and American School of Dance Alumni, she didn't make the final cut for "Cool."

"America" was ready to be filmed, and Irene Sharaff had designed double outfits for all the dancers in "America"—and, in some cases, triples, shoes included. I felt so special on the day the Shark dancers were taken for shoe fittings to Pappagallos, an expensive shoe store on Wilshire Blvd. in Beverly Hills. The salespersons treated us like royalty, and I felt such a sense of belonging. Everyone was so hyped and ramped up to go before the camera when suddenly, overnight, everything changed. We got the word that something had happened to Rita, and production was called to a halt. The press was all over it and said she was inconsolable because of her breakup with her long-time love of her life, Marlon Brando. I remember in the months earlier, he had come on the lot to see Rita, and he looked like an Adonis. He was shooting *The Young Lions* at the time and looked so gorgeous with his bleached blond hair and his trim body. I don't know what caused the breakup, but I do know that Rita was devastated. That was the first time I realized the importance of the "star's" responsibility toward a film production, and how their personal life was exposed for the whole world to see. I was glad that I didn't know the whole story. I think it was about three or four days later that we got the call to resume shooting. I don't remember anyone talking about what had happened. It was as though it never took place.

During the shooting, if anything ripped or got too sweaty, we made a quick change. The lights were so hot and dancing full out every take made the guys sweat like sprinklers. In the original Broadway version, Anita and just her girls danced "America." For the movie version, Jerry choreographed a whole new version that included the guys. It was now a battle between the Sharks and their ladies. We danced to the playback that we had recorded prior to the shoot. The first note of Anita singing "Puerto Rico, my heart's devotion, let it sink back in the ocean" set the number in gear, and the teasing and taunting began.

My heart raced as I got ready to sing my line, "Industry booms in America."

Then Bernardo took over and he and the guys danced with pure testosterone. We teased, flirted, and danced to such a climax we could barely breathe at the end of each take. As soon as we'd hear "CUT," all the make-up and hair people ran toward us with cloths dipped in Sea Breeze, slapping it on our bare arms and touching up our hair. They had to do tons of touch-ups because our make-up sweated off our faces. They placed the wet cloths on the backs of our necks and foreheads. It was the only thing that revived us.

Even though both Jerry and Robert Wise were co-directing, "America" was Jerry's creation. His vision. Mr. Wise, a great filmmaker, was the studio's insurance that this film would be completed. Jerome Robbins was the genius behind *West Side Story*, and the artist that the studio executives couldn't or wouldn't depend on. Bob Wise was easy to work with and void of ego. Jerry was the complete opposite. He was relentless about perfection. We kept doing the coda in "America" over and over again because it had to be just right. It was the last combination that worked up to a final frenzy, and each girl was lifted up on the shoulders of her partner, freezing the end pose. We had been doing this for two weeks, all day, every day. Jerry kept pushing for more. Something was always going wrong. Either one couple got to the end pose before everyone else or someone was too late or the timing was off for Rita and George. Everyone looked like soloists instead of an ensemble. We all had to end on the exact same beat at the exact same time. Not one fraction of a second off. One time Rita's dress just kept slipping right off of George's shoulder until she was practically on the floor before Jerry yelled cut. It was the release we all needed. We laughed so hard that it took an hour to recover.

Finally, on the last take, holding that last pose for dear life, we finally heard, "CUT! THAT'S A LILY!"

When you heard "That's a Lily," that meant it was finally done! No more retakes! We all collapsed onto the ground in a dead heap. Was "America" really in the can for good? We couldn't believe it. A couple of days later it was rumored that Jerry wanted to reshoot the entire thing all over again, and he also wanted to make some set changes.

The studio obviously didn't allow that. I am so grateful that Jerry was there for the shooting of "America." His presence always made you dance better and greater than even YOU thought you could.

"Dance Hall" was next. It is odd that I don't have a vivid memory of any off-screen interaction with the Sharks and Natalie Wood. In her case, Jerry's declaration of separation between the Jets and the Sharks was in full effect. The first time I saw Natalie Wood, I was surprised to see how small she was in stature. She was just a little taller than me. And she was more beautiful in person than all the photographs I had seen in the movie magazines. Her waist measurement must have been 18 inches or less because she looked so tiny. I noticed she always wore a large bracelet on her left wrist. It was large enough to cover her entire wrist bone. Whether we were rehearsing in leotards or costumes, in front of the camera or eating lunch at the commissary, she was never without that bracelet. I later heard stories that she broke her wrist when she was very young and it never healed properly. She made sure on or off camera her crooked wrist would never be revealed. I also remember she wore an amazing perfume that permeated every place she went.

When asked what fragrance it was she merely said quietly, "I'll never tell."

It seemed that it was a special brand that was created just for her. I was too naive to understand the reasons as to why she wasn't about to share her secrets with just anyone. In Hollywood it was always about being the real "original" deal. I guess to Natalie, even being copied was a no, no. Many years later I thought I had finally discovered what the fragrance was. It smelled like Jungle Gardenia but lighter, more delicate.

When Natalie was on the set, there was always a level of excitement that was different than the energy the dancers brought. I guess you could call it "Star" quality. It was the same electricity that you felt when you saw Marlon Brando, or Robert Wagner, Natalie's husband. I think maybe they were separated at the time because when Warren Beatty came to visit her and watch rehearsals, it didn't look like they were just friends. The gossip columns were filled with their romantic involvement while working together on *Splendor in the Grass*. I know there was more drama going on off-screen than on, but I was a horse with blinders on and only focused on the dance.

We were a couple of days away from putting "Dance Hall" on camera. We had been rehearsing the mambo every day, and the competition between the Sharks and the Jets got so thick that it followed me into my dreams at night. Jerry had succeeded in creating the tension between the two gangs, and we all took it seriously. One memorable afternoon with emotions peaking, Jerry came onto the "Dance Hall" soundstage and dropped a bomb.

"I am leaving!" he announced.

"Leaving? What is he talking about?" one person whispered as everyone started to look around at one another for explanations.

"What's happened? An emergency?" I asked Jaime.

No one understood what Jerry was talking about. Probably Howard, Tony, Tommy, Maggie, and those in the inner circle knew of the existing problems between Jerry and the studio, but most of us had no idea how serious those problems were.

"You think any of you are indispensable?" Jerry shouted. "Well you're not!"

I don't remember what else was said because like everyone else, I was in shock. How do you get rid of the parent and keep the child? *West Side Story* was Jerry's baby. It wasn't possible. I soon found out that it WAS true and yes, Jerome Robbins was being fired and was going back to New York. We were all in a state of confusion. We didn't know what we were supposed to do or feel. Were we loyal to Jerry or to the film? With "Cool" and "Officer Krupke" already shot, we set out to rehearse and shoot "Dance Hall."

At first I felt like a passionless minnow swimming around without direction or purpose. Fortunately that wilderness didn't last long. It took about a month to shoot "Dance Hall," and Robert Wise had the horrible job of picking up the pieces. The responsibility of finishing this film was on his shoulders. He had the experience and the sensitivity to walk in the enemy's camp and not be devoured, but the absence of the creator lingered like a ghost.

A day or two later, I remember Mr. Wise calling out in the middle of the gym scene, "Let's have some more salt and pepper."

I asked someone, "What does that mean, 'more salt and pepper'?"

Someone answered, "I think he means spice it up."

I don't think anyone else other than Robert Wise could have handled it better and gotten the results he did. Tony Mordente and Tommy Abbott were asked to take over as assistant choreographers to help him with the dance numbers. Howard quit and left with Jerry. Maggie Banks remained.

When we got to the "Cha-Cha," which was the love exchange between Tony and Maria, Tommy had me replace Suzie as one of the dancers behind Tony and Maria. My partner was Eddie Verso. Carole partnered Tommy, and Joanne partnered Bobby Thompson. Tony Mordente became Natalie's main support, and he made sure she was taken care of and rehearsed thoroughly. He covered the dancing and was absolute in knowing if our performances were perfect or not. Mr. Wise made sure that the coverage was there on film for edit purposes.

The "Cha-Cha," a section that musically takes about three minutes on screen, took us three days to shoot. Natalie looked at the dailies and if she didn't like something, we went back in the next day and reshot it. Either Carole's position behind Natalie had to be changed, so that Carole's gorgeous face ended looking upstage away from the camera instead of downstage, or the couples were not clean and in sync with each other. The "Cha-Cha" was the easiest and the simplest combination, yet the hardest because we had to make it look so easy and effortless. I held my breath every time I made the soutenu ending with my arm intertwining Eddie's. One day we did fifty-two takes on just that same soutenu step. I felt bad for Natalie because she kept falling off her relevé, which is a step that is on half point, and each take kept getting worse.

By the third day, we were all so punchy and giddy that I didn't dare look into Eddie's eyes for fear of seeing them twitching. If they started to twitch, it meant he was about to lose it. His chest and diaphragm would start to quiver and I knew if I made eye contact with him, the dam would burst and I would be lost in a wave of convulsive, gut-wrenching laughter. This always happened when we were supposed to be still, like statues. God forbid if Natalie and Richard's dialogue was perfect, making the scene just right, and we were behind, giggling or losing our balance. Eddie and I were always visible behind them and we couldn't fake it. It was sheer agony.

After the third day, Bob Wise said he had everything he needed. I could inhale again. It was many years later that I heard Mr. Wise and Jerry were in daily phone contact during the actual shooting of "Dance Hall." I guess Jerry was privy to the dailies and gave his notes to Mr. Wise, but in the end, Jerry felt that the magic and the soul of "Dance Hall" had not being captured. In the "Mambo," I thought Gina's rawness and Russ's gymnastics were comparable to Rita and George's passion and fire. For Jerry, I know that being in New York three thousand miles away was not the same as being on the set directing one on one. Not being allowed to father his "child" had to have been devastating for him.

When "Dance Hall" wrapped and all the extra dancers were let go, an eerie quietness fell on the lot like the leftovers of a New Year's Eve party. It was at these times I would jump in my car and go home to Temple City. A feeling of loneliness would come over me, and I knew I had to see my mother. There was something about "going home" that gave me strength. Hope for the next day. Sometimes all I needed was to drive my car into that familiar driveway and walk into that family den that my father built and sit in front of the fireplace that he built from scratch and feel safe. I didn't even have to talk to anyone. My home and family was an oasis for me. I cherished those visits. I remember one visit when I came home with a broken heart. It was before Jerry left the production.

"Mama, I didn't get picked for 'I Feel Pretty.'" I cried.

"Oh Mija," she said, trying to comfort me. "Was that important to you?"

"Yes!" I cried out. "I don't understand." I cried, continuing, "We rehearsed the song a hundred times with Bobby Tucker, and he was always so supportive of my singing. He said I had a wonderful voice. Mama, I really thought I was going to get the part. Why didn't Jerry pick me? Joanne is beautiful and a fantastic dancer, but SHE IS JAPANESE! It's not right!"

After a few minutes my mother quietly said, "Some things are not meant to be."

When the movie came out and I didn't see my name on the credits, I felt rejected all over again. I was later told that the producers only wanted to list three female Sharks and three female Jets. I was the fourth Shark eliminated who did "America," and Patti Tribble was the fourth Jet that was eliminated who did "Cool." It wasn't fair—the absence of my name up there on the big screen made me feel nonexistent. I carried that rejection for decades. Like my mother said, some things are just not meant to be.

I have often thought maybe had I not been chosen to be the fourth girl in "America," would I have been the one to perform "I Feel Pretty" and be listed in the credits? I wonder. What I do cherish are the friendships that I made during that year of filming. Love blossomed. Gina and Bobby Banas were a couple, Suzie's boyfriend Larry, from PA, came out from New York to stay with her and her mother Ethel, and Gus Trikonis and Rita D'Amico became a couple. Andre's fiancé, Sarah Reed, who was a ballerina with Ballet Theater in New York, moved out to California because Andre had decided to make California his home. Carole accepted a marriage proposal to Robert Morse. As for me, I had no love life. Jaime Rogers had made some passes and even Andre, but they were like brothers to me. I had a bit of a crush on Eliot Feld, but he only thought of me as just a friend. I learned how to knit and make lasagna, and loved all the late-night weenie roasts we had at Playa Del Rey and going to the movies at the Gardner Theater. The year of being together with my new family was coming to an end. I had been transformed. My life was never to be the same. What I didn't know was that my journey was just beginning.

After

DID BEING HANDPICKED by Jerome Robbins to be a Shark dancer in the movie *West Side Story* change my life? Was this a "once in a lifetime" opportunity that was orchestrated by God? Did this priceless experience set the bar for anything and everything that followed in my life and career? The answer is YES, YES, AND YES!

After completing the film, my courage had gained momentum, and I made the decision to go to the Big Apple in search of true greatness. I wanted to study under the giants of the dance world and also had hopes of joining Jerome Robbins' company, Ballets USA. I thought it ironic that my newly found *West Side Story* family was staying together in my homeland, and I was going to theirs alone. Jaime, Eliot, Jay, and some others returned to N.Y. after the final wrap, and that helped comfort me. Going to New York City by myself was so ethereal at best. I was born and raised in sunny California, where grass and trees were permanent fixtures. When I first set foot on Manhattan, New York, soil, I soon found myself surrounded by wall-to-wall buildings and cement.

Eliot had arranged for me to stay at his parents' apartment until Yvonne's apartment was available for me to move into. I was very grateful for their hospitality even though I felt we were from two different worlds. We had very little in common. They were Jewish and celebrated Shabbat every Friday night. I was raised a Catholic who always ate fish on Friday nights. I went to a church and they went to Temple. My mother, who always worried about me being so far away, made me promise to thank them for taking me in. I honored that promise two weeks later, when the time came to say good-bye to Mr. and Mrs. Feld. I was surprised to find how detached I felt. I could never bring myself to call them by their first names. Was that my fault? Was it a Jewish/Christian thing? I doubt it. I was raised to believe in God and Jesus and never had any altercations because of my faith. Any prejudice that I grew up with was about the color of my skin, not my religion. If the Felds felt differently, their kindness never made me feel inferior. I guess the only thing that united Eliot's parents and me was Eliot. That was enough for them to welcome me into their home, and I will always be grateful.

Two weeks after my arrival, I made the move into Yvonne's apartment, which was above the unemployment office on 54th Street. I had finally arrived at a stopping place. It was a one-bedroom apartment with a little kitchenette, a bath, and a small living room. Completely furnished with a small portable television and stereo accompanied by a rack of vinyl records that consisted of Frank Sinatra, Tito Puente, Miles Davis, and more. I only had to pay for monthly rent and utilities, thanks to Yvonne's generosity and kindness. Since her apartment was centrally located, I learned my way around the city very quickly and became an expert on traveling the subway and taking the bus.

I attended ballet classes at Ballet Theater and took jazz classes from Matt Mattox and Luigi. Eliot finally returned to New York, and we were inseparable. We went all over the city together, hopping in and out of subways, running to the Joffrey School of Dance, or places that he wanted to show me. We both loved going to the movies. We would see one movie and then quickly run across the street to catch another one. I forget how many times we saw Marlon Brando in *One Eyed Jacks* together. When I was with Eliot, I had a sense of belonging. I didn't feel so alone. Things got even better when Jaime, Eddie, and Jay returned to Manhattan. As my circle of friends got bigger, I started to really feel cocky.

The day I had been waiting for finally came. I was to audition for Jerry's company, Ballets USA. I got to the rehearsal hall two hours earlier. I couldn't believe there were already a hundred dancers standing in line, waiting to register and get a number. I felt like I was auditioning for *West Side Story* all over again. Eddie Verso, who was already hired, gave me the confidence I needed.

"Eddie, why am I so scared?" I asked him.

"Ah, don't worry. Jerry already knows what you can do," he answered.

"But look at Vickie Mazzo," I moaned, continuing, "she looks just like the white fragile swan Jerry wants."

Eddie quickly said, "That's not all Jerry's looking for. Stop with the complaining and just go out there and dance! You'll be great!"

I took his advice and did just that. I danced! When Jerry read off my name and I knew I had made the cut, I couldn't wait to call my family in California and tell them the good news. I was going to be a member of Jerome Robbins' Ballets USA.

That first week of rehearsals was like a faded dream. I was there physically but my head was somewhere else. I was in a state of elevation and my feet never hit the floor. I couldn't believe that I had succeeded in achieving what I came to New York to do. Or so I thought. Again I found myself amongst the best of the best, I was taking class with dancers that I read about in *Dance Magazine*. Patricia Dunn, Wilma Curley, Gwen Lewis (who was married to Jay Norman), as well as Eddie Verso, Jay Norman, Tommy Abbott, and Howard Jeffrey.

Just when I was able to catch my breath, Jerry came into the rehearsal hall and announced, "Get your passports ready. We are going to Spoleto, Italy."

Everyone seemed excited—everyone but me. A fear came over me that was overwhelming. Was it a fear of going to another country, not really knowing if that would make me a brilliant dancer or not? Or was it just a plain and simple lack of faith? Didn't my Heavenly Father orchestrate my steps? Did I not believe in my destiny? Whatever the reason, a blanket of fear covered me completely. Since I was also studying with Matt Mattox and was asked to be a guest soloist in his company, I wondered if I should use that as an excuse not to go to Italy. I couldn't sleep at all that night.

The next morning I felt I was marching to the guillotine to tell Jerry I couldn't go. I almost choked getting the words out. Did Jerry buy my excuse? Did he smell the fear all over me? I believe he did. He could have pressed the issue and devoured me with his wrath. Instead, he said he understood. Three months later, when the company returned to New York, I asked Howard and Tommy to please meet me at Confucius, a popular Chinese restaurant.

"Do you think I will ever dance for Jerry again?" I asked.

They both tried to reassure me that I would.

Then Howard remembered, "You know, there was something strange that happened." He continued, "Pat tore some ligaments in her ankle and there was no one to replace her in *Opus Jazz* so Jerry said, send for Maria."

"But I never got the call," I interjected.

Tommy then said, "That's because the call was never made."

"Why?" I asked.

Tommy shook his head. "I don't know. Jerry suddenly changed his mind."

The decision not to go to Spoleto is one that I have mulled over in my head for years. If I had to do it all over again, would I make the same decision? Sometimes we just don't get second chances. I will never know if I should have taken the road less traveled.

Like my mama always said, "Some things are just not meant to be."

I continued my classes, learned from the best, and one day, the "best" saw me in Matt's jazz class and came over to introduce herself. I already knew who she was before she opened her mouth. It was Lee Becker, the original Anybodys who was in that Los Angeles production of *West Side Story* that changed my life. I was blown away by her compliments of how my dancing reminded her of herself. She said she wanted to work with me and would I be interested in being part of her new dance workshop. Without hesitation I said YES! My days were filled with rehearsals for Matt's concert, but the evenings belonged to Lee. Jay Norman, Jaime, and Eliot were also part of the group. Lee mentored me, introducing me into the art of improvisation. I trusted her with all that I was.

She took me to a higher ground, and I can still hear her voice yelling out, "MARIE, STOP DANCING WITH YOUR BRAIN! DANCE FROM YOUR HEART!"

She was my mentor, and all that I learned about improvisation and creating an original moment, a step, a new birth of movement,

I learned from her. That education would forever be an asset to me when I started to choreograph, act, design sweaters, and write.

While still in New York, I also did two summer stock shows of *West Side Story* in Cohasset, Massachusetts, for Lenny Dale. I was given the role of Anybodys. My hair was chopped off and dyed carrot red, and I danced the best ever. When you love what you are doing, there is only joy. I loved every second being on stage with my new group of friends that consisted of Joe Bennett, Johnny Mineo, Marcia Gregg, Stephan Zima, and my new roommate, Julie Makis, later known as Julie Maginnis, the opera star. Julie was a brilliant opera singer but always wanted to be a dancer. Also Donna McKechnic made her debut in this production. She played a Jet Girl. Even she had no idea where her journey would take her.

When I returned to Manhattan, Lee later asked Eliot and me to assist her on a special work for The Robert Joffrey Ballet Company. Eliot and I had drifted apart and the atmosphere had changed. I didn't seem to fit in this trio. This was a special time for me because as much as I thought I knew as a professional dancer, I found out the hard way that I was very naive in the things of the world. The heaviness that loneliness brings can be an invaluable education. For me, living in New York was the best of times and the worst of times. In retrospect, I discovered that sometimes it's the failures that give you character and make you stronger, not the success.

The Prodigal returned home, war wounds and all, but still alive. Andre, Gina, Gus, and Bert were in Jeff Cory's and Leonard Nimoy's acting classes. They of course said I had to join them and take classes with them, but I was so broke, I knew I had to get some work first. My first job was being half of a dance team. It was for two weeks at Harrahs in Lake Tahoe. Our adagio was part of the chorus number that opened the show. Rosemary Clooney was the opening act for Sammy Davis Jr. They were great. We were terrible.

There were auditions for a short run of *West Side Story* to be done at the Moulin Rouge Theater in Hollywood, staged by Tony Mordente. Chita Rivera, Larry Kert, and Carla Alberghetti were heading the cast, and Tucker, Gus, David, Andre, and Bruce Hoy were also doing it. I joined the cast playing Consuelo, and Hope Clark, Marti Litis, Teri Garr, and Toni Basil were among some of the dancers.

One night during this production, I had this desire to write a letter to Jerry thanking him for creating such a powerful show and what it meant to me to be a part of it as well as the movie. I didn't know if he still harbored a grudge against me for not going to Spoleto with Ballets USA. To my complete surprise, he answered my letter and thanked me for taking the time to write him and wished me the best. Thank you, God, Jerry didn't discard me! I treasured that letter and still have it amongst my most valuable possessions.

After that production, I started acting classes with Jeff Cory and Leonard Nimoy. When Leonard and Jeff split up, most of us followed Leonard to a little theater on Chuenga Blvd. in Burbank. Two important things happened during this wonderful time of putting on plays and studying the Bard. The first happening was I fell in love for the first time in my life with someone that I was certain I would spend my life with forever. I was wrong. The second happening was I met a wonderful friend who everybody loved who, unbeknownst to me, was to become part of my future. His name was Donald Caperton Henley. He was a theatrical co-manager of Pat Boone and the Family. He was a dapper Southern gentleman from Nashville, Tennessee, who drove expensive cars, dressed in expensive suits, and always had a gorgeous tall-legged girl on his arm. I soon discovered he was also a man of great faith in God.

When Andre asked Gina Trikonis and me to go to England to perform in a Beatles Television Special for Producer Jack Good, I jumped at the chance. Our visas had to say we were an "eccentric acrobatic team" in order for us to be allowed into the country. John, Paul, George, and Ringo, who were big fans of the movie, welcomed us and treated us with respect. In the special, we were introduced as The Jets. It was a once-in-a-lifetime experience working, dancing, laughing, and eating side by side with the biggest music phenomenon of all time. These mopheads endeared themselves to us. Experiencing that kind of mania and fan hysteria was like being taken to the circus for the first time. You didn't know where to look first or what you were going to feel because the adrenalin level was so high. The London papers printed, "The Jets from Los Angeles danced like savages." I think that was a true statement. It was raw, down, and dirty. To my knowledge this was, and still is, the only Beatles television special that was ever done. I can't be certain that it was ever aired.

Don and I had been dating seriously for six months by now. It was during this time while still in England that he called me from Los Angeles and proposed to me over the phone. The Beatles and a marriage proposal! I wondered, Does it get any better than this? I of course accepted. We returned to Los Angeles and Jack Good informed Andre, Gina, and I that we were to begin rehearsals immediately for a rock-and-roll television pilot he was producing for ABC called *Shingdig*. Andre was signed to choreograph, and I was to do the double duty of co-choreographing as well as dancing regularly every week. We held auditions, arrived at 10 regular "dancing ponies" of which Gina and I were included, and on September 16, 1964, the live half-hour show was launched.

That was an insane month for me because on September 26, 1964, Don and I got married in a candlelight service. Andre, Leonard Nimoy, and James Hampton were ushers, and Gina and Suzie Kaye, my sisters Barbara and Teri were in the bridesmaid party. After a honeymoon in Acapulco, Mazatlan, and Mexico City, I returned to work.

At one time, for about four episodes, David Winters was hired to choreograph *Shindig*. The *West Side Story* family was still connecting. The *Shingdig* series was like being on a bumper car. Five cameras covered the constant movement as we knocked out ten dance numbers a week. The ten "pony" dancers gyrated nonstop. The show was electrified with guest stars from the Rolling Stones, the Temptations, Marvin Gaye, Tina Turner, Aretha Franklin, Jackie Wilson, James Brown, Neil Sedaka, The Everly Brothers, The Mamas & The Papas, Jackie DeShannon to the Righteous Brothers, The Supremes, Ray

Charles, Jerry Lee Lewis, The Byrds, The Turtles, The Kinks, Smokey Robinson and the Miracles, and the list goes on and on. Every tabloid from *Look* magazine to *Time* did interviews with us and reported on this "wild generation of rock 'n' roll." On January of 1965, *Shindig* was extended to an hour show and ran for over two years.

I continued assisting such choreographers as Jaime Rogers, David Winters, Tony Basil, DeeDee Woods, and Donny McKayle. In 1967, I worked on the film called *Thoroughly Modern Millie* for Producer Ross Hunter and Director George Roy Hill. Herbert Ross wanted me to test for the role of the eighty-year-old Jewish grandmother in the big wedding scene. He said I danced the part like a female Zero Mostel and believed I could pull off the age. George Roy Hill thought I was too young and wasn't in favor of it at all. Ross Hunter ordered the test in support of Herbert Ross, and the next day I reported to the make-up, hair, and wardrobe department at 6:30 A.M. Three, maybe four hours later, I don't quite remember, I went before the camera. The test was great! The word got back to me that Hill thought I looked and played TOO OLD a grandmother, and I would have to play her a little younger. Can you believe that? Only in the movies does such a thing happen. I got paid very well because I had to be in that make-up for three weeks, only able to eat lunch through a straw. The prosthetics were so delicate that I couldn't move my mouth, eyes, or face for fear I would cause the prosthetics to fall off of my face. I also got to play myself as a young dancer in one of the party scenes. Julie Andrews and Mary Tyler Moore were wonderful to all of us, and it was a fun experience for me.

On January 3, 1971, Don and I were blessed with the birth of our firstborn, Youree Goyo Henley. Goyo was short for Gregorio, named after my grandfather. What a beauty he was. He was just one month old when we had that horrific 6.6 Sylmar earthquake. Six months later I was asked to be part of a skeleton group of dancers on a film for Disney called *Bednobs and Broomsticks* that Donald McKayle was choreographing. I was still recovering from that earthquake experience, and the thought of my baby being out of my sight for one second was not agreeable to me. We needed the money and since we already lived in the Valley, this job seemed a godsend. Don brought Youree to the Disney lawn every lunch hour so that I could breastfeed him on my lunch hour. None of us were the worse for it. We worked on that film for almost a month. I remember making blueberry muffins in the morning to take to our producer Bill Walsh, because he said he loved fresh blueberry muffins. Don't ask me why I got up an hour earlier each day to make these muffins. I just did. It made me happy to see Bill Walsh happy when I gave them to him. When Donny asked me to do the Academy Awards on April 15, to be taped at the Dorothy Chandler Theater, it meant my breastfeeding would have to come to a halt. I couldn't say no. Youree, Don, and I got through it and it was fine.

Andre and I stopped working together for professional reasons. The truth of the matter was that he didn't want to share co-choreographer credit with me, and I felt betrayed. I had choreographed over 50% or more of the production numbers we were hired to do, and I felt it warranted recognition. He said no. He would not share the credit, and we ceased to be close friends for almost two years. One day, he called me on the phone and asked for my help on a stage production that he was working on. I knew it must have been difficult for him to ask me. It was the first rock-and-roll version of *Othello* called *Catch My Soul* directed by Jack Good. Jerry Lee Lewis was cast as Iago. I said I would help on the conditions that I would share co-choreographer credit and that I would have complete control and rein over the dance numbers he was needing help with. He accepted my demands. The show premiered at the Ahmanson Theater. It was ahead of its time and didn't do well. I think it closed after a couple of weeks.

Donny remained an important mentor in my life as a dancer. His love, kindness, and scale of perfection went deep into my soul and spirit. The first time I auditioned for him, I didn't get the job. It was an NBC variety show starring Dick Van Dyke. The reason I got the call two days later after the audition was, I think, that someone got ill and I was the next choice in line. That first day of rehearsals I had to prove myself worthy all over again—shades of *West Side Story*. Well, I not only succeeded but I surpassed the level of expectation. I became part of the inner circle of dancers that Donny would have around him. Names like Jerry Grimes, Michael Peters, Roy Smith, Michelle Simmons, Lorraine Fields, Bill and Jackie Landrum, and Carolyn Dyer. We were all at our peak of brilliance coming together as Donny's company like a well-oiled machine. We did all the Bill Cosby specials, more Dick Van Dyke specials, and later the Lesley Uggums series. I later toured with Donny's company as a soloist.

After a year of soul-searching and re-grouping, Don returned to management for Pat Boone and the Family as well as Debby Boone, who was on the rise. It was in the year 1974 that my life took a sudden turn. I was five months pregnant when Don had his first heart attack. He was 39 years old. The night before his open-heart surgery, I had a miscarriage and it was Andre and Sarah who took me to the hospital. Don recovered from a successful heart surgery, and because of the miscarriage, it was discovered that I had a rare cancerous uterine mole and was immediately treated as an outpatient at UCLA. Two years later, I was given a good bill of health.

Andre and I mended our fences and continued to work together as co-choreographers for the *Andy Williams*, *Jim Nabors*, *Danny Thomas* and *Tiny Tim* specials, as well as *Laugh-In* and numerous television variety shows, films, and stage, working with everyone from Elvis Presley, Sonny & Cher, to Tom Jones. We continued to watch our families grow up together.

Don and I had resigned ourselves to the idea that maybe we would only have one child in our lives. Seven years later on May 6, 1978, our second son Raphael Jordan was born. Don's health seemed stable and my life seemed complete. We also had a cottage business as a hobby and had opened a country store in Big Bear Lake called "The Mother Lode," which my parents and aunt ran for us. They lived in Big Bear, and even though we had a cabin there, our home base was still in Los Angeles. I was also doing the Leslie Uggums series with Donny for CBS.

In 1980 I was asked to choreograph a stage production of *Jane Heights*, directed by Roy Christopher. It was a comedy that combined *Wuthering Heights* and *Jane Eyre*. I didn't want to do it because it was a comedy and I didn't think I could do it. Drama was my cup of tea. Don thought I would do a great job, and my training and discipline as a dancer helped me to overcome my fear. I received the Drama Critic's Award for best choreography that year. I was more surprised than anyone. I also continued to choreograph the *Pat Boone* specials in Israel and his family road shows as well as Debby Boone and Dottie West. I also created my own sweater-designing business under The Mother Lode label, and our lives seemed to be in a definite transition.

One morning in January of 1983, I experienced an urging desire to go see Shirley Boone at her home. It had to have been God because I felt led by a force that was beyond my own understanding. That morning my life as I knew it changed as Shirley led me to the Lord and I was filled with the Holy Spirit. All of my life I had been raised to believe that God was real. He was always there for me as a child, a teenager, a young adult, and a wife and mother. But now this was different, deeper in my soul, and I know now He was going before me and preparing my steps. He knew I would need more of Him to continue my journey.

On September 3, 1983, the eve of our move to make Big Bear Lake our permanent home, my beloved husband Don of nineteen years suffered a fatal heart attack at the young age of forty-eight. I was forced to face a life without him and the duty of raising our two sons Youree and Raphi, ages twelve and five years old, alone. I realized I had to return to Los Angeles in order to find work. Also Raphi was under a neurologist's care as he had experienced two grand mal seizures at the age of four that the doctors did not have a clue as to why. My world, at best, was in a constant whirlwind.

After relocating, I was hired by Producer/Dancer Gary Menteer and Producer David Duclon to choreograph a tap number for twelve youngsters on NBC's *Punky Brewster*. I choreographed three shows, and they liked me so much that I was asked to stay on as a stand-in. Youree was in junior high and Raphi was starting first grade. I worked as a stand-in for over two years. Unfortunately the take-home pay, which was under $400, was not enough to make mortgage payments and feed and clothe two boys. I knew I had to seek a more lucrative job. The stage manager on *Punky*, David Wader, and the script supervisor Shiela Lauder suggested that I think about joining the Directors Guild of America and become a stage manager. I already knew about multiple cameras and timing because of all the variety shows I had done.

My first question was, "What does it pay?"

When David told me, I immediately set my goals. *West Side Story* had shown me that all things are possible. Why not this?

In 1987 I became a member of the DGA, The Directors Guild Of America. David Duclon was producing a new show with Mathew Perry called *Boys Will Be Boys* and asked me to come on as a DGA stage manager. I started out as a second stage manager, sometimes a third, all the while learning the craft and gathering experience, making my way up the food chain and earning my days to become a first stage manager. I have worked in television as a stage manager and assistant director on such shows as *Punky Brewster, Good Morning, Miss Bliss, Saved by the Bell, Saved by the Class: New Class, California Dreams, Night Court, Growing Pains, Evening Shade, The Homecourt, Wings, USA High, Los Beltrans, Viva Vegas, One World,* and *All About Us*, to name just a few.

In April of 1993, I was diagnosed with breast cancer and received radiation every day for seven and one half weeks, never once getting sick or missing a day of work on *Saved By The Bell*. This cancer has not returned. In 1998 I was diagnosed with a low B-cell MALT lymphoma and am currently treated as an out-patient at UCLA.

I served for two years from 1998 to 2000 as the chair of the DGA AD/SM/PA Council and continue now to serve on the council. I served for six years as co-chair of the DGA Latino Committee and co-chaired the Latino Sub-Committee for the Student Film Awards and the Mentor Outreach Sub-Committee. I take pride in being one of three Latinos nominated by my peers to serve from 2005–2007 as a second alternate on the Directors Guild National Board.

My sons have followed in the business. Youree is a line producer and just finished a film entitled *Somewhere* for Director Sophia Coppola. He also works in commercials, music videos, and documentaries. On March 31, 2007, he married Emily Skinner, also a producer in commercials, and on September 21, 2009, they became the proud parents of Olive Skinner Henley, my first grandchild. My second son Raphael, known as Raphi, is a hip-hop artist and music producer. He goes by the name of Shames Worthy. Perfecting his craft since the early '90s, he's already been featured on over thirty full-length albums. On April 17, 2010 Raphi married Celina de la Rocha and is getting ready to release his latest CD. I am so very proud of both of them and consider myself blessed and highly favored.

On November 9, 2009, the DGA National Board Committee officially notified me that I was to be awarded the Franklin J. Schaffner Achievement Award to be given at the 62nd annual DGA Awards Dinner on Saturday, January 30, 2010. This is a huge honor and makes a big statement for Latinas, and women in general. Although still active in television, I also serve as a vice president on the board of Shirley Boone's WE WIN Ministries, which stands for "We empower women in need."

I don't think any of us saw the foreshadowing of how enormous the film *West Side Story* would be. History was in the making, and we didn't have a clue. That year of filming, I found a new "family" that would be with me for years to come. Who knew then the place this film would hold in the hearts of millions, in the world of cinema, the ten Academy Awards it received—who knew? The lasting friendships that were birthed have embraced joy, love, loyalty, wrath, laughter, cooking, and breaking bread together. Our *West Side Story* family has weathered together marriage, divorce, childbirth, drug and alcohol abuse, sickness, and death. We have lost dear friends, but I remember them as if they were still here among us, walking and dancing with me. The friendships that are still with me now are very much a part of the fabric of my life. I am thankful and grateful to the fans whose lives were changed because of this film. I will never forget the privilege I was granted.

I am also enjoying another career. It is as a writer. I love the process. To me, it is the closest thing to choreographing. You start creating with just one gesture, a few bars of music, maybe an idea. The improvisation takes over and the creator begins to "see" what no one else sees. For me, it's the same with the written word. An idea, a sentence, takes on a life of its own and where it goes, where the character wants to dance, starts to form and the journey is set in motion. I love it. I have just completed my memoir, which is called *Did You Hear Me Say Goodbye*, and my hope and dream is to get published. I believe in dreams and reaching for the brass ring. After all, it's dreams that have brought me to this very point in my life. FOR SUCH A TIME AS THIS.

Maria Henley

Program Photos

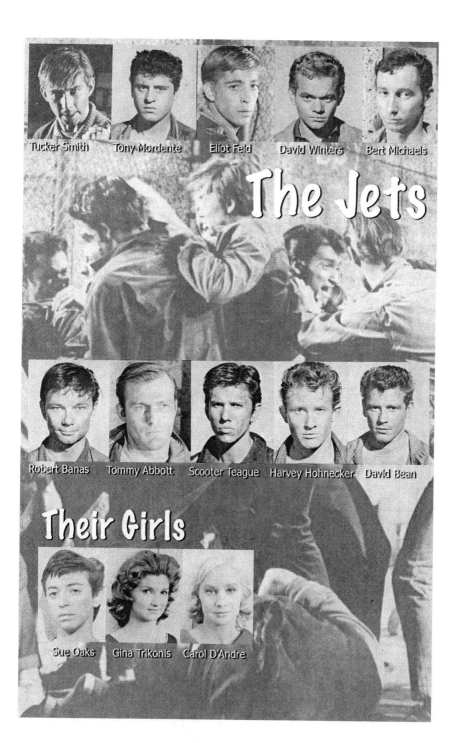

Tucker Smith Tony Mordente Eliot Feld David Winters Bert Michaels

The Jets

Robert Banas Tommy Abbott Scooter Teague Harvey Hohnecker David Bean

Their Girls

Sue Oaks Gina Trikonis Carol D'Andre

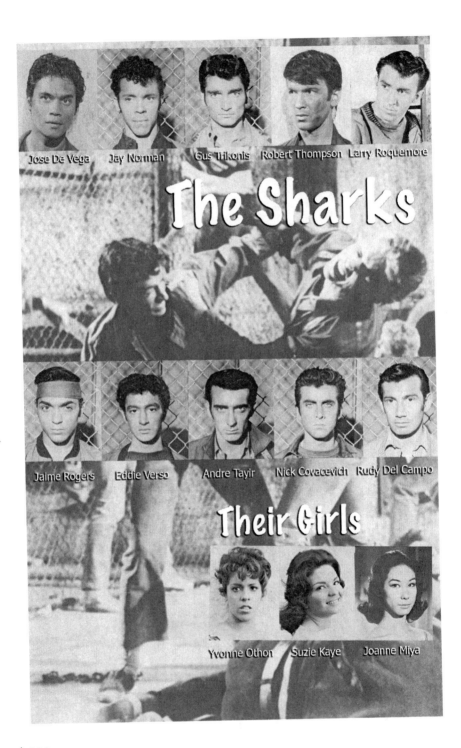

Jose De Vega Jay Norman Gus Trikonis Robert Thompson Larry Roquemore

The Sharks

Jaime Rogers Eddie Verso Andre Tayir Nick Covacevich Rudy Del Campo

Their Girls

Yvonne Othon Suzie Kaye Joanne Miya

Snapshots – Before!

Robbins & Wise

A VERY SPECIAL Tribute to two highly gifted gentlemen, "Big Daddy," Jerome Robbins, and "Mr. Cool," Robert Wise, who joined hands as directors to embark on an unbelievable journey, nurturing, molding, and guiding this film to the greatness it now enjoys. Both these gentlemen in their own rights as director and choreographer have achieved remarkable, tremendous acclaim for their works of artistic endeavor, and have won many outstanding awards for film and Broadway stage. They complemented each other with the experience and knowledge they both brought to bear and articulated the story with overwhelming spectacular visuals and explosive, dynamic dance and song. Did they know that they had a tiger by the tail, or was this just another musical about a Broadway show? I think not. You might have thought "two directors spoil the film." In this case they presented a film that only two men with such tenacity and passion could complete and deliver the perfect motion picture. It's not every day you start a film with two pros, one of film and one of stage, that share their talent and ride the same train. Both with the same objective...give the audience something to remember. Could they share that title that usually goes to one man and one man only? Well, they did, and did it with a stroke of genius. Their names will live on as "Trendsetters" that had the guts to do this film together. We can only sing and dance their praise for their guidance and talent, which made this film what it is today..."Outstanding!"

Jerome Robbins	**Robert Wise**
1918–1998	**1914–2005**

In Memory

WE DEDICATE THIS book in memory of those who no longer share the bright lights and dance floor. Their words are no longer spoken; we don't see those smiling faces, or their wonderful wit and warm friendship...a deep emptiness exists. They were part of this close family and will not be forgotten for their tremendous contribution to this film. They gave of themselves with sweat and physical effort, never complaining, never stopping, never asking "Why?" but "Let's do it again till it's right." Unfortunately, they deprived us of their very own personal experiences and up-front accounting of what went on behind the making of this great film classic. We hope we were able to fill in some of those gaps and bridge their experiences with some of ours.

Jets

Tucker Smith (Ice) Tommy Abbott (Gee Tar) Scooter Teague (Bid Deal)

Patti Tribble (Jet Girl)

Sharks

Robert Thompson (Luis) Jose De Vega (Chino) Rudy Del Campo (Del Campo) Andre Tayir (Chile)

Susie Kaye (Rosalia) Linda Dangcil (Shark Girl)

Acknowledgments

I would like to thank Carole D'Andrea's Mom and Dad. I had the best dance partner in the world...Tony Mordente.

While filming, my parents Sam and Evie showed up at the public barrier where Lincoln Center now stands. How proud they must have been, and somehow they knew how proud I was of them. Love you - Mom and Dad...Bert Michaels

Thanking my Mother for all the tap lessons, El Monte to N. Hollywood three times a week. She played piano as my accompanist, for anyone who'd watch. At 102, she still plays the piano and entertains like we did 65 years ago......David Bean

I would like to thank Ken Bennett and Titusz Bankuti...Harvey Evans

Thanking my wonderful parents, Marian and Joseph Banas for their encouragement, support and guidance...Robert Banas

I thank my amazing daughter Christina Huntington for all her help and razor sharp insights and Rachelle Benveniste, who awakened my writer's muse and gave me a voice...Gina Trikonis

Thank you to my parents Jessica and Patrick D'Andrea, who perished in a car accident, for providing me with dance lessons. I have felt their love and presence throughout this blessed career they afforded me...Carole D'Andrea

Karen Verso for writing down my ramblings of my stories....Eddie Verso

I wish to thank the Lester Horton Dancers who gave me my dance foundation and especially Don Martin...Nick Covacevich

My gratitude to my mother and father Mitsue and Mark Miyamoto who gave me their love of art, to Eugene Loring wo gave me dance as my first language, and to Chris Iijima with whom I found my song... Nobuko Miyamoto

First, I thank my Lord Jesus Christ. Second, my mother Juanita Jimenez for her unconditional love and support in making me believe I could do the impossible. Third, Rachelle Benveniste for giving me my writing voice...Maria Jimenez Henley

A Special Thanks to:
Jeremy Lott - Clips and Stills MGM
Maggie Adams - VP Arts & Digital Asset Management MGM
Gina Trikonis - Manuscript Assistant
Christina Huntington - Administrative Support
Jonathan Ade - Technical Support
Eden Banas - Artistic Support
Outskirts Press - Overall support
Witnout their help this book would not have been possible.

Credit: Courtesy of MGM Media Licensing

Technical support: Jonathan Ade

Copyright filing and helpful support: Cristina Huntington

Maggie Adams – MGM VP Asset Management

Manuscript Assitant: Gina Trikonis

CPSIA information can be obtained at www.ICGtesting.com
Printed in the USA
LVOW071651290512

283769LV00013B/61/P